BULLETIN OF THE JOHN RYLANDS LIBRARY

*Higher Learning and Civic Cultures of Knowledge:
Manchester 1824–2024*

Guest Editor: H. S. Jones

VOLUME 100 NUMBER 2, AUTUMN 2024

BULLETIN OF THE JOHN RYLANDS LIBRARY

ISSN 2054-9318 (Print)
ISSN 2054-9326 (Online)

Established in 1903

Members of the Editorial Board 2024

Chair: David Matthews
Editors: Fred Schurink and Rachel Winchcombe
Editorial Assistant: Emma Nelson

Editorial Board
Guyda Armstrong
Paul Fouracre
Roy Gibson
John Hodgson
David Law
Phyllis Mack
Janette Martin
John Morgan
Walter Pohl
Lynda Pratt
Ingrid Rembold
Carsten Timmermann
Huw Twiston Davies

Subscriptions

To subscribe please contact: Manchester University Press Journals Subscriptions, 176 Waterloo Place, University of Manchester, Oxford Road, Manchester, M13 9GP, UK
Tel: +44 (0)161 275 2310
manchesterhive@manchester.ac.uk
https://www.manchesterhive.com/view/journals/bjrl/bjrl-overview.xml

The *Bulletin* is published twice a year. The subscription prices for 2024 are:
Institutions (print and online) £235/$360/€285
Institutions (online only) £200/$295/€235
Individual (print only) £81/$120/€91

The complete archive of the *Bulletin of the John Rylands Library*, from its first issue in 1903 to Volume 80 (1998) is now available to purchase from Manchester University Press. The archive complements the current subscription product (1999 to date), and can be purchased on a one-time basis or as an annual subscription. To obtain pricing information, please contact manchesterhive@manchester.ac.uk.

BULLETIN OF THE JOHN RYLANDS LIBRARY

VOLUME 100 NUMBER 2 AUTUMN 2024

Higher Learning and Civic Cultures of Knowledge: Manchester 1824–2024

CONTENTS

Introduction: Higher Learning and Civic Cultures of Knowledge: Manchester 1824–2024   1
H. S. Jones

'Not in the college but city': Networks of Higher Learning in Manchester before 1824   11
Heather Ellis

Aftershocks of Peterloo: Manchester Mechanics' Institution and Mutual Improvement   33
Rachel Johnson

The Owens College Extension of 1870–73: Rethinking the Origins of the Civic University Tradition in England   53
H. S. Jones

Lancashire Trade, University Work: The University of Manchester and the Regional Economy, c.1930–39   75
Chris Godden

Servicing the State: Municipality and the Military Industrial Complex   97
Richard Brook

Forging the Future with the White Heat of the Past? Legacies of 'the Tech', and the Making of the Manchester Institute of Science and Technology, 1966–74   125
Erin Beeston

Introduction: Higher Learning and Civic Cultures of Knowledge: Manchester 1824–2024

H. S. JONES, UNIVERSITY OF MANCHESTER

Foundations

The occasion for this special issue of the *Bulletin of the John Rylands Library* is the University of Manchester's celebration of its bicentenary in 2024. This celebration has caused some surprise among nineteenth-century historians, familiar as they are with the foundation of Owens College in 1851 as the great landmark in the history of higher education in the city. But 1824 saw the foundation of two institutions that were precursors, of a sort, of the present University. One was the Manchester Mechanics' Institution, one of a swathe of mechanics' institutes that came into being in the 1820s and after, in response to the perceived need to bring 'useful knowledge' within the reach of the urban working class.[1] The other was Turner's School of Medicine, also known as the Pine Street School, one of the ancestors (but not, in fact, the oldest) of the Royal School of Medicine, and hence of the Medical School established at Owens College in 1872. One of the objections to a focus on centenaries and the like is that they prioritise a quest for origins, and a teleological framing, of which professional historians are rightly critical. The Manchester Mechanics' Institution was undoubtedly, like its counterparts elsewhere, a culturally important innovation; and indeed the mechanics' institutes, which were much studied by historians in the 1970s, deserve more scholarly attention than they have latterly received.[2] Whether they are illuminated by being treated as incipient universities is more questionable, with the notable exception of Birkbeck, whose distinctive mission remains indebted to its predecessor, the London Mechanics' Institution of 1823.[3]

There were over 700 mechanics' institutes in Britain by the middle of the nineteenth century, not just in the big cities, but in northern and midland towns such as Alnwick, Keighley, Wakefield and Wolverhampton. They awarded no qualifications; they promoted no research; they had no professors. They had 'members' rather than students. For these reasons, the Manchester Mechanics' Institution is better understood not diachronically, as an embryonic university or even an embryonic school of technology, but synchronically, in relation to other kinds of knowledge institutions that flourished in the cultural life of early nineteenth-century Manchester: other subscription societies such as the Literary and Philosophical Society (founded 1781), the Portico Library (1806), the Royal Manchester

Institution (1823) and the Athenaeum (1835).[4] That is the first rationale for this special issue. We seek an alternative to celebratory teleologies by studying the University's precursor institutions in connection with the wider civic culture of knowledge in their time.

The 1824 'foundation' is placed in a wider context in the first two articles. Heather Ellis makes a compelling case for severing the history of higher education from a hermetic focus on universities. There was, she argues, a rich history of higher education in Manchester which can even be traced back to John Chorlton's first iteration of a Manchester Academy in the 1690s. This history certainly embraces the Manchester Academy of 1786, the successor to the Warrington Academy and the direct institutional ancestor of what is now known as Harris Manchester College, Oxford.[5] But this history also enfolds bodies such as the Manchester Literary and Philosophical Society, the Portico Library, and the Royal Manchester Institution, as well as the Mechanics' Institution and the Infirmary too. From this point of view, the Mechanics' Institution certainly forms part of a wide-ranging history of higher education in Manchester, but it was equally certainly not a starting point. The same could be said of Turner's School of Medicine: like the founders of the Mechanics' Institution, Thomas Turner was an active member of the Manchester Literary and Philosophical Society, and in fact it was at the Society that he first started lecturing on anatomy and physiology in the autumn of 1822. It was the success of these lectures that persuaded him to set up a school of medicine, initially in a house in Pine Street, close to the Infirmary.[6]

What is particularly striking about Ellis's article is that it shows that this cluster of institutions – dissenting academies, the Manchester Literary and Philosophical Society, the Portico Library, the Mechanics' Institution – all had their roots in an Enlightenment conception of polite learning as belonging properly to the public sphere. This understanding was commonly contrasted with the kind of 'monastic' learning that was thought to prevail at Oxford and Cambridge. Variants of that binary – the polite versus the clerical or monastic – are familiar enough in the literature on English and continental Enlightenments, but Ellis breaks new ground in showing its potential to open up a much wider history of higher education.[7] In particular, she notes that this was not a simple battle of the ancients and the moderns. Exponents of a 'modern' and urbane, even urban, conception of higher education did not by any means reject the classics, but they did approach the classical authors in a different spirit.

Rachel Johnson's article complements Ellis' by focusing on the early years of the Mechanics' Institution. It traces its origins to the specific context of the rise of liberalism to ascendancy in Manchester in the wake of Peterloo. One conventional narrative about the mechanics' institutes holds that their distinctive mission was to provide a technical instruction grounded in the fundamentals of natural science for the benefit of the industrial workforce, but in practice they rapidly deserted this mission in favour of an elementary education decorated with a smattering of high culture, and as they did so they increasingly attracted a clientele of artisans and shopkeepers rather than mechanics. In the historiography of the 1970s, this constituted 'failure': a failure of Britain to develop an indigenous tradition of technical instruction of the kind that Germany in particular would later develop. But Johnson shows that these facts can be construed very differently, so as to draw out the institutes' vibrancy rather than their rapid decline. She builds on a body of very recent work which has suggested that the mechanics' institutes, far from belonging to an organised movement, really owed much more to their specific urban contexts than to their counterparts in other towns and cities. In the aftermath of Peterloo, Manchester's Liberal elite was possessed of a new-found confidence and self-consciousness, and this inspired the wave of institution building of which the Mechanics' Institution was an important part.

The Civic Idea at Work

While a focus on 1824 distorts the nature of the Manchester Mechanics' Institution, it also has the effect of obscuring from view other 'foundation moments'. These include the establishment of Owens College in 1851; the foundation of the federal Victoria University in 1880; the creation of the independent (Victoria) University in 1903; and the creation of the Technical School in 1883. Later foundation moments include 1956, when the College of Technology (a municipally run institution for over sixty years) achieved independence from the Manchester Corporation as a university college; 1966, when it was renamed the University of Manchester Institute of Science and Technology (UMIST); 1994, when UMIST achieved degree-awarding powers; and 2004, when UMIST merged back with the Victoria University to establish a formally new University of Manchester. I have argued elsewhere for the importance of the dissolution of the federal Victoria University as a key moment in the invention of the civic university.[8] In my own article in this issue I make the case for another foundation moment: the 'extension' of Owens College in 1870–73, a movement that saw the college expand, reform its governance, and relocate to the site of the present-day campus in Chorlton-on-Medlock. A key feature of the extension movement was that it created a new and deeper connecton between the College and the wider civic culture: in particular, the culture of the commercial, industrial and professional bourgeoisie. It was really the moment when the idea of the (English) civic university was born. As my article shows, the extension movement self-consciously framed a constitution that would help realise the twin objectives of academic self-government and accountability to civic opinion; and the institutional forms defined in that constitution remained the norm for English civic universities until the end of the twentieth century.

In addition to offering what we hope is a new account of the knowledge cultures of Manchester at a number of key moments in the long history of the University and its antecedents, the articles collected here aim to explore the civic-ness of the civic university. The question of which was 'the first civic university' in England is a sensitive question in which the *amour propre* of several universities is at stake.[9] But it is also an unimportant one for historians, as distinct from university marketing departments. All we claim here is that Manchester was and is one of the most notable and important of the civic universities, and that it, and its predecessors, were important sites for the formation of a clear vision of what it meant to be a civic university. This story calls for rediscovery, for the idea of the civic university has experienced a rather sudden and unexpected vogue since around 2015, manifest in a Civic University Commission, Civic University Agreements, and a burgeoning academic literature. This last is overwhelmingly contemporary in focus.[10] William Whyte's *Redbrick*, the one really indispensable history of the civic universities, had the skill or good fortune to be published just as this vogue was getting under way.[11] But Whyte, whose focus was on social and architectural histories, was not primarily concerned with the historical emergence of the *idea* of the civic university.

In the early phase – the first half of the nineteenth century – the concept of the civic university did not really exist. Universities were still widely regarded as part of an *ancien régime*. They were confessional, and served as finishing schools for the sons of the aristocracy and the gentry, as well as providing a liberal education for aspiring Anglican clergy. Universities and industrial cities belonged to different worlds. The idea of a civic university only began to form when middle-class opinion began, from the 1860s onwards, to show some interest in formal higher education. But viewed in this context, the striking thing about the idea of a civic university is that it was something of a fusion of opposites, even an oxymoron.

The central issue at stake in the historical literature on the civic universities concerns the extent to which they were intended to serve economic needs, and especially the needs of the local economy. Michael Sanderson, in a series of important and influential works, set out to emphasise the importance of the university–industry nexus. He suggested that Owens College was weakened by John Owens's stipulation that the education offered at his college should mirror that offered at the existing universities.[12] For Sanderson, the historian John Seeley, speaking in 1887, was 'patently wrong' to think that what drove the new higher education was 'a demand for knowledge, not for training'.[13] But Sanderson recognised that some civic colleges – Manchester and Liverpool, most notably – were characterised by their educational breadth, and were strong in the humanities as well as in the physical sciences and technology; he also recorded, but did not make the connection, that these were the best endowed and most successful of the civics.[14] Subsequent work has generally attributed more importance to 'a prevailing tone of municipal improvement and civic pride', in Anthony Howe's words.[15] This was the kind of spirit that also infused the projects of creating more dignified civic spaces in the city centre – in Manchester and in other industrial cities – from the 1860s onwards.[16] Owens moved out of the city centre, it is true: but in doing so it vacated cramped premises in an obscure part of town for a spacious site where it could maximise its public visibility.[17] Sir Thomas Bazley, cotton spinner, former Cobdenite MP, and personification of the Manchester mercantile community, insisted in 1877 that in pressing for a university, the Manchester business community did not want an institution 'secretly devoted to calico'.[18] It wanted something worthy of the civic dignity of a great industrial city.

The period when the civic colleges began to flourish in England, and then were transformed into civic universities, was also an enormously important moment in university history globally. In particular, it was the moment when American universities first emerged as international leaders: the decade after the end of the Civil War saw the foundation of two pioneering new kinds of university, Cornell and Johns Hopkins, and the start of the remarkable presidency of Charles W. Eliot at Harvard; it was also the start of the proliferation of the land grant universities (of which Cornell was one, though a rather untypical one) which became such a distinctive feature of the American system. In this new wave of American universities, as in the English civics, we find a synthesis of the pre-modern idea of the university with the needs – especially the economic needs – of modern life. In the United States, however, the archetypal public university, even if located in one or more cities, is a *state* university, not a civic one in the English sense; and while the land grant universities had a strongly technical and practical focus, the emphasis in the first wave was on supporting agricultural innovation rather than industry.

Manchester and the other English civics were not land grant universities, and not only because they rarely got a land grant. Integration with the needs of the local economy came slowly. When Walter Moberly (no technocrat) became Manchester's vice-chancellor in 1928 (so his obituary recalled forty-five years later), the university was 'renowned for its enterprise in research and for the distinction of its scholars'; but while it was respected in the local area for its 'independence and integrity', its aims were not well understood or appreciated, and it was not 'fully integrated in the industrial and business community surrounding it'.[19] It was Moberly's achievement, and that of his successor John Stopford, to get the people of Manchester to 'look upon it as their own university'.[20] That was the realisation of the vision of those who had led the campaign for university status in 1880 (when it was partially successful) and in 1903, when it finally came to fruition in the independent University of Manchester. What this meant in practice is teased out in Chris Godden's article. It was not just chemistry and engineering and others of the physical and technological sciences that had the potential to impact on the regional economy. The Faculty of Commerce and Administration – the ancestor of the later Faculty of Economic and Social Studies – had a long-standing focus on the problems of the regional economy dating back to its first dean, Sydney Chapman. Under Henry Clay and John Jewkes, this kind of 'realistic economics' became something of the hallmark of the faculty, and it was characterised by a deep engagement not just with the city of Manchester but also with its industrial hinterland. 'My realism was primarily derived from Lancashire', wrote Chapman in an unpublished autobiography.[21]

Godden suggests that the Economic Research Section had significant impact, at least in informing the understanding of the economic problems confronting policymakers. Jewkes and his colleagues received good coverage from the *Manchester Guardian*, which under a succession of editors (Scott, Crozier and Wadsworth) had close links with the University. The other initiative Godden discusses was only ambiguously successful. This was the attempt to develop the study of Chinese, with a particular focus on the Chinese economy and Britain's trade links with China. Boxer Indemnity Funding permitted the creation of four academic positions in Chinese Studies at four leading universities, and whereas the other three were focused on different aspects of the humanities, the post at Manchester was earmarked for the study of the Chinese economy. This probably reflected both Manchester's growing reputation for a 'realistic' approach to economics, and the perceived benefits to the Manchester business community of an enhanced understanding of China. The appointment of E. W. Mead as Reader in Chinese Language and Social Economy was short-lived, however, since it was brought to an end by the outbreak of war in 1939. As with the Economic Research Section, Mead's principal external partners were the Chamber of Commerce (to which Jewkes had once been assistant secretary), the Manchester Statistical Society, and of course, the *Manchester Guardian*.

Civic University, Civic Decline?

The final two articles, by Richard Brook and Erin Beeston, provide two connected perspectives on the early years of the chartered College of Technology and UMIST: appropriately, since it is through UMIST that the present-day University of Manchester traces its ancestry back to the Mechanics' Institution of 1824. Thinking about the relationship between academy and city in the postwar period poses some distinct challenges, for the civic tradition in British universities was certainly in decline in this period, as, indeed, was British civic culture in a wider sense.[22] Manchester, still economically vibrant in the interwar period, experienced most of the second half of the twentieth century as a period of decline.[23] UMIST – as it was renamed in 1966 – has an intriguing place in this history. It was, after all, a municipal institution from 1892 until 1956, at the same time as being, from 1905, the Technology Faculty of the Victoria University of Manchester. It had some claim to be an important civic university in its own right, but, if the civic universities generally were perceived as being in decline in the 1960s, UMIST, by contrast, was blessed with the backing of Whitehall, and seemed to stand for a vision of a dynamic, high-tech future.[24]

UMIST's campus – the subject of Richard Brook's contribution – has a notable place in the architectural history of British higher education. It was the most important campus development between the University College of North Staffordshire (subsequently Keele) in 1949 and Sussex (and then the other 'new universities') from 1958 onwards. Whereas those new universities were all located at a distance from urban centres, and, in a clear symbolic departure from the civic tradition, were often named after counties rather than cities, UMIST's was very much a city centre campus, much more so than the Victoria University's 'Owens' campus.[25] UMIST was something of a hybrid institution, directly funded by the University Grants Committee from 1956, but also part of the Victoria University; set up as part of a *national* plan driven by a sense of the *nation*'s urgent need for more technologists, it had (even more than the rest of the Victoria University) strong local and civic roots, in that it had until 1956 been owned and run by the Manchester Corporation. One of the distinctive features of the campus masterplan, as demonstrated by Brook, was its explicit attempt to create a readily permeable interface between campus and city. In an era of civic decline, it was an architectural reaffirmation of the civic tradition.

The expansion of science and engineering in British universities in the aftermath of the Second World War was a key dimension of what David Edgerton calls the 'warfare state': a state geared to military preparedness rather than, or alongside, the welfare of its citizens.[26] But Edgerton's emphasis is overwhelmingly on the role of central government, whereas Brook's article provides a case study of how local authorities and civic actors interacted with, participated in, and benefited from the warfare state. Although the College of Science and Technology was, from 1956, funded by central government and freed from the control of the city council, its development was, crucially, the product of partnership between central and local authorities. It is a story that powerfully demonstrates the operation of the warfare state at the civic level.

Vivian Bowden – the head of the Manchester College of Science and Technology and then of UMIST from 1953 to 1976 – emerges from Brook's article as a visionary figure. But what kind of vision inspired him? Was it really a civic vision, when UMIST had such a strongly national mission? These are questions explored by Erin Beeston's article. Bowden was at the forefront of the 'white heat of technology'; indeed, as a recently elevated life peer, he was Harold Wilson's first appointee to the position of minister of education and science, charged with driving the re-orientation of the educational system towards science and technology. But Beeston's article demonstrates, rather strikingly, that Bowden's work at UMIST was shaped by a future-oriented vision which nevertheless made copious and creative use of Manchester's own scientific and industrial heritage. He was a notable advocate of the creation of what is now the Museum of Science and Industry, and also insistent on the importance of having a Department for the History of Science and Technology at UMIST.[27] Bowden is often twinned with C. P. Snow as a philistine and a technocrat, but in Beeston's account he absolutely does not fit David Edgerton's influential model of the anti-historian technocrat.[28] This article also has rich implications for ways of thinking about the relationship between UMIST and a city that, by the end of Bowden's time, was in the depths of industrial decline.

Conclusion

Together, these six articles are intended to offer a range of perspectives on the porous interface between academy and city over a century and a half. At a time when the idea of the civic university is once again coming into fashion, and every university is discovering its own distinctive civic mission, there is a case for historians to re-visit ways in which that civic mission has been understood historically. Today, advocates of the renewal of the civic university grapple with an analogous tension between civic and global engagement. Thus, the University of Bristol aspires to be 'a model global civic institution powered by our sense of place and connections to communities'.[29] Internationally, the idea of the 'glocal university' has gained traction to capture the idea of building a global brand on the basis of a grounding in place. In working out how to connect the global and the local in practice they could do worse than to consider the way in which Vivian Bowden in the 1960s wrestled with the analogous tension between UMIST's municipal past and its national, government-defined mission to shape the industrial future.

Notes

1. Among the more notable were the Edinburgh School of Arts (1821), and the Glasgow, Liverpool and London mechanics' institutes (1823).
2. Some of these bodies were known as mechanics' institutions, and others as mechanics' institutes; Manchester's fell into the first category. It is usual to refer to them in the plural as mechanics' institutes.
3. As shown by Joanna Bourke, *Birkbeck: 200 Years of Radical Learning for Working People* (Oxford: Oxford University Press, 2022).
4. For the contemporary sense that the Mechanics' Institution was a similar kind of institution to the Athenaeum, see Oxford, Bodleian Library, MS Bryce 55, fol. 71v (R. D. Darbishire to James Bryce, 11 July 1865). As Darbishire saw it, the Athenaeum was 'a newsroom and Library and general meeting of middle class young men' and the Mechanics' Institution 'a similar institution for perhaps older men of somewhat narrower incomes'.
5. On this history, see Barbara Smith (ed.), *Truth, Liberty, Religion: Essays Celebrating Two Hundred Years of Manchester College* (Oxford: Manchester College, 1986).
6. Stella Butler, 'Thomas Turner (1793–1873), Surgeon and Founder of Pine Street School of Medicine', *Oxford Dictionary of National Biography*, https://doi.org/10.1093/ref:odnb/27871 [accessed 6 September 2024].
7. For example, J. G. A. Pocock, 'Conservative Enlightenment and Democratic Revolutions: The American and French Cases in British Perspective', *Government and Opposition*, 24 (1989), 81–105.
8. H. S. Jones, 'T. F. Tout and the Idea of the University', in C. M. Barron and J. T. Rosenthal (eds), *Thomas Frederick Tout (1855–1929): Repositioning History for the Twentieth Century* (London: Institute of Historical Research, 2019), pp. 73–87.
9. The University of Birmingham boldly made this claim in its centenary history: see Eric Ives, Diane Drummond and Leonard Schwarz, *The First Civic University: Birmingham 1880–1980: an Introductory History* (Birmingham: Birmingham University Press, 2000).
10. John Goddard and Paul Vallance, *The University and the City* (Abingdon: Routledge, 2013); John Goddard, 'The Civic University and the City', in Peter Meusburger, Michael Heffernan and Laura Suarsana (eds), *Geographies of the University* (Cham: Springer, 2018), pp. 355–74; Liz Todd, Simin Davoudi, Mark Shucksmith and Mel Steer, 'The Civic University: Introduction', in Mel Steer, Simin Davoudi, Mark Shucksmith and

Liz Todd (eds), *Hope under Neoliberal Austerity* (Bristol: Bristol University Press, 2021), pp. 147–52, and other contributions to the same book; Julian Dobson and Ed Ferrari (eds), *Reframing the Civic University: An Agenda for Impact* (Cham: Palgrave, 2023).

11 William Whyte, *Redbrick: A Social and Architectural History of Britain's Civic Universities* (Oxford: Oxford University Press, 2015).

12 Michael Sanderson, *The Universities and British Industry, 1850–1970* (London: Routledge & Kegan Paul, 1972), p. 62.

13 *Ibid.*, p. 82.

14 Birmingham, once it acquired university status, could be classed in this company too.

15 Anthony Howe, 'The Business Community', in Mary B. Rose (ed.), *The Lancashire Cotton Industry: A History since 1870* (Preston: Lancashire County Books, 1996), p. 116. This draws on Howe's argument in his earlier work, *The Cotton Masters* (Oxford: Clarendon, 1984).

16 On these projects, see Simon Gunn, *The Public Culture of the Victorian Middle Class: Ritual and Authority in the English Industrial City, 1840–1914* (Manchester: Manchester University Press, 2000), pp. 50–4; see also Patrick Joyce, *The Rule of Freedom: Liberalism and the Modern City* (London: Verso, 2003), pp. 144–82.

17 On this point, see Stuart Jones, 'James Bryce's Manchester', in Stuart Jones (ed.), *Manchester Minds: A University History of Ideas* (Manchester: Manchester University Press, 2024), p. 68; on light and visibility in liberal management of urban space, see Chris Otter, *The Victorian Eye: A Political History of Light and Vision in Britain, 1800–1910* (Chicago: University of Chicago Press, 2008).

18 Thomas Bazley, 'Shall Manchester Have a University?', *Fortnightly Review*, 2 (1877), 122.

19 'Sir Walter Moberly. Educational Statesman', *The Times* (2 February 1974), p. 14.

20 *Ibid.*

21 Manchester, John Rylands Library, Eng. MS 1318 (Sydney Chapman, 'Autobiography').

22 For a classic narrative, see Tristram Hunt, *Building Jerusalem: The Rise and Fall of the Victorian City* (London: Weidenfeld & Nicolson, 2004), especially the epilogue. More recent work has stressed the vibrancy of civic life in the interwar period, but agrees in seeing a pattern of decline after 1945: see Charlotte Wildman, 'Urban Transformation in Liverpool and Manchester, 1918–1939', *Historical Journal*, 55 (2012), 119–43; Charlotte Wildman, *Urban Redevelopment and Modernity in Liverpool and Manchester, 1919–1939* (London: Bloomsbury, 2016), pp. 21–48; Tom Hulme, *After the Shock City: Urban Culture and the Making of Modern Citizenship* (Woodbridge: Boydell, 2019).

23 The theme of 'decline' in British history is much debated: see Jim Tomlinson, 'Thrice Denied: "Declinism" as a Recurrent Theme in British History in the Long Twentieth Century', *Twentieth Century British History*, 20 (2009), 227–51.

24 I develop this point in Stuart Jones, 'Civic University and Civic Decline', in Jones (ed.), *Manchester Minds*, pp. 153–8.

25 In the terminology of the 2004 merger, the two ancestor institutions were the Victoria University of Manchester and UMIST. That was true enough for the period 1994–2004, but when imposed (as it was) on the pre-1994 history it is misleading. The two

campuses had historically (even in the 1970s and 1980s) been known as 'Tech' and 'Owens'.

26 David Edgerton, *Warfare State: Britain, 1920–1970* (Cambridge: Cambridge University Press, 2006), especially pp. 145–90.

27 This was transferred to the Victoria University of Manchester in 1986, as the Centre for the History of Science, Technology and Medicine, under which name (remarkably, in an era of incessant name changes) it still survives. But, having been located in the Victoria University's Faculty of Science from 1986 until 2004, it has subsequently been institutionally housed with the life sciences, in what is now the Faculty of Biology, Medicine and Health. This signals something of a move away from its old UMIST-inspired mission.

28 On anti-historians and technocrats, see Edgerton, *Warfare State*, pp. 191–229.

29 University of Bristol, 'Our Mission', www.bristol.ac.uk/university/strategy/mission/ [accessed 30 July 2024].

'Not in the college but city': Networks of Higher Learning in Manchester before 1824

HEATHER ELLIS, UNIVERSITY OF SHEFFIELD

Abstract

This article explores in what ways and to what extent it is possible to talk about 'higher learning' and 'higher education' in Manchester before 1824, the date formally chosen by the University of Manchester to mark its foundation. It considers diverse sites and institutions, revealing a complex, interconnected web of knowledge spaces – dissenting academies, teaching hospitals, learned societies, independent libraries and individual initiatives – which complicate existing narratives of the development of higher education in the city that usually focus on the origins of the university. In the early nineteenth century, with Manchester rapidly becoming the 'world's first industrial city', we see emerging at the same time a vibrant urban educational landscape, with no parallel in the British Isles at that time.[1] In contrast to England's ancient universities which remained, for the most part, closed and private entities until the mid-nineteenth century, Manchester's educational culture was self-consciously diffused, civic and participatory, strongly influenced by the city's prominent dissenting communities. Excluded from Oxford and Cambridge, Manchester's Unitarians, in particular, sought to shape the city's educational culture according to the Enlightenment ideal of polite learning as a public endeavour. While civic participatory models have been foregrounded by historians of knowledge and ideas in recent years, this article considers, for the first time, how such models influenced the history of educational cultures in Manchester.

Keywords: Manchester; higher education; higher learning; literary and philosophical societies; dissenting academies

It is important to note, at the outset, that this article makes the case for a history of higher learning and education that looks beyond the university. In a sense, this is obvious from the title, since the date that it invokes was chosen to represent the foundation of the University of Manchester. Building on recent historiographical developments, it argues that the history of higher education ought not to be limited to the history of the university, an institution fixed in space and time. Any definition must embrace a wider range of institutions, of which some were of short duration, and others have exercised a lasting influence until the present day.[2] A history of higher learning (rather than simply of universities) invites researchers, for example, to look more closely at the (frequently blurred) boundaries between secondary and tertiary education in the past. Until the middle of the nineteenth century, for instance, Scottish universities recruited students who were on average between fourteen and sixteen years old, an age more usually associated with secondary education.[3] As H. S. Jones notes in his own contribution to this special issue, the 'fundamental binary' was between elementary and higher education for much of the nineteenth century.[4]

Higher learning, as a term, also encourages a focus on the specific activities and practices that constitute it – teaching, research and the training of future researchers – rather than on a particular institutional context. In so doing, alternative, frequently neglected spaces carrying out specific aspects or functions of higher learning are thrown into greater relief. Another risk when telling the story of higher learning in Manchester before 1824 is that of reading developments in the city and surrounding area solely through the lens of the emergence and spread of the research university, which is usually considered the central story in the development of modern higher education. It is not the only one, however. As William Whyte has written, 'the development of higher education in the early nineteenth century cannot be reduced to a simple story in which the forces of progress ... inevitably and irresistibly created a new and modern sort of university'. There were rather, he continues, 'a multitude of competing visions' which could provide the basis for 'an alternative history of higher education'.[5] While it is clear in hindsight that the University of Manchester would come to dominate the history of higher learning and higher education in the city, it is important not to lose sight of the rich and diverse educational landscape, flourishing against the background of Manchester's unprecedented growth as the world's first industrial city, which preceded it and from which it emerged.

For much of the eighteenth century in England and France, universities like Oxford and Cambridge were widely condemned as intellectually stagnant and 'monkish', isolated from the cut and thrust of national life.[6] Intellectual innovation and reform in higher learning and education took place elsewhere. According to the Irish playwright, Oliver Goldsmith, in 1759, 'the true intellectual forum was the city, where the members of this larger university, if I may so call it, catch manners as they rise, study life, not logic, and have the world for correspondents'. The best universities, Goldsmith argued, were those that interacted with urban life most intensely, 'where the pupils are under few restrictions; where all scholastic jargon is banished; where they ... live not in the college but city. Such are Edinburgh, Leyden, Gottingen, Geneva.'[7] In what follows, I would like to keep in mind this idea of the city – here the city of Manchester – as one of these 'larger universities'.

Manchester Collegiate Church and Chetham's Library

Manchester Collegiate Church had, since its foundation in 1421, been a centre of education for the surrounding population. However, it was during the English civil war that efforts were made to locate a northern university there. The proposal, made in 1641 by a group of local inhabitants, asked Parliament to establish a university for the north of England in Manchester; it was anticipated that the old College buildings would form the core of the new university, likely supported by the clergy from the Collegiate Church. This proposal never came to fruition, however, since it faced opposition from a competing bid from York and was ultimately overshadowed by other parliamentary matters.[8] The foundation of Chetham's Library in 1653, in the same college buildings that had been intended to form the core of this northern university a decade earlier, marks the real beginnings of higher learning in Manchester prior to 1824. It is an institution that holds the distinction of being the oldest surviving public library in Britain, and its establishment can be attributed to Humphrey Chetham (1580–1653), a prosperous merchant, banker and landowner from Manchester. In his will, Chetham made provisions for the foundation of a library, as well as a school for forty poor boys.[9]

Before the library's establishment, independent study was difficult in the north of England. In response, the twenty-four feoffees (or governors) appointed by Humphrey Chetham set out to amass a substantial collection of books and manuscripts that encompassed a broad spectrum of knowledge, rivaling the libraries of prestigious institutions like Oxford and Cambridge. Indeed, in 1670, the Manchester-born Master of Jesus College, Cambridge, John Worthington, declared the library to be 'better than any library in Cambridge'.[10] Chetham's will of 1651 stipulated that the library should be accessible to 'scholars and others well affected', and he instructed the librarian to demand nothing from anyone entering the premises.[11] Chetham's Library continued to play an important role as a centre for private study in Manchester and the surrounding area in succeeding centuries, particularly for the region's dissenting community. At the turn of the seventeenth and eighteenth centuries, the author James Clegg noted the significant advantage enjoyed by those studying under the Presbyterian minister and tutor John Chorlton, whose house in Manchester was near to Chetham's Library.[12] Almost a century later, in 1794, the chemist John Dalton, who was at that time Mathematics Professor at the newly opened Manchester Academy, referred to Chetham's Library as one of the most attractive features of Manchester as a place of learning.[13]

Under the terms of Chetham's will, the sum of £200 was also allocated for the provision of five small libraries of books, designed to be 'chained upon desks or to be fixed to the pillars or in other convenient places'. They were to be located in the parish churches of Manchester and Bolton and in the parochial chapelries of Gorton, Turton and Walmesley. The feoffees or trustees were instructed to purchase 'godly Englishe Bookes ... for the edification of the common people'. The library at Gorton was the first of the five to be completed, containing fifty-one works.[14] At the time, chained libraries such as these constituted one of very few educational resources available to local people.

Dissenting Academies

Following the Uniformity Act of 1662, obtaining degrees from the ancient English universities of Cambridge and Oxford, became challenging for men (women being excluded in any case) who were not practising members of the Church of England. Until the Oxford University Act of 1854, the University of Oxford required a religious test for admission, comparable to joining the Church.[15] Similarly, at the University of Cambridge, a statutory test was necessary to obtain a bachelor's degree. During this period, English Dissenters – Nonconformist Protestants who did not conform to the beliefs of the Church of England – faced difficulties pursuing degrees at English universities. As a result, many Dissenters attended dissenting academies instead.[16]

While religious reasons were paramount, the geographical availability of university education also played a role in reducing the access of dissenters to higher learning. The establishment of Durham College by Oliver Cromwell aimed to challenge the educational monopoly of Oxford and Cambridge and provide university-level teaching to students in the north of England, although it ultimately failed due to political changes following the restoration of the monarchy in 1660.[17] However, Richard Frankland, who founded Rathmell Academy, the oldest nonconformist educational institution in the north of England, and who supported the Durham College project, continued to campaign for an independent university in northern England.[18] The need for this was felt especially acutely by dissenting communities who were strongly represented in northern English towns such as Manchester. According to the diary of James Clegg, upon the death of Richard Frankland on 1 October 1698, Clegg was sent to Manchester to invite John Chorlton, an old student of Rathmell Academy, to deliver Frankland's funeral sermon. Chorlton, born in Salford in 1666, had studied at Rathmell under Frankland's guidance. Five years later, he became a colleague of the respected Presbyterian minister Henry Newcome in Manchester, witnessing the construction of the Cross Street Unitarian Chapel, which was consecrated in 1694. Chorlton preached Frankland's funeral sermon, but declined the subsequent request to continue running Rathmell Academy.[19]

Chorlton's refusal was not absolute, however. Instead of relocating to Rathmell, he 'set up teaching university learning in a great house in Manchester'. Eleven of Frankland's students from Rathmell Academy, including James Clegg, completed their studies under Chorlton. Another student of the early Manchester Academy was Thomas Dixon, who followed Chorlton as a tutor, succeeding him and his assistant James Coningham. Chorlton faced opposition from ecclesiastical authorities, but the threat of prosecution at the Assizes was avoided through the support of powerful local individuals.[20] After Chorlton's death in 1705, his colleague James Coningham, a graduate of the University of Edinburgh, continued the work of the Academy in conjunction with his ministry at Cross Street Chapel until he moved to London in 1712. At that point, Dr Thomas Dixon, known for his theological and medical expertise, established his own academy in Whitehaven in Cumbria, taking up the mantle after the first iteration of the Manchester Academy.[21]

In July 1754, a circular was issued from Manchester, announcing a project to establish a new academy in Warrington, located about fifteen miles away. The primary reason for this initiative was given as 'the total deficiency of Academies in this part of the country'.[22] The goal was to address the need for qualified ministers for

Nonconformist churches, as well as to provide education for lay individuals pursuing other professions, including commerce. The plan involved the formation of a body of trustees who would oversee the establishment and supervision of the academy. The proposed academy aimed 'to unite in the best manner the advantages of the public and more private methods of education', providing at the same time 'for the extensive learning of our youth and the security of their morals'. Those preparing for careers in the learned professions or in commerce would not only gain 'some knowledge of the more useful branches of literature'; they would be led 'to an early acquaintance with, and just concern for, the true principles of religion and liberty, of which great interests they must in future life be the supporters', while for those aiming at ministerial office it would be 'an invaluable advantage to have them educated where they may freely follow the dictates of their own judgments in their inquiries after truth, without any undue bias imposed on their understanding'. With the need for a new academy established on these grounds, appeal was made to the generosity 'of all friends of Religion, Liberty and Learning'. John Seddon, the minister of the Nonconformist congregation at Sankey Street Chapel in Warrington, played a prominent role in spearheading the project. To garner further support for the new academy in Warrington, extensive correspondence was carried out with influential Nonconformists across the country.[23]

After considering the competing claims of Manchester and Ormskirk, the academy was eventually established in Warrington. Promises of subscriptions were received from various cities with strong dissenting communities, including Manchester, Liverpool, Birmingham and Warrington. By April 1755, the total amount pledged reached nearly £300, indicating significant support for the project. Amid the support received for the establishment of the Warrington Academy, there was some criticism from supporters based in Leeds, where it was proposed that higher education could be adequately obtained at Glasgow University. These suggestions did not deter the progress of the project, however. On 30 June 1757, the first general meeting of subscribers took place in Warrington. It was decided that annual subscribers contributing two guineas and donors contributing twenty guineas would form the body of trustees. Lord Willoughby of Parham was appointed as the president, John Lees of Manchester as the vice president, Arthur Heywood of Liverpool as the treasurer, and John Seddon as the secretary. At that point, the promised annual subscriptions amounted to £469 5s.[24]

Housing arrangements were made for the tutors, who would also serve as boarding masters for the students. The terms for boarding were set at £15 for students with a two-month vacation period, or £18 for those without a vacation, with additional charges for amenities such as tea, washing, fire and candles. The tutors were to receive a salary of £100 per year, and the academy covered their rent and taxes. In December 1758, these salaries were increased to £120 and later to £135. Warrington Academy opened in October 1757 and enjoyed a prosperous and successful thirty years of activity under famous tutors such as John Aikin and Joseph Priestley.[25] Despite this, however, the academy faced numerous challenges that ultimately led to its downfall. The institution accumulated significant debt related to its buildings, and internal issues, such as a lack of discipline, further exacerbated the situation. These difficulties weighed heavily on the academy's administrators and supporters, leading to a sense of profound discouragement. In January 1783, during a general meeting of trustees, it was determined that the academy could no longer sustain itself and it was decided that it would close its doors at the end of the current academic session.[26]

On 29 June 1786, the Warrington Trustees referred to the 'intended' establishment of a new academy in Manchester. By that time, however, plans for the new foundation were already well underway. A meeting had taken place on 22 February 1786, at Cross Street Chapel in Manchester, where Dr Thomas Barnes and Ralph Harrison, both ministers of the chapel, were appointed as tutors for the new academy. Following this decision, a committee was formed on 1 March 1786, and on 26 March Harrison delivered a sermon 'on the occasion of the establishment of the Academy', which was subsequently published.[27] The individuals involved in these decisions were largely the same group of influential figures from the north of England who had been supportive of Liberal dissent. Among the fifty-four Warrington trustees who voted for the dissolution, seventeen had also signed the invitation to Barnes and Harrison, and twelve of them were members of the new committee.[28]

Dr Thomas Percival FRS, a well-known physician in Manchester and a member of the Cross Street congregation, served as the chairman and, along with the two minister-tutors, exerted significant influence in securing the foundation and shaping the policies of the new academy. The opening statement in the printed record of the first meeting gives us an insight into its aims and aspirations: 'a very respectable meeting of gentlemen was held this 22nd day of February, 1786, when it was unanimously agreed, after due deliberation, that an Academy should be established in Manchester, on a plan affording a full and systematic course of education for divines, and preparatory instruction for other learned professions, as well as for civil and commercial life. This institution will be open to young men of every religious denomination, from whom no test, or confession of faith, will be required.'[29] In an address given in Cross Street Chapel on the morning of 14 September 1786, and subsequently published together with Ralph Harrison's sermon, Thomas Barnes declared his hopes for the new Academy to the assembled congregation. From his words, we can see that, although based in Manchester, he viewed the academy as part of a much wider international network of higher education free from religious barriers and controls:

> You are erecting a Temple, on the front of which you will inscribe no name of any distinguished human leader, either in science or theology. You will dedicate it 'to Truth! to Liberty! to Religion!' When you turn your eyes towards it, you will breathe forth the dying Patriot's fervent aspiration (*Esto Perpetua!*). You will pray that it may flourish, with increasing honour, to many future generations. Nor will you confine your good wishes to this Seminary: you will also pray that the sacred cause to which it is devoted may extend its influence abroad with glorious success; and that the holy light of truth, of reason, and of righteousness, may shine over all the nations of the earth with growing lustre, even to meridian day.[30]

To the published version of Barnes's address was added a statement listing the reasons for the establishment of the Academy, and several resolutions designed to form its constitution. The 'expediency, and even necessity' of the Manchester Academy was explained by the fact that, with the closure of Warrington, there was 'no place of education for youth, on the liberal and extensive plan proposed' within more than a hundred miles of Manchester. In addition, it was urged that 'the great populousness of this vicinage, the opulence of its inhabitants, the number and respectability of the Dissenters and the increasing taste for learning, insure both adequate support and a constant succession of pupils'. They also had an eye to the relative security of the city, 'remarkable for a well-regulated police, and for a serious attention to the duties of public worship; and that the industry, ingenuity and enterprising spirit which characterise the people cannot fail to influence by example, and may catch the minds of youth by a secret and powerful sympathy'.[31]

In a second circular, published later the same year, the announced programme of studies included a five-year course for Divinity students and a shorter course for others. Thomas Barnes was assigned the following subjects: Hebrew, Logic, Ontology and Pneumatology, Ethics, and the elements of Jurisprudence. Additionally, he was to teach the 'Evidences, Doctrines, and Precepts of Christianity, Ecclesiastical History, Jewish Antiquities, and the duties associated with the Pastoral Charge'. It continued,

> Through the greatest part of this course particular attention will be paid to Scripture Criticism, and to the composition and delivery of sermons. For this purpose the students will be employed, every week, in analysing the best printed sermons, in preparing schemes of their own subjects proposed by their Tutor, and in Elocution. Whilst thus engaged, they will enjoy opportunities of attendance on the other Professors, for the acquisition of the several branches of science essential to a Liberal Education.[32]

From this we see that it would be incorrect to describe the Manchester Academy as simply a religious seminary for Dissenters. Harrison, as 'Professor of the Classics and Polite Literature', would teach Latin and Greek, and 'illustrate his lectures with observations on the History, Mythology, Manners and Philosophy of the Ancients'. For Polite Literature, a course of lectures each session would deal with a range of different subjects including 'the Theory of Language, particularly the English, Oratory, Criticism, Composition, History and Geography'. A third professor was to be appointed to teach Mathematics and Natural Philosophy.[33]

According to V. D. Davis, the historian of Manchester Academy, the system of discipline prescribed for residential students was not dissimilar to those under which students at Oxford and Cambridge had to live. Clearly, moral supervision was to be as important as academic oversight in the new academy:

> No student shall be allowed to be out of his lodgings, without leave from the Conductors of the Academy, after ten o'clock.

> No student shall be permitted to ride out of town, or to be in a Tavern or Inn, without leave from Dr Barnes or Mr Harrison.
>
> All games of chance shall be strictly prohibited.
>
> It shall be earnestly recommended to the students, to use great plainness in dress, and economy in expenses. And it is hoped that Parents and Guardians will second so important an advice by their allowances and influence.
>
> Every student, except where an exemption is particularly requested by their friends, shall, when the public buildings are completed, regularly attend morning and evening prayers at the Academy.[34]

The initial period of the Academy's existence was marked by a sense of optimism, and during the first eleven years under Dr Barnes's leadership, a total of 135 students were enrolled. Among them, twenty were specifically preparing for the ministry, and four of these were firmly committed to joining the Church. A significant number of the eighty-eight students destined for 'Commerce' resided in Manchester. Additionally, there were twelve students studying Law and eleven pursuing Medicine. An important milestone in these early years was the appointment of the famous chemist and subsequent developer of atomic theory, John Dalton, as Mathematics Professor in 1793. In the prospectus of August 1798 of the 'Academical Institution or New College at Manchester', Dalton's subjects were described as including, 'with Mathematics and Geography, Natural Philosophy and Chemistry, theoretical and experimental'.[35]

A letter written by Dalton in February 1794 to his cousin, Elihu Robinson, presents a vivid picture of life at Manchester Academy some eight years after its foundation. It provides important details about the layout of the original academy buildings (which are now lost), the accommodation, charges and daily routine of tutors and students:

> Our Academy is a large and elegant building in the most elegant and retired street of the place; it consists of a front and two wings; the first floor of the front is the hall where most of the business is done; over it is a library with about eight thousand volumes; over this are two rooms, one of which is mine; One of the wings is occupied by Dr Barnes's family, he is one of the tutors, and superintendent of the seminary; the other is occupied by a family who manage the boarding and seventeen In-students with two tutors, each individual having a separate room, etc. Out-students from the town and neighbourhood at present amount to nine, which is as great a number as has been since the institution; they are of all religious professions; the tutors are all Dissenters. Terms for In-students forty guineas per session (ten months); Out-students twelve guineas. Two tutors and the In-students all dining, etc., together in a room on purpose: we breakfast on tea at 8 1/2, dine at 1 1/2, drink tea at 5 and sup at 8 1/2; we fare as well as it is possible for anyone to do ... My official department of tutor only requires my attendance upon the students twenty-one hours in the week but I find it often expedient to

prepare my lectures previously. There is in this town a large library, furnished with the best books in every art, science and language, which is open to all, gratis; when thou art apprised of this and such like circumstances, when thou considerest me in my private apartment, undisturbed, having a good fire and a philosophical apparatus around me, thou wilt be able to form an opinion of whether I spend my time in slothful inactivity of body and mind.[36]

In June 1800, Dalton retired from the Academy, leaving the Divinity tutor George Walker (of whom more later) with the sole responsibility for the institution. On receiving Dalton's resignation, the trustees made the decision to temporarily reduce the scope of the Academy. They decided not to make any further appointments, allowing Walker to continue as the Divinity tutor while also permitting him to accept a few lay students, so long as this did not interfere with his care for the others. Walker continued for two more years, before ultimately resigning at the end of the session in June 1803. It was determined at the annual meeting of trustees in March 1803 that the funds of the institution would continue to be used for the education of young men for the ministry among Protestant Dissenters. This led to the question of where this education could best be carried out, and the decision was made to relocate the college to York.[37]

The Manchester Infirmary

The Manchester Infirmary was founded on 27 July 1752, and the construction of a new hospital to house it was begun in 1753 and completed in June 1755. The infirmary was primarily intended for the treatment of patients, employing initially three physicians and three surgeons including Charles White, who would go on to be a founding member and vice president for twenty-three years of the Manchester Literary and Philosophical Society. It also had a significant teaching function, however. Its first student was John Daniel, who was taken on in 1754 as an apprentice to the apothecary based at the hospital. By 1790, the institution had a staff of six physicians and six surgeons. The organised admission of medical pupils began in 1793. The fee for the first six-month session was five guineas, and for two subsequent sessions three guineas, with extra fees payable to surgeons for attendance at operations. The infirmary was equipped with a library in 1791 for the benefit of its medical staff and students.[38] Many of the physicians and surgeons employed by the infirmary went on to enjoy positions at the centre of Manchester's intellectual life in the late eighteenth and early nineteenth centuries. As well as carrying out research in their respective medical fields of interest, they also became prominent members and officers of the city's learned and scientific societies, in particular the Manchester Literary and Philosophical Society, where they presented papers on a wide range of subjects including art and literature as well as the natural and physical sciences.

The Manchester Literary and Philosophical Society

The period between 1780 and 1840 saw the establishment of numerous smaller learned societies in towns and cities throughout the British Isles. These societies, often referred to as 'literary and philosophical societies', also began to flourish in the United States and other parts of the British Empire, contributing to the widespread growth of these organisations during the same era.[39] Closely intertwined with the history of the Manchester Academy and Dissenters in the city more broadly is the foundation (in 1781) and the subsequent history of the Manchester Literary and Philosophical Society, an institution that was profoundly concerned with the promotion of what, I contend, may be legitimately described as a culture of higher learning within Manchester and its surrounding area.[40] Thomas Percival, whom we have already met as chairman of the committee responsible for overseeing the establishment of the new Manchester Academy in 1786 and as a prominent member of the Cross Street Chapel congregation, became the society's first president.

It is worth focusing on Percival's own higher education trajectory, since it is typical of many of the prominent members and officers of the Manchester Literary and Philosophical Society in the first forty years of its existence. After completing his student years at the Warrington Academy, Percival proceeded to Edinburgh and then to Leiden, where he studied and graduated in medicine. While his father had been in business in Warrington, other members of his family, including his grandfather and an uncle, were doctors in the same town. Following his studies, Percival initially began his medical practice in Warrington but later, in 1767, settled in Manchester, where he would spend the remainder of his life. In 1765, two years before his move to Manchester, Percival was elected as a Fellow of the Royal Society. He is recognised as a pioneer in the field of town sanitation in Manchester, and as one of the earliest proponents of factory legislation. Notably, in 1781, the first meeting of the Manchester Literary and Philosophical Society took place at his house, and he served as its president until his death.[41]

The links between the Manchester Academy, the dissenting community in the city, and the Manchester Literary and Philosophical Society were strong during the early years of the latter. In addition to Percival as president, Thomas Barnes served as the secretary of the society for several years, alongside Thomas Henry, a chemist who also attended Cross Street Chapel. There were also strong links with the Manchester Infirmary, with several prominent members holding posts there – most notably, Charles White, one of the first surgeons at the infirmary as well as a founding member of the Manchester Literary and Philosophical Society, who would go on to be its vice president for some twenty-three years.[42]

The literary and philosophical societies have rarely been discussed as educational institutions or as bodies seriously interested in the theory and practice of education.[43] However, higher education and learning, in particular, were a regular feature of their debates. Unsurprisingly, perhaps, given the significant overlap in personnel, many of the attitudes expressed reflect those we have already encountered in the dissenting academies. A consistent feature of their debates about higher education was a determination to present themselves and their attitudes as being directly opposed to those that they thought prevailed at Oxford and Cambridge. This is perhaps clearest in papers presented to the society (and subsequently published in their *Memoirs*), which discussed Classical learning – not a field of inquiry often associated with the Manchester Literary and Philosophical Society, which has usually been viewed by historians as a crucible of the industrial revolution.[44]

Members of the Manchester Literary and Philosophical Society did not dismiss knowledge derived from reading ancient authors in general. Their criticism was directed towards a specific approach to Classical writers, which they associated with the cloistered world of Oxford and Cambridge. They believed that the Classics should be approached with an open and practical mindset, just like any other subject of study. According to George Gregory, an Anglican clergyman who presented a paper to the society in November 1793, the value of a Classical education for men of science depended entirely on the attitude and perspective with which it was approached; instead of the 'senseless definitions ... introduced by the School of Aristotle', he wrote, 'facts [must be] appealed to with confidence, as the only basis of solid argument'. For Gregory, Classical sources were only valuable in so far as they were investigated according to the 'more logical and less confused method of investigating truth [which] has been adopted of late years'.[45]

While admitting that the scientific significance of ancient writers had reduced in importance with the growth of modern discoveries, their work, Gregory claimed, was still valuable to contemporary men of science:

> Whoever expects to find in the ancients the perfection of science will be disappointed, but this will not warrant in us a total rejection of all the assistance which may be derived from this source ... I should wish to see the ancients studied for their matter, as well as for their language – But the information which they convey, is too commonly made a secondary consideration. The attention of youth is directed to the elegant latinity of Caesar and of Horace, not to the facts, observations, or precepts, which are contained in these valuable authors.[46]

Gregory advocated the approach he believed to be followed by men of science in France and Germany, who learned modern languages and studied works of modern science at the same time as ancient authors. 'They make themselves masters not only of the ancient, but of the modern languages', he wrote, 'they can converse with the well-informed of other nations, and they can read their works'. The type of education that Gregory was proposing was broad and open, embracing all subject areas, but it also proceeded with a due regard for scientific method. Men educated in this way 'are less likely to be the slaves of prejudice than the cloistered pedant', wrote Gregory.[47]

It is worth taking a moment to reflect on the origins of this particular attitude towards the Classics. As highlighted by Arnold Thackray in 1979, and evident in the case of Percival, many influential early members of the Manchester Literary and

Philosophical Society had received their education either at dissenting academies, particularly Warrington, or at Scottish universities, most commonly Edinburgh and Glasgow.[48] Significantly, these institutions fostered a different approach towards Classical authors compared to the ancient English universities of Oxford and Cambridge. The disdain expressed by members of the Manchester Literary and Philosophical Society towards the meticulous focus on 'niceties of language' associated with Classical studies at Oxford and Cambridge closely resembles similar sentiments expressed by notable figures at Scottish universities. For instance, in 1825, George Jardine, Professor of Rhetoric and Logic at Glasgow, declared that 'we do not, in this part of the kingdom, attach to classical learning that high and almost exclusive degree of importance which is ascribed to it elsewhere; thinking it of greater consequence to the students, to receive instructions in the elements of science, both mental and physical, than to acquire even the most accurate knowledge of the ancient tongues; of which all that is valuable may, it is thought, be obtained without so great a sacrifice of time and labour'.[49]

We see precisely this approach recommended in a paper introducing 'A Plan for the Improvement and Extension of Liberal Education in Manchester', which was read to members of the Manchester Literary and Philosophical Society in April 1783 by Thomas Barnes himself, and proposed the establishment of a 'College of Arts and Sciences' in the city.[50] Although ultimately unsuccessful, ceasing operations within a few years of its inception, the plan for the college reflected what Barnes perceived to be a real need in the city, namely a particular course of scientific studies designed for commercial life as well as for the professions of the law, medicine and divinity, and in this view he was strengthened by the existing members of the Manchester Literary and Philosophical Society.

Together with Thomas Percival, Charles White, Thomas Henry and various others, Barnes proposed a course of liberal education, which was intended to be compatible with the needs of commercial life. Lectures on 'Practical Mathematics, Chemistry, and the Fine Arts' were accordingly advertised, while Barnes proposed to give a course of lectures on the 'origin, history, and progress of arts, manufacturers, and commerce, the commercial laws and regulations of different countries, the nature of commutative justice; of oaths, contract, and other branches of commercial ethics'.[51] Significantly, Barnes viewed a thorough Classical training as an essential (though not exclusive) part of the education of young men who were to be engaged in commerce and industry. Once again, however, it was the attitude taken towards the Classics which mattered most. As Barnes made clear, 'the shreds and fragments ... which a boy picks up, in conning over the Latin and Greek authors are not surely deserving of the name of regular and systematic science. He must move from mere linguistic analysis to a systematic study of the content and information contained in the ancient authors. It is surely desirable, that he shall *now* rise, from words to things ... All that he has yet been doing, is preparatory to real knowledge. Language, of itself, is but a scaffolding to science.'[52]

Thus, as part of the curriculum for his new College, Barnes proposed a proper training in 'the LEARNED LANGUAGES ... which shall connect occasional remarks, on the history, mythology, philosophy, common manners, jurisprudence, &c. of ancient times, with the authors which shall be read'. In other words, it was not the grammar of the ancient languages which was to be studied, but rather the information the works contained. This can be seen by his clear focus on the different areas of knowledge to which ancient authors were held to contribute: 'history, mythology, philosophy, common manners, jurisprudence'. Under the same plan, students were also to be introduced to modern writers on similar subjects: history, law, logic, morals, belles-lettres, natural philosophy, chemistry, mathematics.[53]

Here, once again, we see the close links with the Manchester Academy, for this curriculum was very similar to the one developed for that institution when it was established three years later in 1786. It was even proposed that students at the academy who wished to study a wider array of subjects, including Chemistry, Anatomy and Physiology, would be able to attend lectures in these subjects provided by the new college. No less a person than Charles White, founding member and long-term vice president of the Manchester Literary and Philosophical Society, together with his son Thomas, delivered one of the earliest (if not the earliest) series of lectures outside London in connection with the new college.[54] This particular series was on Anatomy, and was delivered at the society's premises in 1783. White also began to carry out instructional anatomy lectures from his house in King Street in 1787, which is reminiscent of John Chorlton's decision to provide a course in 'university learning' from a private house in Manchester in the final years of the seventeenth century, as a successor to the Rathmell Academy which closed in 1698.[55]

As well as reading the Classics for the information they contained and in combination with modern authors, members of the Manchester Literary and Philosophical Society also recommended studying Classics in a context very different to that in the ancient universities: in conversation, in society, in the world. One paper presented in 1796 by the prominent abolitionist, Thomas Gisbourne, entitled 'On the benefits and duties resulting from the institution of societies for the advancement of literature and philosophy', argued that societies like the Manchester Literary and Philosophical Society placed a wide range of men and women who would not normally have access to universities 'within the reach of libraries stored with the information, ancient or modern, of which [they] stand in need'.[56] Such societies 'bring literature and philosophy from the college and the closet into public view', Gisbourne wrote, 'into the walks of common life, into scenes which would otherwise have been merely the haunts of business or of dissipation; and subject numbers to the influence and enrich them with the treasures of learning and science, to whom little was previously known of either but the name'.[57] This is perhaps one of the clearest articulations of the Manchester Literary and Philosophical Society's role as an institution of higher learning and education by one of its own members in the early years of its existence.

Another member of the teaching staff at the Manchester Academy to read papers to the Manchester Literary and Philosophical Society on the subject of higher education and learning was George Walker, Professor of Theology and head of the Academy from 1798 until its removal to York in 1803. He was also a future president of the Manchester Literary and Philosophical Society. In stark contrast with the image of Classical scholarship as the work of isolated pedants, a paper read by Walker on 15 November 1799, entitled 'A Defence of Learning and the Arts, against some charges of Rousseau', identified the ideal scientific persona with Cicero's definition of urbanity; while Cicero's *urbanitas* was closely connected with learning, it was nonetheless located in the cultured context of the *urbs* or city. The 'scientific man', Walker wrote, was he 'who has studied man as well as books, which alone deserves the name of true science'. Such a man was 'possessed of more nice discernment, more accuracy in weighing everything in the scale of sober judgement, more facility in resolving, combining, comparing, deciding'. He stressed that he did not 'ascribe this praise to the verbal critic, the mere mathematician, or the simple sciolist of any form'.[58] It was this view of ancient authors, as connected with civility and urbanity, which prompted early members of the Manchester Literary and Philosophical Society to recommend the Classics explicitly as part of an education designed for young men who were to pursue careers in industry and commerce. In so doing, they participated in a wider discussion in late eighteenth-century Britain about the need for learning to be grounded in social interaction, conversation and within a wider urban educational culture.

Connections between the Manchester Literary and Philosophical Society and Other Manchester-based Educational Initiatives

In its early years, the Manchester Literary and Philosophical Society built strong connections with a wide range of educational institutions across the city. We have looked in detail at some of these – the proposed 'College of Arts and Science', which was itself an offshoot of the society; the Manchester Academy, formed just three years after the society and led by some of its most prominent officers and members; and the Manchester Infirmary, which had been an important centre of medical training since the late 1750s. Another example is the Portico Library, which was established as a result of a meeting of Manchester businessmen in 1802, which resolved to establish an 'institute uniting the advantages of a newsroom and a library'.[59] A visit by four of the men to the Athenaeum in Liverpool had inspired them to develop a similar institution in Manchester. The Liverpool Athenaeum was founded in 1797 to ensure the up-to-date provision of newspapers and pamphlets, and to create a library for the use of the merchants and professional men in the city. For the Portico Library in Manchester, money was raised through 400 subscriptions from prominent Manchester families, and the library opened in 1806. Charles White, John Dalton and other leading members of the society were among the Library's most important supporters.[60]

By the end of the eighteenth century, several artists were offering tuition in drawing and painting in Manchester. In 1783, William Green, later a famous lakeland artist, opened an afternoon school for drawing and painting, which by 1786 had moved to his home in Brazennose Street. He continued to run a drawing school with his half-brother Hartley until he left Manchester for London in 1796.[61]

In December 1802, William Craig initiated an ambitious project to establish an 'Academy on a plan something like that of the Royal Academy, for the gratuitous instruction of one hundred young men, in the different departments of Drawing and Designing'. Craig's plan differed somewhat from that of the Royal Academy, however. The prospectus put forth by Craig stressed the artistic aspects of drawing, highlighting its role as an 'elegant amusement'.[62]

It also emphasised the potential commercial benefits arising from advancements in mechanics and manufacturing. Membership was limited to one hundred subscribers, each paying an annual subscription of a guinea, which entitled them to nominate a pupil for three months. This membership structure was designed to attract manufacturers and individuals involved in artistic trades so that they could utilise the academy as a training ground for their workers. The academy was exclusively open to men, and there were ambitious plans for an annual exhibition and the acquisition of a collection of antique casts. The initiative garnered support from the aristocracy, with the Earl of Wilton serving as the president; the subscribers included representatives from prominent mercantile and banking families such as the Hardmans and the Heywoods, who were also closely involved with the Manchester Literary and Philosophical Society. Despite operating in 1805, however, the academy closed shortly afterwards, for reasons that are not entirely clear.[63]

Other independent teaching establishments were successfully opened in Manchester in the early years of the nineteenth century. In 1814, the Manchester-based surgeon and prominent member of the Literary and Philosophical Society, Joseph Jordan, opened a school of anatomy in Bridge Street. Initially, teaching focused only on anatomy and took the form of lectures, demonstrations and dissections. Following a move to a larger premises in 1816, however, Jordan was joined by other teachers and the school offered a broader range of subjects. Just three years after the school first opened, the Society of Apothecaries recognised its lectures as acceptable in counting towards their members' diploma, the membership of the Royal College of Surgeons.[64] A few years later, in 1822, another Manchester surgeon, Thomas Turner, began lecturing on anatomy and physiology using rooms belonging to the Manchester Literary and Philosophical Society, of which he was a member. Following the success of these lectures, Turner established a school of medicine at a house in Pine Street, close to the Infirmary where he had previously worked as a house surgeon. Considered the first complete school of medicine outside of London, Turner persuaded other members of the society, including John Dalton (then president) to support his venture and even offer lectures at the school.[65] Once again, we see the closely interwoven and overlapping nature of the connections between different knowledge and educational institutions in early nineteenth-century Manchester.

The Royal Manchester Institution was founded on 1 October 1823 at a public meeting held by Manchester merchants, local artists and others keen to dispel the image of Manchester as a city lacking in culture and taste. The Institution was intended to hold regular art exhibitions, collect works of fine art and promote the arts generally. The initiative behind it came not this time from members of the

Manchester Literary and Philosophical Society, but from the growing community of artists in the city. The proposal to establish an art academy attached to the institution, which would admit pupils free of charge, proved particularly contentious. Many artists derived a significant part of their annual income from teaching painting and drawing. Charles Calvert, at the third public meeting, opposed an academy because it would 'eventually prove highly detrimental to the Professional Tutors in Art'. Accordingly, the proposal to establish an academy was rejected following a show of hands.[66] At the same meeting, however, plans emerged for a general educational institute attached to the institution, not only for 'opening a channel through which the works of meritorious artists may be brought before the public', but also for the 'encouragement of literary and Scientific pursuits'. The membership structure within the organisation was established through a hierarchy of governorships. For a payment of forty guineas, one could acquire a hereditary governorship that could be passed down to descendants. Alternatively, a life governorship could be obtained for twenty-five guineas, and an annual governorship could be secured by a payment of two guineas per year. The governance of the society was entrusted to a council elected by governors from within the membership. It is worth noting that the institution was not conceived of solely as a space for male socialisation, despite the prevailing homosocial nature often associated with artistic activities at this time. While governorships were limited to men, all governors were granted the privilege of bringing their wives and immediate family members to attend lectures, exhibitions, and other educational activities organised by the society.[67]

Until the early 1820s, however, most of the (higher) educational projects sponsored by the Manchester Literary and Philosophical Society were targeted at the middle and upper classes of the city, providing commercial, legal and liberal education to the sons of the city's growing industrial and mercantile elite. Its support for, and involvement in, the establishment of the small Manchester Mechanics' Institution in 1824 (the subject of a separate article in this special issue) was a departure from this pattern, with the overarching aim being to instruct artisans in the basic principles of science, especially mechanics and chemistry, through part-time study. Several prominent Manchester residents, including many leading figures in the Manchester Literary and Philosophical Society, met in the Bridgewater Arms on the High Street on 7 April 1824, to establish the Mechanics' Institution.[68] While the Manchester Mechanics' Institution was one of several such institutions founded around that time, the particular culture of the institution was also very much rooted in the particular social, cultural and educational matrix of Manchester, as Rachel Johnson demonstrates in her article in this special issue.[69] Peter Ewart, a millwright and engineer, and then Vice President of the Manchester Literary and Philosophical Society, took part in the meeting, as did the then-President, John Dalton. William Henry, who had been apprenticed to Thomas Percival at the Manchester Infirmary and who was a former secretary of the society, was also present, and the meeting was convened and chaired by two more leading Manchester Unitarians and members of the society, George William Wood and Sir Benjamin Heywood.[70]

Conclusions

When tracing the history of higher learning in Manchester, it is vital to go further back in time than the establishment of the city's first university. I have argued that the history of higher education and higher learning should not be reduced to the history of universities, something that has too often been the case. If higher education is instead defined as any effort to learn or study beyond the normal limits of secondary education (assuming that something akin to secondary education existed for even a limited section of society, as it did in Manchester in the period considered here), then we are freed from the institutional constraints of the university. Other spaces become potential sites of interest in such a history. These include public libraries, private houses, dissenting academies, hospitals and learned societies, all of which, in the case of Manchester, combined to create a rich and varied landscape of higher learning and education in the rapidly developing city prior to 1824.

The dissenting community, in particular the congregation at Cross Street Chapel and their wider links to northern dissenting networks, were instrumental in many of these efforts. Together, they created a distinctive alternative to traditional higher learning at Oxford and Cambridge. Inspired by the curriculum of the Scottish universities (where many of them were educated), they emphasised the value of natural sciences, modern languages and economics alongside classics and mathematics. This is especially clear in the foundation of Warrington and then Manchester Academies and the appointment of professors to teach chemistry, practical mathematics and modern languages. Through the crucial role they played in the early history of the Manchester Literary and Philosophical Society and the opportunities this offered for research and discussion of the latest developments in science and the arts, Manchester's dissenters extended their educational influence beyond formal learning institutions. They also became important sponsors and supporters of a wide range of other educational initiatives in the city, including the establishment in 1824 of the Manchester Mechanics' Institution, which is now looked back on as marking the foundation of the University of Manchester.

Notes

1. Robina McNeil, 'Manchester: Symbol or Model for the World?', in Adrian Green and Roger Leech (eds), *Cities in the World: 1500–2000*, 3 (Abingdon: Routledge, 2017), p. 151.
2. See, for example, Heather Ellis, 'Beyond the University: Higher Education Institutions Across Time and Space', in Tara Fitzgerald (ed.), *Handbook of Historical Studies in Education: Debates, Tensions and Directions* (Singapore: Springer International Handbooks of Education, 2020), pp. 1–17; William Whyte, *Redbrick: A Social and Architectural History of Britain's Civic Universities* (Oxford: Oxford University Press, 2015); Tamson Pietsch, *The Floating University: Experience, Empire, and the Politics of Knowledge* (Chicago: University of Chicago Press, 2024).

3 Robert D. Anderson, *European Universities from the Enlightenment to 1914* (Oxford: Oxford University Press, 2004), p. 12.
4 H. S. Jones, 'The Owens College Extension of 1870–3: Rethinking the Origins of the Civic University Tradition in England', *Bulletin of the John Rylands Library*, 100:2 (2024), 53–74.
5 William Whyte, *Redbrick: A Social and Architectural History of Britain's Civic Universities* (Oxford: Oxford University Press, 2015), p. 28.
6 Anderson, *European Universities*, p. 35.
7 Oliver Goldsmith, *An Enquiry into the Present State of Polite Learning in Europe* (London: J. Dodsley, 1759), p. 186.
8 Ian Atherton, 'Manchester Collegiate Church, 1558–1660', in Jeremy Gregory (ed.), *A History of the Collegiate Church and Cathedral, 1421 to the Present* (Manchester: Manchester University Press, 2021), p. 114.
9 Edward Baines, *History of the County Palatine and Duchy of Lancaster Vol. II* (London: Fisher, Son, & Co., 1836), p. 367.
10 Matthew Yeo, *The Acquisition of Books by Chetham's Library, 1655–1700* (Leiden: Brill, 2011), p. 229.
11 *Ibid.*, p. 228.
12 V. D. Davis, *A History of Manchester College: From its Foundation in Manchester to its Establishment in Oxford* (London: Routledge, 2016), p. 27.
13 *Ibid.*, p. 25.
14 Andrew Cambers, *Godly Reading: Print, Manuscript and Puritanism in England, 1580–1720* (Cambridge: Cambridge University Press, 2011), p. 141.
15 Heather Ellis, *Generational Conflict and University Reform: Oxford in the Age of Revolution* (Leiden: Brill, 2012), p. 31.
16 On the wider history of dissenting academies, see the ongoing work of the Dissenting Academies Project (www.qmul.ac.uk/sed/religionandliterature/dissenting-academies), in particular, the forthcoming monograph edited by Isabel Rivers and Mark Burden, *A History of the Dissenting Academies in the British Isles, 1660–1860* (Cambridge: Cambridge University Press). Older historiography on the dissenting academies includes Irene Parker, *Dissenting Academies in England: Their Rise and Progress and Their Place Among the Educational Systems of the Country* (Cambridge: Cambridge University Press, 1914); Herbert McLachlan, *English Education Under the Test Acts Being the History of the Nonconformist Academies, 1662–1820* (Manchester: Manchester University Press, 1931); J. W. Ashley Smith, *The Birth of Modern Education: The Contribution of the Dissenting Academies, 1660–1800* (London: Independent, 1954).
17 Joseph Thomas Fowler, *Durham University: Earlier Foundations and Present Colleges* (London: F. E. Robinson, 1904), pp. 19–21.
18 Davis, *A History of Manchester College*, p. 22.
19 *Ibid.*, p. 27.
20 *Ibid.*, p. 28.
21 *Ibid.*, p. 28.
22 *Ibid.*, p. 30.

23 *Ibid.*, p. 30.
24 *Ibid.*, p. 31.
25 *Ibid.*, p. 31.
26 *Ibid.*, p. 40.
27 Ralph Harrison, *A sermon preached at the dissenting chapel in Cross-Street, Manchester, March 26, MDCCLXXXVI, on occasion of the establishment of an academy in that town* (Warrington: W. Eyres, 1786).
28 Davis, *A History of Manchester College*, p. 45.
29 *Ibid.*, p. 47.
30 *Ibid.*, p. 48. Barnes's address was appended to and published alongside Ralph Harrison's sermon.
31 *Ibid.*, p. 48.
32 *Ibid.*, p. 49. This circular, originally published in 1786, is preserved in *The Monthly Review; or Literary Journal*, 80 (January–June 1789), pp. 719–22.
33 Davis, *A History of Manchester College*, p. 49.
34 *Ibid.*, p. 49.
35 *Ibid.*, p. 50.
36 *Ibid.*, p. 51.
37 *Ibid.*, p. 56.
38 Edward Mansfield Brockbank, *The Foundation of Provincial Medical Education in England and of the Manchester School in Particular* (Manchester: Manchester University Press, 1936), pp. 57–8.
39 J. W. Hudson, *The History of Adult Education* (London: Longman, Brown, Green and Longmans, 1851), pp. 166, 174, 213, 215, 218. On literary and philosophical societies in general, see Trevor Fawcett, 'Self-Improvement Societies: The Early 'Lit. and Phils'', in *Life in the Georgian Town: Papers Given at the Georgian Group Symposium* (London: Georgian Group, 1986), pp. 15–25.; Jon Mee and Jennifer Wilkes, 'Transpennine Enlightenment: The Literary and Philosophical Societies and Knowledge Networks in the North', *Journal of Eighteenth-Century Studies*, 38 (2015), 599. See also Jon Mee, *Networks of Improvement: Literature, Bodies and Machines in the Industrial Revolution* (Chicago: Chicago University Press, 2023).
40 On the history of the Manchester Literary and Philosophical Society, see Arnold Thackray, 'Natural Knowledge in Cultural Context: The Manchester Model', *American Historical Review*, 79 (1974), 672–709; Heather Ellis, 'Classical Authors and "Scientific" Research in the Early Years of the Manchester Literary and Philosophical Society, 1781–1800', *Intellectual History Review*, 32 (2022), 473–501; Mee, *Networks of Improvement*, pp. 41–66.
41 *Biographical Index of Former Fellows of the Royal Society of Edinburgh 1783–2002* (Edinburgh: The Royal Society of Edinburgh, July 2006), p. 728.
42 Stella Butler, 'White, Charles (1728–1813)', in Lawrence Goldman (ed.), *Oxford Dictionary of National Biography* (Oxford: Oxford University Press, 2004), https://doi.org/10.1093/ref:odnb/29238 [accessed 26 September 2024].
43 Heather Ellis, 'Beyond the University: Higher Education Institutions Across Time and Space', in Tara Fitzgerald (ed.), *Handbook of Historical Studies in Education: Debates,*

Tensions and Directions (Singapore: Springer International Handbooks of Education, 2020), pp. 1–17.

44 On the relationship between the literary and philosophical societies and the Industrial Revolution, see Peter M. Jones, *Industrial Enlightenment: Science, Technology and Culture in Birmingham and the West Midlands, 1760–1820* (Manchester: Manchester University Press, 2017), pp. 110, 113, and Joel Mokyr, *The Enlightened Economy: Britain and the Industrial Revolution, 1700–1850* (London: Penguin, 2009), p. 33.

45 George Gregory, 'On the Uses of Classical Learning', *Memoirs of the Literary and Philosophical Society of Manchester*, vol. 4, Part 1 (1793), p. 109. See also Ellis, 'Classical Authors and "Scientific" Research', 473–501.

46 Gregory, 'On the Uses of Classical Learning', 127.

47 *Ibid.*, 129.

48 Thackray, 'Natural Knowledge in Cultural Context', 690.

49 Michael J. Morris, '"A Manly Desire to Learn": The Teaching of the Classics in Nineteenth Century Scotland' (PhD thesis, Open University, 2008), p. 39.

50 Thomas Barnes, 'A Plan for the Improvement and Extension of Liberal Education in Manchester', *Memoirs of the Literary and Philosophical Society of Manchester*, vol. 2 (1785), p. 19.

51 *Ibid.*, p. 45.

52 *Ibid.*, p. 31.

53 *Ibid.*, p. 38.

54 Ann Félicité Tuxford and Willis J. Elwood (eds), *Some Manchester Doctors: A Biographical Collection to Mark the 150th Anniversary of the Manchester Medical Society* (Manchester: Manchester University Press, 1984), p. 69.

55 Brockbank, *The Foundation of Provincial Medical Education in England*, p. 37.

56 Thomas Gisbourne, 'On the benefits and duties arising from the institution of societies for the advancement of literature and philosophy', *Memoirs of the Literary and Philosophical Society of Manchester*, vol. 5, Part 2 (1798), p. 72.

57 *Ibid.*, p. 76.

58 George Walker, 'A Defence of Learning and the Arts, against Some Charges of Rousseau', *Memoirs of the Literary and Philosophical Society of Manchester*, vol. 5, Part 2 (1802), p. 457.

59 Nicholas Joseph Frangopulo, *Tradition in Action: The Historical Evolution of the Greater Manchester County* (Wakefield: E. P. Publishing, 1977), p. 82.

60 Tinsley Pratt, *The Portico Library, Manchester: Its History and Associations* (Manchester: Sherratt & Hughes, 1922).

61 Mary Elizabeth Burkett and J. G. Sloss, *William Green of Ambleside: A Lake District Artist, 1760–1823* (Kendal, Cumbria: Abbot Hall Art Gallery, 1984), p. 17.

62 Holger Hoock, *The King's Artists: The Royal Academy of Arts and the Politics of British Culture, 1760–1840* (Oxford: Clarendon Press, 2003), p. 91.

63 James Moore, *High Culture and Tall Chimneys: Art Institutions and Urban Society in Lancashire, 1780–1914* (Manchester: Manchester University Press, 2018), p. 68.

64 Brockbank, *The Foundation of Provincial Medical Education*, p. 87.

65 Stella Butler, 'Turner, Thomas (1793–1873), surgeon and founder of Pine Street School of Medicine', in Goldman (ed.), *Oxford Dictionary of National Biography*, https://doi.org/10.1093/ref:odnb/27871 [accessed 26 September 2024]; see also Jones, 'The Owens College Extension of 1870–3', 53–74.
66 Moore, *High Culture and Tall Chimneys*, p. 73.
67 *Ibid.*, p. 74.
68 Mabel Phythian Tylecote, *The Mechanics' Institutes of Lancashire and Yorkshire before 1851* (Manchester: Manchester University Press, 1957), p. 129.
69 Martyn Walker, *The Development of the Mechanics' Institute Movement in Britain and Beyond: Supporting Further Education for the Adult Working Classes* (Abingdon: Routledge, 2017). For more on the Manchester Mechanics' Institution, see Rachel Johnson, 'Aftershocks of Peterloo: Manchester Mechanics' Institution and Mutual Improvement', *Bulletin of the John Rylands Library*, 100:2 (2024), 33–52.
70 Tylecote, *The Mechanics' Institutes*, pp. 129–30.

Aftershocks of Peterloo: Manchester Mechanics' Institution and Mutual Improvement

RACHEL JOHNSON, ROYAL NORTHERN COLLEGE OF MUSIC/UNIVERSITY OF SHEFFIELD

Abstract

Manchester's Mechanics' Institution, established in 1824, has during the past two hundred years been co-opted into narratives increasingly remote from the essence of its foundations. A substantial body of literature has evaluated the Mechanics' Institution with a focus on 'social control', and has routinely privileged the history of 'science', narrowly conceived. Such histories have tended to conclude the Mechanics' Institution 'failed'. Detailed archival study, focused on the first ten years of the Mechanics' Institution's existence, tells a different story. This article places the foundation and early years of this institution within the story of Manchester and the broader history of working-class education. It explores some of the tensions and concerns underpinning its establishment, in particular the impact of the Peterloo Massacre, on Manchester's Liberal nonconformist leadership. It then traces a rapid movement from fear and distrust between different elements of Manchester's industrial society towards an environment where deeper levels of mutual support and understanding became possible.

Keywords: Manchester; mechanics; Liberalism; reform; education; elephant

The Manchester Mechanics' Institution was established at a meeting at the Bridgewater Arms on 7 April 1824. Its stated purpose, at its foundation, was 'to instruct Mechanics and Artisans in various Sciences, and their practical application to the Arts'.[1] This article examines this cornerstone, the political and social circumstances out of which it emerged, and the rapid changes to the institution's objectives during its earliest years. It looks in particular at the effect that the Peterloo Massacre had on Manchester Liberalism, and the direct impact this had on the Mechanics' Institution. In doing so it contextualises and complicates the history of the institution, assessing shifts in leadership and management, and identifying a mutuality which arose out of conflict and distrust, leading towards a transformation of relationships between different elements of this new and changeable industrial society.

The existing history of mechanics' institutes is dominated by a substantial body of literature dating from the 1960s and 1970s – texts that have emphasised paternalistic aspects of leadership and management, and adopt a 'social control' narrative. They focused on the scientific objectives of mechanics' institutes, and routinely dismissed them as failures for not delivering the education they initially planned to the mechanics and artisans they initially targeted. Brian Simon argued, in 1960, that mechanics' institutes were used by businessmen 'to instil their own doctrines'.[2] Richard Johnson wrote, in 1970, that 'the early Victorian obsession with the education of the poor is best understood as a concern about authority, about power, about the assertion (or the re-assertion?) of control'.[3] Edward Royle, writing in 1971, stated that power struggles within institutions meant that 'mechanics' institutes failed, and a potentially useful instrument of adult education was wrecked by ideological and class warfare'.[4] In 1977, Steven Shapin and Barry Barnes aimed 'to show how the founders of British Mechanics' Institutes thought a scientific education would aid in the social control of those artisans who were their designated target'.[5]

This historiography addresses important components of the history of Manchester's Mechanics' Institution. During the period of its establishment, there were national concerns about the 'lower orders', particularly in the manufacturing districts. The Member of Parliament Robert Slaney spoke in the House of Commons, in February 1833, about the need for 'safety valves', without which 'the working classes will fly to demagogues and dangerous causes'.[6] Benjamin Heywood, founding chairman (and later president) of the Manchester Mechanics' Institution, followed this line of thought in his Presidential Address at the Institution's annual meeting in 1836: 'the communication of moral instruction … to those great masses of men, who are now beginning to think and act for themselves, and whose influence on the general condition of society is every year becoming more important, is not only an act of justice, but a measure of safety'.[7] Narratives concerning the top–down hierarchy of the Mechanics' Institution, its educational priorities and its ultimate 'failure' have persisted. Taking the stated foundational aim of the institution as its starting point, the University of Manchester's website emphasises these aspects of its own history: 'the Mechanics' Institution was formed by industrialists who thought that artisans should learn basic sciences at evening classes. Its first building was near St Peter's Square. At times the Institute struggled because students had little basic education; primary schooling was not made compulsory in England until 1870. Artisans worked long hours and many saw little advantage in science studies.'[8]

These dominant narratives investigate and evaluate undeniably important aspects of the mechanics' institute movement's history. However, by focusing on 'science', and by centring narratives around what may count as 'successes' or 'failures' on the basis of historical and mid-twentieth century interpretations, such histories have tended to neglect substantial aspects of institutional life. The literature has also embedded some problematic wording within the discourse, such as 'establishment' and 'elite'.[9] The group of men who came to play central roles in this process (and they were all men) frequently described and perceived themselves as 'middle class', and while they recognised themselves as holding positions of authority, they did not describe themselves as 'elite'. Ideas about and conceptions of an emergent middle-class identity during the 1820s and 1830s are evasive, based as they are on individual actors' self-perceptions, which can only ever be partially gleaned from the archives. Where possible, this article aims to use language used by Manchester's men, from the archives, apart from when using specific language from specific items of scholarly literature in specific contexts.[10]

The historiography of the mechanics' institute movement has only recently been challenged. Helen Hudson Flexner's PhD thesis (2014) provides a nuanced analysis of the members of the London Mechanics' Institution and their occupations, which supports substantial working-class engagement, including evidence that student autonomy was encouraged.[11] Martyn Walker's book on the development of the mechanics' institute movement challenges the notion that mechanics' institutes 'failed' by drifting away from scientific and technical education; he has provided evidence that they did, in fact, retain a substantial focus on science and technical subjects, setting strong foundations from which technical and vocational education continued to develop into the twentieth century and through to the present day.[12] Helen Hudson Flexner has highlighted the 'sweeping generalisations' made in existing literature about the function and clientele of mechanics' institutes, critiquing how they have been imagined as 'identikit bodies', and has emphasised that mechanics' institutes cannot be understood without looking at specific examples within specific social and cultural contexts.[13]

Joanna Bourke's recent book for the bicentenary of Birkbeck, which began life as the London Mechanics' Institution, further develops this approach.[14] Some of the specifics of the early years of the London Mechanics' Institution are striking in their similarities to the early years of the Manchester Mechanics' Institution; some of the specifics are equally striking in their differences. One notable point of commonality between London and Manchester is that previous accounts about the success (or otherwise) of mechanics' institutes tend to refer back to their founding objectives, which were rarely met. In both London and Manchester, the founding objectives were almost immediately rewritten, and continued to be adapted as these institutions encountered and responded to the needs of their members.[15] Conversely, while the London Mechanics' Institution included mechanics and other working men in its management from the start, a fact that Bourke notes was particularly radical, this was not the case in Manchester, where anxiety regarding granting the membership autonomy and independence remained acute for some time.[16]

The early history of the Manchester Mechanics' Institution, therefore, cannot be abstracted from the parallel history of Manchester, or from the individual experiences of its founding members and subscribers. While it was part of a broader mechanics' institute movement, Manchester's Institution had unique origins and a distinctive identity. To understand these, we must go back, not to 1824, but to 1819 and the momentous events which occurred on St Peter's Fields in Manchester. The Peterloo Massacre catalysed a sea-change in the political landscape of Manchester, affording the emergent Liberal middle class the opportunity to capitalise on the groundswell of public opinion. The identity of Manchester Liberalism was fundamentally shaped by Peterloo, and in particular by the struggle to shape the narrative of Peterloo. The Mechanics' Institution's development during its first decade was therefore determined more by the aftermath of the massacre than by the actions and decisions made at contemporary mechanics' institutes. In turn, the Mechanics' Institution came to play an important role in the shaping of Manchester's new society.

Industrial Manchester is commonly regarded as a Liberal city – the home of the Anti-Corn Law League, an advocate for free trade and a free press, and instrumental in the passage of the 1832 Reform Bill. From the passing of this bill, when Manchester first achieved parliamentary representation, until 1868, its Members of Parliament were all Whigs, Liberals or (in the case of John Bright) Radical. Less familiar is how different Manchester's politics looked just a few years earlier. Prior to 1819, as Michael Turner has noted, a 'select Tory-Anglican circle' had kept a firm hold on local affairs for several decades.[17] To the alarm of members of this circle, the situation suddenly and rapidly changed. Calls for reform accelerated, gaining momentum from 1816 before exploding in 1819. The *Manchester Mercury*, a Tory newspaper, repeatedly expressed serious concern about the revolutionary potential of the reform movement, thinly concealed under layers of dismissiveness, sarcasm and satirical writing. Typical of the language used is the Editorial of 22 June 1819:

> The worshipful tribe of *itinerant Reformists* have not altogether abandoned their public performances. Yesterday, about twelve o'clock, a number of people assembled on the vacant site of ground in the vicinity of St Peter's Church, and surrounded a stage upon which a slender assemblage of the *professors of political oratory* were assembled ... They terminated their proceedings about three o'clock, and the people quietly dispersed, after bearing some most inflammatory language, and the proposition of a string of seditious resolutions.[18]

Events came to a head on 16 August 1819, when the peaceful gathering planned to take place at St Peter's Fields ended so disastrously. The day began with a carnival atmosphere, following patterns established over the years at rush processions and wakes in the region.[19] Samuel Bamford, one of the leading members of the Radical reform movement, wrote: 'it was deemed expedient that this meeting should be as morally effective as possible ... We had frequently been taunted by the press, with our ragged, dirty appearance at these assemblages ... and we concluded that, for once at least, these reflections should not be deserved.'[20] This fact was recognised by some among Manchester's middle class. John Benjamin Smith, then a young businessman but later chairman of the Anti-Corn Law League and Member of Parliament for Stockport, recalled that 'it seemed to be a gala day with the country people who were mostly dressed in their best and brought with them their wives, and when I saw boys and girls taking their father's hand in the procession, I observed to my Aunt: "These are the guarantees of their peaceable intentions – we need have no fears".'[21]

Given the increasingly feverish build-up of anti-Radical petitions, pamphleteering and press commentary in advance of the gathering, much of the Tory establishment could not accept that it might be a peaceful procession. There was serious concern that the Radicals would be armed, and that the gathering posed a threat to peace, property and life. The Reverend Edward Stanley described the people he saw prior to the meeting as 'sullenly peaceful' – a phrase markedly contradictory to accounts by Bamford and his fellow Radicals – and asserted that 'Hunt and Carlile are dangerous people, and any mob under their control must be dangerous'.[22] In consequence, the volunteer Manchester Yeomanry, backed up by the regular military, were called upon by the magistrates to disperse the crowd. Stanley recorded how, 'in much disorder and with scarcely the semblance of line, their sabres glistened in the air, and on they went, direct for the hustings ... and with a zeal and ardour which might naturally be expected from men acting with delegated power against a foe by whom it is understood they had long been insulted with taunts of cowardice, continued their course, seeming individually to vie with each other which should be first'.[23] Stanley's attempt to justify the actions of the Yeomanry could not mask the reality: with no warning, a minimally trained, untested and allegedly drunken militia charged into a peaceable and largely defenceless crowd, out of control of their sabres and their horses, slashing at and riding down men, women and children indiscriminately.[24]

While initially there were strenuous efforts to suppress reporting – the *Times* correspondent John Tyas was arrested – and to whitewash the whole affair, Tory attempts to control the narrative were ultimately unsuccessful. A sizeable proportion of Manchester's middle class, and of the country as a whole, were deeply shocked by the events which had taken place. As John Benjamin Smith described, 'the dispersion of a legally convened meeting by military force aroused a general indignation ... These proceedings produced a deep impression on the minds of thoughtful men, who began to think we were on the brink of despotism, and that the time had arrived when the country should be no longer ruled by Landowners and Boroughmongers, but by representatives chosen by the people.'[25] The influential reformer and journalist Archibald Prentice made similar observations about the growth of middle-class support for reform, and the effect Peterloo had at accelerating the cause: 'a deep sympathy for the oppressed and injured reformers prevailed amongst the middle classes ... It was a healthful sign of the times, which should not be passed over in silence; for sympathy with reformers gave the promise of co-operation in the work of reform; and from this period may be dated a marked and favourable change in the current of public opinion.'[26]

Over the following decade, Manchester's Liberal middle class rapidly gained powers previously held by the Tory elite. The *Manchester Guardian* was established as a direct result of Peterloo, amplifying the voices of the reformers and increasing the circulation and political legitimacy of their views. This was accompanied by increasingly prominent calls for positive action, for the provision of opportunities for social and moral 'improvement' for all classes, and for activities that would promote social cohesion. The first major institution to be developed out of this tumult was the Royal Manchester Institution (RMI). The RMI was established in 1823 'for the Promotion of Literature, Science, and the Arts'.[27] It was organised by and intended for the elite of the city, and aimed to foster closer relationships between members of Manchester's propertied class. The legacy of Peterloo is clearly visible in the pamphlets and press commentary surrounding its creation. Its initial proposals emphasised that:

> An Institution, such as this, would, moreover, serve as a point of union for the enlightened and liberal part of this widely scattered, and, in some respects, unconnected population ... besides the direct benefits which it would confer upon the community, [the Institution] would have the pleasing effect of removing prejudice, or softening the asperity of party feeling, and of fixing the public attention upon an object, with regard to which vehement differences of opinion can hardly be expected to arise.[28]

These proposals evidence the need its founders identified to create an institution that was set up in a way that would limit opportunities for conflict in the short term, and reduce conflict in the longer term.

The year after the RMI's foundation, the Mechanics' Institution was established. It was one of the earliest of a network of mechanics' institutes developed by philanthropists around the country for the education and improvement of the working man.[29] One of its first tasks was to secure land upon which to construct its own building, and to secure funds for that end. Its first purpose-built premises, on Cooper Street, opened in 1827 (this building no longer survives). In 1856, the institution moved to a new building on Princess Street, which does still exist. Its webpage proudly proclaims that, of the 'hundreds' of mechanics' institutes established around the same time, this one alone 'has survived to date as an autonomous body'.[30] The background to this claim is not clear; the name of the 'Manchester Mechanics' Institute' has been retained, but it currently exists primarily as a conference centre.[31] This building is perhaps best known today as the birthplace of the Trades Union Congress, who held their first meeting here in 1868.[32]

The overlap between the founding committee of the RMI and that of the Mechanics' Institution is remarkable. So too is the overlap between these individuals and the membership of Manchester's Literary and Philosophical Society, further explored by Heather Ellis in this volume. Equally striking is the overlap between these individuals and the prominent voices from Manchester's Liberal response to Peterloo. The founding committee of the Mechanics' Institution (below) was comprised of men typical of the leadership of Manchester's civic and philanthropic organisations during the 1820s and 1830s; they were predominantly Liberal and dissenting, in many cases Unitarians worshipping at the Cross Street or Mosley Street Unitarian Chapels. Members of these chapels held key positions within the Literary and Philosophical Society, Manchester Statistical Society, Manchester Guardian, RMI, Mechanics' Institution and Athenaeum.[33] The Manchester Guardian, established by the Unitarian John Edward Taylor, positioned itself as the of Liberal reform.[34] Its consequent support for the Mechanics' Institution and other institutions is evident in the column inches devoted to them throughout their early decades. Benjamin Heywood (1793–1865), banker and philanthropist, was the founding Chairman, later styled President, of the Mechanics' Institution until 1841; he was also a Vice-President of the Manchester Athenaeum at its foundation, and served as President of the RMI in 1840. The philanthropist George William Wood (1781–1843), a partner in a hat-making business and a Member of Parliament from 1832, was concurrently Chairman of the RMI, a Vice-President of the Athenaeum, and a Director of the Mechanics' Institution. William Fairbairn was named as the institution's first Secretary. The founding committee were as follows:[35]

'At a numerous meeting of Gentlemen friendly to the Establishment of a Mechanics Institution in Manchester held on Wednesday the 7th of April 1824 at the Bridgewater Arms; Benjamin Heywood, Esq. in the Chair'

Mr John Kennedy [McConnel & Kennedy cotton mills]	Mr John Pooley [cotton-spinning mill owner]
Dr William Henry [physician and chemist]	Mr James Murray
Mr George William Wood [businessman, MP from 1832]	Mr Richard Roberts [Sharp, Roberts & Co.; engineer]
Mr Thomas Sharp [Sharp, Roberts & Co., manufacturers of equipment including locomotives]	Mr William Fairbairn [Engineer; Fairbairn & Lillie]
Mr Benjamin Heywood [banker, MP from 1831]	Mr Thomas Hopkins
Mr Peter Ewart [engineer]	Mr John Davies [chemist]
Mr Robert Hyde Greg [textile manufacturer, owner of Quarry Bank Mill]	Mr William Williams [Peel & Williams engineering firm]
Mr James McConnel [McConnel & Kennedy cotton mills]	Mr Lawrence Buchan
Mr Henry Houldsworth, jun. [influential cotton spinning family]	Mr Jonathan Cocker [iron works owner]
Mr Thomas Hoyle [calico printing; Mayfield print works]	Mr David Bellhouse [builder]
Mr Henry Marsland [cotton mills and bleach works; MP from 1835]	Mr Joseph Brotherton [cotton mills owner; Swedenborgian minister; MP from 1832]

The leadership of the Mechanics' Institution during its early years was sensitive to allegations that the institution was failing to attract mechanics and artisans. They regularly published lists of subscribers, designated by profession, in their annual reports. They also tended to champion notable achievements within the institution by individuals who aligned closely with the founding objectives (for example, in relation to annual prizes in 1834), while also continuing to emphasise to as broad

TRADES, &c.		TRADES, &c.	
Architects	1	Brought Forward	249
Attorneys	2	Joiners and Builders	22
Basket-makers	1	Leather Factors	1
Bleachers	1	Letter-press Printers	1
Block-cutters	1	Mechanics and Machinists	27
Booksellers, Binders and Stationers	5	Merchants and Manufacturers	44
		Makers-up	3
Bricklayers	1	Millwrights	4
Brush-makers	1	Overlookers	8
Cabinet-makers	6	Packers	1
Callenderers	2	Painters	5
Calico-Printers	12	Paper-makers and Stainers	1
Carvers and Guilders	3	Pattern Drawers	5
Chemists and Druggists	7	Pawnbrokers	2
Clerks	94	Plumbers and Glaziers	2
Clock and Watch-makers	2	Publicans and Malsters	3
Colliers	3	Reed-makers	1
Coopers	3	Salesmen	4
Corn Dealers	6	Schoolmasters and Ushers	11
Cotton Spinners	31	Shopkeepers	2
Common Brewers	2	Silkmen and Manufacturers	5
Drapers	7	Smiths	4
Draughtsmen	1	Spindle-makers	1
Dressers and Finishers	3	Stay-makers	1
Drysalters	1	Stone-masons	6
Dyers	5	Surgeons	12
Engineers	6	Surveyors	7
Engravers	14	Timber Merchants	1
Fanlight-makers	1	Tinplate-workers	1
Fustian Cutters	2	Tool-makers	2
Grocers and Tea Dealers	8	Upholsterers	1
Hair Dressers	1	Umbrella-makers	1
Hatters	6	Warehousemen	27
Iron Founders and Dealers	9	Weavers	3
Jewellers	1	Wire Drawers	3
Forward	249	Total	471

Number and Classification of Subscribers, 1st May, 1828.

Figure 1 List of subscribers published in Annual Report of 1828.

an audience as possible the range of activities they offered and the benefits they brought, in the hope of recruiting more subscribers from their target audience. The list of subscribers published in the Annual Report in 1828 (Figure 1) highlights the diversity of members' occupations. 'Mechanics' and 'artisans' evade precise definition, and how individuals chose to define themselves further complicates the picture, but the MMI's membership evidently consisted of a broad cross-section of Manchester's industrial workforce.

The 1834 annual report prize list and commentary emphasised limits in the prior education of prizewinners and how far they had come, with the information delivered by Benjamin Heywood as part of his Address to those present at the annual meeting, and published as part of the report.[36] Thomas Farnworth, for example, 'knew nothing of drawing' before joining the Mechanical Drawing Class. Heywood said that Farnworth was a journeyman when he joined the class, and 'now he works on his own account: his diligence in availing himself of the instruction he has received here has not merely, he says, been of great service to him as a designer, but has enabled him to effect some valuable improvements in the machinery used in his business, for which he has made his own drawings and superintended the construction of the machines'.[37] The first prizewinner in the architectural drawing class, said Heywood, 'had not the slightest knowledge of drawing when he entered the class, 3½ years ago; he was, until lately, only a journeyman, but the execution of this and other similar drawings has brought him into notice, and he has lately commenced business on his own account'.[38] In the mathematical classes, the first prize

> for the solution of questions in Algebra, Trigonometry and Fluxions, has been awarded to *Isaac Newton*, a journeyman cotton-spinner, who entered the Institution ignorant of the rule of three. His diligence and earnestness to improve himself are most exemplary; he speaks very gratefully of the value this institution has been to him, and says he owes all he knows to it, beyond the mere rudiments of education. His acquirements have now enabled him to open an evening school.[39]

Isaac Newton also won a French prize. John P. Spencer, who won the grammar class prize, was 'not only indefatigable in his own improvement, but in assisting the teacher in his instruction of the other pupils'.[40] John Jerom, a clerk and second prizewinner in grammar, 'knew nothing of grammar when he entered the class; by his own exertion to improve himself, he has already advanced himself considerably in the world'.[41] Many of these prizewinners, including Isaac Newton (in 1834) and John Jerom (in 1836), went on to be elected to the Mechanics' Institution's committee.

When looking at the activities that these subscribers had access to, existing histories tend to state that the Mechanics' Institution's broadening of its activities and objectives during its early history was a deviation from its founding objectives. The reality does not appear to be quite so clear-cut. Heywood's initial 'Address' (1825) included references to how the institution was designed to support amusement, broader 'useful knowledge', and leisure.[42] Activities beyond 'science' were therefore fundamental to the institution's work from its establishment. The library was particularly important at this very early stage of existence, offering 'books of history, voyages and travels, and other works of amusement and instruction, for the benefit of those who may take a less lively interest in scientific subjects, or who may wish to become acquainted with other branches of useful knowledge'.[43] The prominent place of the library in the early annual reports, at the top of the front page, reflects the pride that the directors took in this part of their activities. This impression is heightened by the extensive pages in the minute book during the early years of the institution, listing every book purchased for the library as well as every book donated.

Classes and lectures were slower to become established, but this seems inevitable given that the directors first needed to have their building constructed. In its earliest years, classes were offered in mathematics, and in mechanical and architectural drawing, alongside lectures on various scientific topics. The 1828 annual report included reports and syllabuses for Nicholson's lectures on mechanics and Davies's lectures on chemistry, and reports for Cottam's arithmetic and mathematics classes, Chapman's mechanical drawing class, and Hadfield's architectural drawing class. Cottam had mastered the art of exceedingly polite criticism, writing in his report:

> I cannot conclude this report without bearing testimony to the respectful conduct and the attentive application of the students in general; at the same time, I cannot but regret that many have remained so short a time in the class, as not to make that progress which those have done who have steadily persevered for a longer period. I trust, however, that no one has left the class without deriving benefit proportionate to the time he has attended.[44]

It is fascinating to trace from this starting point the variations in classes and activities at the Mechanics' Institution during its early years. They rapidly expanded into a diversity of activities deemed appropriate by the committee for working-class leisure, from gardening to gymnastics, and classes soon included subjects as diverse as vocal music and figure, flower and landscape drawing. The rapidity with which schedules shifted away from initial conceptions of science appropriate for artisans should not be surprising, when the other interests and activities of committee members are considered. Comparing the Mechanics' Institution's committee with the membership of Manchester's Literary and Philosophical Society is particularly striking. In 1831, George William Wood was vice-president of that society, John James Tayler was secretary, Benjamin Heywood was the treasurer, and the list of ordinary members represents a roll call of Manchester's leading manufacturers and civic figures: Hugh Hornby Birley, James and Samuel Darbishire, William Fairbairn, Robert Hyde Greg, Henry Houldsworth, Alexander Kay, the McConnels, John Potter, Archibald Prentice, the Reverend J. G. Robberds and Absalom Watkin. John Dalton was at that time the president.[45] Manchester's leading citizens were fully supportive of, and personally engaged in, intellectual sociability, individual improvement and the pursuit of knowledge.

The variations in activities were accompanied by variations in the wording of the institution's aims. In 1835, a *Sketch of the Objects and Advantages of the Manchester Mechanics' Institution* was published and included in the annual report, which began:

the object of the Institution is to instruct the Working Classes in the principles of the arts they practice, and in other branches of useful knowledge, excluding party politics and controversial theology. At a small expense, the Workman may not only acquire a more thorough knowledge of his business, and a greater degree of skill in the practice of it; but he will also be better qualified to advance himself in the world, and be better entitled to secure to himself and his family the means of comfort and enjoyment.[46]

Under the heading of 'Lectures', it stated that 'Monday and Friday Evenings are set apart for Lectures on a great variety of useful and interesting objects; such as the various branches of Natural Philosophy, Mechanics, Chemistry, Electricity, Geography, Geology, Botany, Astronomy, Physiology, Natural History, and General Literature'. A list of evening classes is included:

EVENING CLASSES

Annual Report (1835)

Evening	Class	By Whom Taught
Tuesday	Grammar	Mr James Turner
	Architectural Drawing	Mr James Knox
	Vocal Music	Mr A. Ward
	German	Mr Charles N. Weiss
Wednesday	Arithmetic	Mr S. E. Cottam
	Mechanical Drawing	Messrs Hadfield and Lewis
	Elocution and Composition	Mr James Turner
Thursday	Figure, Landscape, and Flower Drawing	Mr Chas. Calvert
	Latin	Mr A. M. Dougall
Saturday	Writing	Mr I. P. Hemm
	Algebra and Geometry	Mr S. E. Cottam
	French	Mr L. A. J. Mordaque

The Mutual Improvement Society meets every alternate Thursday evening – Mr JOHN STANFIELD, Honorary Secretary.

In 1836, the annual report proudly announced there had been eighty-nine lectures during that reporting year, and the diversity of subject matter in both classes and lectures is impressive (Table 1).

Based on these facts and figures, and on the enthusiastic communication captured in the printed annual reports, the Mechanics' Institution would appear to have experienced steady growth and expansion in its membership, its educational work, and its social activities. Deeper analysis of the reports and the minute books reveals some conflicts and concerns, however, from both the directors towards the subscribers and from the subscribers towards the directors. The shifting

TABLE 1
Details of lectures in 1836 (taken from the *Annual Report* (1836), pp. 13–14).

No.	Subject	Delivered by
2	Acoustics	Mr Robert Addams
2	Electro-Magnetism	Mr Robert Addams
5	Meteorology	Dr Dalton
6	Animal Physiology	Mr Greaves
7	Art of Reading	Mr F. B. Calvert
8	Modelling and Casting in Plaster, &c	Mr Bally
4	Optics	Mr Addams
1	Music	Mr A. Ward
5	On the Radiated Classes of Animals	Dr R. E. Grant
3	Heraldry	Mr Newton
8	Arithmetic, Theory of	Mr S. E. Cottam
1	Atomic Theory	Dr Dalton
8	Philosophy of the Atmosphere	Mr Sweetlove
3	Steam Navigation	Dr Lardner
6	Mechanics Applied to the Arts	Rev. H. Moseley
4	Electricity	Mr S. E. Cottam
8	History and Construction of the Steam Engine, and its application to the Arts	Mr C. F. Partington
8	Chemistry	Mr Hemming

89 Lectures since the 23rd February, 1835

perspectives and prejudices identifiable between 1824 and 1836 reveal important and underexplored facets evident within this phase of Manchester's development into an industrial city. Howard Wach argued the 'industrial middle-class elite' felt themselves to be in a position of 'stewardship' over their city and its inhabitants.[47] He explained that 'the textile merchants, manufacturers, bankers, and medical and legal professionals composing this "elite" were acutely conscious of their status as both local notables and the vanguard of a newly reconfigured system of production'.[48] However, it appears that in Manchester in the 1820s, the apparently genuine philanthropic intentions of the new Liberal leadership were tempered by ongoing anxiety about potential revolutionary activities, exacerbated by a lack of understanding or of mutual experiences across class boundaries.

For starters, there was a deliberate distinction from the outset between subscribing members and honorary members. The first printed set of rules, dated 28 July 1824, communicated that donors of ten guineas or more would become honorary members of the institution for life. Only honorary members were invited to attend the annual general meeting, and early annual reports were explicitly and repeatedly addressed only to the honorary members.[49] This caused some discontent among the subscribing members (who paid five shillings quarterly). In 1832, a meeting was organised between the subscribers and the directors, soon after the annual general meeting, so that the annual report could be shared with the subscribers too.[50] This turned out to be the start of a fundamental change within the institution, explored further in this article.

Heywood's own preconceptions about Manchester's working classes are particularly evident in his aforementioned Address, which was written for and distributed to parts of the population that the Mechanics' Institution wished to recruit as subscribing members.[51] The Address was didactic, patronising and frequently demonstrated a lack of awareness of the interests and needs of the working classes that it was directed towards. 'You will be pleased with the lectures', he asserted; 'you will very soon become interested in the subjects which will here engage your attention ... Your wives and your children will necessarily share in your improvement ... you will be better, as well as happier men.'[52] There is a striking difference between the tone of this speech and the tone he used when addressing the honorary members in other texts.

As well as evidence of limited understanding of who the subscribers actually were and what they wanted, together with evidence of the deliberate separation of classes within the Mechanics' Institution, the record is peppered with evidence of serious concern within the leadership about what might happen if the subscribers were given too much power. There were recurring anxieties around relinquishing control to the subscribing members, or even to giving subscribing members a voice. The institution's rules expressly excluded party politics and controversial theology. The library had its own rules and resolutions, the first publication of which was dated 3 September 1824. The very first point of these was a resolution that also insisted 'that works on Party Politics and Controversial Theology be excluded from the Library, as inconsistent with the objects of the Institution'; this was immediately followed by a second resolution, 'that, to guard against the possible introduction of immoral works, all Books presented to the Institution be subjected to the approval of the Directors, before they are placed in the Library'.[53]

After 1828, there was a gradual move towards allowing subscribing members to have greater involvement in institutional committees. At the meeting in May 1832, Heywood asserted in his Address:

> We have been told that [limited attendance by the working classes] is mainly attributable to a defect in our constitution, whereby the subscribers are withheld from all share in the management, this being retained by the honorary members, who can neither sufficiently know nor provide for the wants of the general body. But this is not the fact – those who established the Institution, conceived that, in its infancy, it would need their care and direction, but they had never any thought of retaining its exclusive management. In the year 1829, five of the subscribers were selected by the directors to assist them in the management – in the following year these five were chosen by the subscribers themselves, and in the next year, the election, from their own body, of one half of the board of directors was assigned to them. So it continues now, and at almost every meeting of the board, the directors chosen by the subscribers from amongst themselves, constitute a majority.[54]

These claims add gloss to a story that, when comparing the printed reports against the handwritten minutes, is rather conflicted. The texts of subcommittees are not preserved in the minutes, but judging by the number of subcommittee meetings held between 1828 and 1834 concerning rules and regulations, this topic was hotly debated. Requests for changes put forward by the membership were frequently discussed, but not agreed by the directors. Proposals put forward by the directors, including a proposed 50:50 division of directors between honorary and subscribing members, were not agreed by the membership. Such discord was alluded to by Heywood later in the same Address, with these suggestive lines: 'how little of personal intercourse and kindly feeling is there between the labouring classes and those of us, who, in the course of providence, are placed in circumstances above them, and of how many evils is this alone the cause. Let us break through this unnatural barrier, and thereby become ourselves active instruments in the physical and moral improvement of our poorer brethren.'[55]

In early 1834, an agreement was finally reached, and the outcome was reported at the annual meeting:

> The Directors rejoice to inform you that a bill for a reform in the management of the Institution having passed their own board *unanimously*, and having been sent up to the honorary members for consideration, has been approved by them, and will come into operation in the ensuing month. It removes that part of the distinction which was obnoxious, between the honorary members and the subscribers ... The Directors will hereafter be elected wholly by and from the general body.[56]

Similar debates and conflicts can be found played out in relation to the establishment and development of the Mutual Improvement Society. The fact that the subscribing members of the Mechanics' Institution gained such confidence and assertiveness so close to 1832 cannot be a coincidence. This early history of the society encapsulates the major shifts in perspectives and perceptions that occurred in the early 1830s, coming to a head at the same time that the determination of the subscribing members to achieve parity in the institution's leadership reached its zenith. On 6 February 1833, the directors of the Mechanics' Institution received a letter signed by 147 subscribers. On 21 February 1833, documents concerning the establishment and rules of a Mutual Improvement Society were inserted in the minutes.[57] Benjamin Heywood later said about this proposal that 'many and earnest were the objectors to the establishment of this Mutual Improvement Society. We were told of the discord it would inevitably introduce into the Institution; that it would soon become a low debating club, composed of ignorant declaimers, or noisy and brawling disputants, who would bring discredit upon themselves and upon the Institution.'[58]

As with requests to modify rules, regulations and leadership, debates at committee level as to whether or not this society was appropriate appear to have become heated. There were subcommittee discussions, some backwards and forwards between committees, and a condition on the formation of this society was that a set of rules specifically for the Mutual Improvement Society were written by the directors, to be agreed to before the society could start to function. Despite this behind-the-scenes disagreement, it was announced in the annual report in 1834, in a neutral tone, that:

> A society has been formed amongst the members, which meets on every alternate Thursday evening, and which is called the Mutual Improvement Society. It has for its object, to facilitate the acquisition of useful knowledge and to promote social intercourse amongst the members. One of the members reads a paper on some subject of interest which has occupied his thoughts, and general conversation upon it ensues. It now consists of upwards of seventy members.[59]

Subjects of conversation within the Mutual Improvement Society between its establishment in 1833 and the 1834 annual meeting were listed in the report on the latter.[60]

1.	The Philosophy of Apparitions	John Jerom
2.	Emigration	R. A. Phillips
3.	The Moral Influence of the Drama	H. Stanley
4.	City Missions and Provident Societies	T. Bigland
5.	The Necessity of the Introduction of an Improved System of Education among the Poor	R. A. Phillips
6.	Virtual Velocities	Edmund Clarke
7.	The Philosophy of a Candle	S. E. Cottam
8.	On Sound	S. E. Cottam
9.	The Evils of the Poor Laws	R. A. Phillips
10.	Antipathies and Prejudices	John Stanfield
11.	A Diary of a Ten Days' Tour in Scotland	John Spencer
12.	Intemperance and its Remedy	Thomas Dutton
13.	On the Advantages resulting from Education	Samuel Kershaw
14.	The Pleasures and Advantages derivable from the Study of Botany	Isaac Franklin
15.	Advantages to be Derived from the Study of the Dead Languages	Richard Sargeant
16.	Animal Magnetism	Philip Taylor
17.	Trip to Liverpool	John Jerom
18.	Christmas and its Customs	John Stanfield

Although hard-won by the subscribing members, the direct contact between different classes within the institution necessitated by combined directorships, open meetings and subscriber-led societies appears to have rapidly, permanently and positively altered relationships between the previously distinct groups. There are numerous indications of these changes in the record. By 1834, the semantics of the annual report had shifted. These texts were now addressed to the members, who attended these meetings alongside honorary members and a more balanced committee. An excerpt from the annual report for 1834 effectively highlights the change: 'on Tuesday evening, February 25th, 1834, the members of the Mechanics' Institution held their first annual meeting for transacting the general business of the

Institution, and for the election of Directors for the ensuing year, by ballot, from their own body. On this occasion a considerable number of the members attended to avail themselves of the new privilege.'[61]

Once the new committee had been elected, the published list of directors included their professions.[62] The occasion was clearly momentous for all parties, since an equivalent list does not appear to have been issued for previous lists of directors at the Mechanics' Institution, and it does not seem to have been repeated. The institution described its new form of leadership thus:

BENJAMIN HEYWOOD, Esq., PRESIDENT

Mr JOHN DAVIES, VICE-PRESIDENT

DIRECTORS

Mr Edw. Norris, merchant	Mr Isaac Newton, spinner
Mr I. Shimwell, manufacturer	Mr Wm Johnson, surveyor
Mr Benj. Fothergill, merchant	Mr R. A. Phillips, clerk
Mr P. Ewart, jun. merchant	Rev J. G. Robberds, minister
Mr Jas. Brackenbury, solicitor	Mr S. D. Darbishire, solicitor
Mr I. A. Franklin, optician	Mr W. Birmingham, merchant
Mr John Stanfield, clerk	Mr William Hewitt, clerk
Mr John P. Spencer, clerk	Mr Jno. Taylor, schoolmaster
Mr William Langton, banker	Mr R. Armstrong, civil engineer

The growing friendly relations across the social hierarchy of the Institution are also apparent in the activities undertaken and the tone in which they were reported. Heywood's Address of 1834 provides a wonderful example. He described a visit to Liverpool by a group including himself, 'between 30 and 40 in number, by the early train on the railway', where they were met by the president and secretary of the Liverpool Mechanics' Institution. Heywood gave a brilliant account of what was clearly the highlight of his day: 'we went first to the Zoological Gardens; one of our party read to us the descriptive account of the animals, as we stood round their respective enclosures, and I must not omit to mention, among other gratifications there, a ride upon the elephant'.[63]

Another striking example of Heywood's changing perspectives may be found in his vivid description, in 1836, of the Mutual Improvement Society's festive 'supper party' the previous Christmas. He described, with warmth, his place in the gathering of around eighty people, highlighting in particular the alignment between the conviviality he experienced at these gatherings and his own perceptions of high moral standards: 'it has been my privilege to be present at all the festive meetings of the Mutual Improvement Society . . . I can say, with all sincerity, that I have never been in any company where the proceedings were marked with more good feeling and good taste – where the spirit and harmony of the evening were more uninterruptedly preserved, and where the sentiments expressed and the mode of expressing them, were more pleasing.'[64] The contrast in tone between Heywood's addresses to the Mechanics' Institution's membership in the 1830s, and the tone of his addresses to its membership and potential membership in the 1820s, is striking. The shift from 'you' in his original 1825 Address to 'I', 'our' and 'we' is particularly notable. There is a clear progression in these reports from entrenched differences between classes to mutual understanding, and from separation to connection and collegiality.

This early history of Manchester's Mechanics' Institution leads to a re-evaluation of the history of adult education and the historiography of industrial reform. It highlights the tremors and aftershocks that seismic events such as Peterloo had across all aspects of the societies in which they occurred, resulting in some quite unexpected cultural changes. No one could have predicted, in the conflicted fragmented political world of Manchester in 1819, that a mere fifteen years later, a man who had just served as Member of Parliament for Lancashire would be riding an elephant in Liverpool with members of Manchester's working classes. The history of the Mechanics' Institution contains an element of 'social control', grounded in politics, but 'social control' was only ever one part of a more complex picture. 'Mutual improvement' looks to be a more accurate descriptor for how these early years of a new institution played out in practice. Conceptions around the diffusion of knowledge at the beginning of the nineteenth century were made possible by collegiality and community, mutually beneficial interactions and an openness to finding different ways not just of learning, but of living in a new society.

Notes

1 'Rules of the Manchester Mechanics' Institution' (1824), in *Report of the Directors of the Manchester Mechanics' Institution* (Manchester: Printed by R. Robinson, 1828), p. 23. Minutes and annual reports are held at the Manchester Mechanics' Institution archive at Manchester, University of Manchester Archives, GB 133 MMI, MMI/2.
2 Brian Simon, *Studies in the History of Education* (London: Lawrence & Wishart, 1960), p. 216.
3 Richard Johnson, 'Educational Policy and Social Control in Early Victorian England', *Past & Present*, 49 (1970), 119.
4 Edward Royle, 'Mechanics' Institutes and the Working Classes, 1840–1860', *Historical Journal*, 14 (1971), 306.
5 Steven Shapin and Barry Barnes, 'Science, Nature and Control: Interpreting Mechanics' Institutes', *Social Studies of Science*, 7 (1977), 32.
6 Peter Bailey, *Leisure and Class in Victorian England: Rational Recreation and the Contest for Control, 1830–1885* (London: Methuen, 1987), p. 36.
7 Benjamin Heywood, 'Presidential Address to the Manchester Mechanics' Institution Annual Meeting', *Manchester Mechanics' Institute Annual Report* (1836), p. 5. The statement is a quotation from a contemporary commentator, but Heywood did not state his source.
8 'History of UMIST', *The University of Manchester*, www.manchester.ac.uk/discover/history-heritage/history/umist/ [accessed 25 February 2024].

9   This is sometimes addressed in the literature, such as in Richard Trainor, 'Urban Elites in Victorian Britain', *Urban History Yearbook*, 12 (1985), 1–17; more frequently, the terminology is used and re-used without comment or definition.
10 For a detailed exploration of this issue, see Dror Wahrman, *Imagining the 'Middle Class': The Political Representation of Class in Britain, c.1780–1840* (Cambridge: Cambridge University Press, 1995).
11 Helen Hudson Flexner, 'The London Mechanics' Institution: Social and Cultural Foundations 1823–1830' (PhD thesis, University College London, 2014).
12 Martyn Walker, *The Development of the Mechanics' Institute Movement in Britain and Beyond: Supporting Further Education for the Adult Working Classes* (London and New York: Routledge, 2017).
13 Helen Hudson Flexner, 'The London Mechanics' Institution', pp. 9–10.
14 Joanna Bourke, *Birkbeck: 200 Years of Radical Learning for Working People* (Oxford: Oxford University Press, 2022).
15 See *Ibid.*, p. 42.
16 *Ibid.*, pp. 22–4.
17 Michael Turner, *Reform and Respectability: The Making of a Middle-Class Liberalism in Early Victorian Manchester* (Manchester: Chetham Society, 1995), p. 3.
18 'Editorial', *Manchester Mercury* (22 June 1819).
19 Robert Poole, 'The March to Peterloo: Politics and Festivity in Late Georgian England', *Past & Present*, 192 (2006), 109–53.
20 Samuel Bamford, *Passages in the Life of a Radical* (London: Frank Cass & Co., 1967), pp. 176–7.
21 F. A. Bruton (ed.), *Three Accounts of Peterloo by Eyewitnesses Bishop Stanley, Lord Hylton and John Benjamin Smith* (Manchester: Manchester University Press, 1921), p. 66.
22 *Ibid.*, pp. 21 and 41 respectively. Stanley viewed the events of the day from the house occupied by the magistrates – entirely unexpectedly from his perspective, since he happened to have business with the owner of the house. He was cautiously critical of the actions of the magistrates and Yeomanry, but still used language as per the above to describe the Radicals.
23 *Ibid.*, p. 15.
24 M. L. Bush, *The Casualties of Peterloo* (Lancaster: Manchester Centre for Regional History, 2005).
25 Bruton (ed.), *Three Accounts*, pp. 71–4.
26 Archibald Prentice, *Historical Recollections of Manchester Intended to Illustrate the Progress of Public Opinion from 1792 to 1832* (London: Frank Cass & Co., 1970; originally published 1851), p. 170. Prentice (1792–1857) was an influential reformer and journalist. He visited St Peter's Fields as the crowds arrived, and although he did not witness the cavalry charge, he did witness its aftermath. He was instrumental in raising awareness of the atrocity (he and John Edward Taylor wrote the two accounts published in London papers the day after it happened, while the *Times* journalist remained in detention) and he was part of the relief fund committee.
27 Manchester, Manchester Archives and Local Studies, M6/1/79/1 (Mr G. W. Wood's Copy of the Exchange-Herald's Pamphlet relating to the Public Meeting of 1 Oct. 1823).

28 William Robert Whatton, *An Address to the Governors of the Royal Institution of Manchester* (Manchester: Henry Smith, 1829).
29 Mabel Tylecote, *The Mechanics' Institutes of Lancashire and Yorkshire before 1851* (Manchester: Manchester University Press, 1957).
30 'Our History', *Mechanics' Conference Centre*, www.mechanicsinstitute.co.uk/our-history/ [accessed 24 February 2024].
31 It appears to have changed function, and ownership, multiple times since the 1860s, usefully summarised in an article by Michael Herbert, 'The Manchester Mechanics' Institute', *Manchester's Radical History*, 11 November 2011, https://radicalmanchester.wordpress.com/2011/11/11/the-manchester-mechanics-institute/ [accessed 24 February 2024].
32 'Our History', *TUC*, https://www.tuc.org.uk/about-tuc/our-history [accessed 13 October 2024].
33 Howard Wach, 'A "Still, Small Voice" from the Pulpit: Religion and the Creation of Social Morality in Manchester, 1820–1850', *The Journal of Modern History*, 63 (1991), 426–7. See also Ellis, in this volume, for connections between earlier initiatives and the Cross Street Chapel.
34 John Edward Taylor (1791–1844), businessman, editor and publisher, was a trustee of Cross Street Chapel and the son of a Unitarian minister.
35 Manchester, University of Manchester Archive, GB 133 MMI/1/1 (Minute Book 1824–83).
36 Benjamin Heywood, 'Address', *Annual Report* (1834), pp. 11–12.
37 *Ibid.*
38 *Ibid.*
39 *Ibid.*
40 *Ibid.*
41 *Ibid.*
42 Benjamin Heywood, *An Address to the Mechanics', Artisans, &c. by Benjamin Heywood* (Manchester: Robinson and Bent, 1825).
43 *Ibid.*
44 *Annual Report* (1828), p. 17.
45 *Memoirs of the Literary and Philosophical Society of Manchester*, second series, vol. 5 (London: Baldwin & Cradock, 1831), pp. 566–7.
46 *Annual Report* (1835), p. 32.
47 Wach, 'A "Still, Small Voice"', 426–7.
48 *Ibid.*, 425.
49 *Annual Report* (1828), p. 24.
50 Manchester Mechanics' Institution report (May 1832).
51 Heywood, 'Address' (1825).
52 *Ibid.*, pp. 9, 15.
53 Printed in the *Annual Report* (1828), p. 25.
54 *Manchester Mechanics' Institution Report* (May 1832), p. 8.
55 *Ibid.*
56 *Annual Report* (1834), p. 8.

57 Minutes (6 February 1833), p. 52; (21 February 1833), p. 54.
58 *Annual Report* (1834), p. 7.
59 *Ibid.*, p. 5.
60 *Ibid.*, pp. 5–6.
61 'Election of Directors', *Annual Report* (1834).
62 *Annual Report* (1834).
63 *Ibid.*
64 *Annual Report* (1836), p. 6.

The Owens College Extension of 1870–73: Rethinking the Origins of the Civic University Tradition in England

H. S. JONES, UNIVERSITY OF MANCHESTER

Abstract

This article demonstrates that the 'extension' of Owens College, Manchester – the ancestor of the University of Manchester – in 1870–73 represents an important and misunderstood moment in the history of English civic universities. The new model of governance instituted by the extension movement subsequently became normative for the civic universities, and remained largely in place throughout the twentieth century. The reformers set out to devise a model of public accountability appropriate for a public institution as distinct from a private trust. The article centres on the relationship between James Bryce and the lay leaders of the extension movement, and explores the connections between the Owens College reform, the Taunton Commission's inquiry into the endowed grammar schools, and contests over the control of three major educational foundations in Manchester (Chetham's Hospital, Manchester Grammar School and Hulme's Charity).

Keywords: Civic universities; endowments; liberalism; university governance

Introduction

The institutional forms of universities have usually been slow to change, and the changes they do undergo have commonly been disguised in terminology that emphasises their antiquity.[1] They award 'degrees' conferred by chancellors, and they are run by vice-chancellors (in Italy, 'magnificent rectors') and senates. These institutions thus bear the imprint of the political assumptions, and sometimes political struggles of particular moments in the past. A crucial but much misunderstood moment in the formation of English civic universities was the 'extension' of Owens College, Manchester, in 1870–73. This was the moment when the institutional forms took shape that continued to govern the University of Manchester right up until 2004. This reform was of much more than local significance, however: because the governance arrangements introduced in the Owens College constitution of 1870–71 were adapted, with minor modifications, for use by the federal Victoria University established in Manchester in 1880, they were also inherited by its descendants when the federal university was dissolved in 1903. This meant that they governed not just the Victoria University of Manchester, as it was formally known, but also the universities of Liverpool and Leeds. The University of Birmingham, whose foundation in 1900 helped precipitate the break-up of the federal

Victoria University, also borrowed extensively from its model of government.[2] This model thus became normative for English universities created in the twentieth century and remained so until the 1960s, and survived in the civic universities into the twenty-first century.

It is therefore important in the diachronic history of English universities. Indeed, it had some significance for world universities too, as the northern civic universities were emulated from Dundee to Calcutta. Indian universities were profoundly shaped by the Sadler Commission (1917–19), whose members included three veterans of the dissolution of the Victoria University in 1903.[3]

This article demonstrates that the innovations that underpinned the reconstitution of Owens College can best be explained as expressions of a particular conception of liberal reform forged in the context of the wider political battles of early and mid-Victorian Britain, and inflected in some quite specific ways by the politics of Manchester in particular. The story of the reshaping of this civic college thus offers an important example of how enduring institutional forms are shaped by the contingent circumstances of their creation.

The Owens College Extension

Owens College had been established in 1851, in fulfilment of the terms of the will of the cotton merchant John Owens (1790–1846), who left a sum of almost £100,000 for the instruction of young men 'in such branches of learning and science as are now and may be hereafter taught in the English universities'.[4] After a faltering start, student numbers were increasing by the early 1860s, and overtook those of University College, London. By 1865, the College had concluded that its existing premises in Quay Street were inadequate for its needs, and had set up a Buildings Committee to identify a new location. This was the beginning of the campaign for the College's 'extension', a process that came to fruition in 1870–73.[5] This is a moment that has tended to be written out of university history, both the pre-history of the University of Manchester and the wider history of universities, partly because the label 'extension' seems to imply an incremental process of expansion rather than fundamental reconstitution. The institutional innovations that occurred, then, are often conflated in the literature either with the founding of Owens College in 1851, or with the founding of the federal Victoria University in 1880.[6]

The process of 'extension' comprised two principal elements. Legally, it entailed the incorporation of a new body, the Extension College, by means of an Act of Parliament of 1870, followed in 1871 by a further Act that enabled the amalgamation of the Extension College with the existing Owens College (which had never been incorporated), and the establishment of a new scheme of government. This procedure enabled the new College to escape some of the prescriptions of John Owens's will, notably the government of the College by a close trust appointed in the first instance by Owens himself and thereafter self-renewing; and, after extended parliamentary debate, the restriction of the College to male students, although women were not in fact admitted until 1883.[7]

In parallel with the legal reconstitution of the College, an extensive fundraising campaign was launched to finance the purchase of land and the construction of new buildings, and the endowment of new professorial chairs. This was imperative, not least because the trustees of John Owens's will were not empowered to spend endowment funds on the purchase of buildings. The campaign raised more than £200,000, and a further legacy of over £100,000 from the German-born engineer Charles Beyer meant that the original endowment was more than quadrupled.[8] This campaign depended on forging much closer bonds between the College and the business and professional communities of Manchester and the wider region. This was made possible by the new governance arrangements, which were intended to ensure the accountability of the College's governors to 'public opinion', a concept much invoked by the extension movement.

The new scheme of government was thus crucial in creating a new kind of relationship between Owens College and the city's mercantile elite. The only existing study of the extension, by W. H. Chaloner, ignored the significance of the new constitution.[9] But eight decades after it was introduced, it was celebrated by a Manchester Vice-Chancellor, Sir John Stopford, who told the university's Court of Governors that that constitution was a 'daring experiment' which had decisively shaped the theory and practice of English universities. He was clear what the innovation was: whereas Owens's will placed college government entirely in the hands of the trustees that he had himself in the first instance nominated, the constitution of the reorganised college established a delicate balance by distributing powers among lay governors, academics and alumni.[10] In particular, that constitution established the tripartite structure that remained substantially intact in Stopford's university: the Court of Governors, the supreme governing body, consisting overwhelmingly of laymen; the Council, the executive body, with a lay majority but including the principal and two professorial representatives; and the Senate, consisting of the principal and the professors, with de facto jurisdiction over strictly academic matters.[11]

The constitution was drafted by a figure of some importance in British intellectual and political history. James Bryce was then at the start of a many-sided career. As a scholar, he was a jurist, a historian, a political scientist, an Americanist, a geographer, an early practitioner of the study of race relations and of international relations, and a founding fellow (and early president) of the British Academy. As a public man, he was a Member of Parliament, a cabinet minister, a humanitarian campaigner, an ambassador and a serial chair of commissions of inquiry and the like. He was an indefatigable traveller and a mountaineer of some distinction. His association with Owens College is understandably submerged under the avalanche of his many other activities. Still, he was Professor of Jurisprudence from 1870 to 1875, and a part-time lecturer for three years before that. The fact that he drafted the new constitution is known in the literature, but has never been commented upon. Why was he commissioned to draft it? When he did so he was not yet a professor at the College, but merely a part-time lecturer assisting the Professor of Jurisprudence, Richard Christie; and he was much less experienced as a lawyer than several members of the Extension Committee, including Christie himself and the

Unitarian solicitor Robert Dukinfield Darbishire, a key creative force behind the movement. Bryce did not live (and never lived) in Manchester.[12]

The Extension College's constitution committee commissioned Bryce to draft a constitution for the College in June 1869. There is little evidence bearing on how he came to be appointed, but we do have the instructions issued to Bryce by the constitution committee. We also have the draft that Bryce produced, and the amendments made first by the constitution committee and then by the Owens trustees, and of course, the agreed text, which varied only slightly from Bryce's draft.[13] The central feature of that text is the tripartite division in the governance of the College, with power distributed among three distinct bodies: the Court, the Council and the Senate. These powers were not formally separate, for the members of the Council were elected by the other two bodies, eight by the Court, two by the Senate, the other two being ex officio members; Senate consisted of the professors, who were appointed by Council; while Senate and Council had (limited) representation on the Court. Importantly, lay governors predominated, and, equally, lay members elected by the Court from its own membership greatly outnumbered the academic members on Council. There was also representation in the Court for former students of the College (designated 'associates', not 'graduates', since the College did not award degrees in its own right). This was a status that had come into being in 1858, with strict criteria for admission; but now, for the first time, the associates had a formal role in governance.

This tripartite academic polity merits attention, for this was the model that was adopted by the federal Victoria University and thereafter by most English civic universities of the first half of the twentieth century.[14] It institutionalised the role of laymen (meaning, in this context, non-academics) in university governance, while at the same time planting the seeds of academic self-government in the civic universities. Given how enduring this model proved, it is reasonable to ask where Bryce derived the idea of this separation of powers, whether it was his conception, and what problems it was designed to address.

To explore where Bryce may have derived the idea, the first question to ask is what precursors this system had. Delicate equilibria were by no means a novelty in themselves in university history. Oxford and Cambridge had historically been constituted according to a kind of Gothic federalism in which the parts (the colleges) had grown in power at the expense of the whole (the university). Indeed, Bryce himself would later analyse the universities of Oxford and Cambridge as federal structures in the appendix to the first volume of his *American Commonwealth*, entitled 'The federal system of the English universities'.[15] Graduates (strictly, Masters of Arts) were powerful, and constituted the supreme governing body, Convocation, while week-to-week executive power was wielded by the Hebdomadal Board (later, the Council) consisting of the College heads. Colleges, meanwhile, were democracies of the fellows constituted as the governing body, chaired by the head; while the head, elected by the fellows but well-nigh irremovable once elected, held executive power in his hands via the appointment of fellows to the College offices.[16] The reforms of the 1850s clipped the wings of Convocation and transferred the bulk of its powers to the revived House of Congregation, composed of the resident dons; and they diminished the powers of the heads both by ending their monopoly of membership of Council, and by somewhat constraining their executive omnipotence within their own college. In that respect, the tendency of Victorian reforms in Oxford – and much the same was true of Cambridge – was to strengthen the academic democracy, or the omnipotence of the dons.[17] There was no 'lay' (non-academic) element unless the Masters of Arts in Convocation (most of them country clergy) could be conceived in that way; Convocation was certainly a counterweight to academic self-government, although a much-diminished counterweight after the Oxford University Act of 1854.

A more obvious counterpart to Owens College was University College, London; much more so than the University of London.[18] Owens recruited its first two principals from University College, and was indebted to its model in several important respects, not least its refusal of religious tests.[19] But in terms of governance University College did not offer many usable lessons. True, it had a Council and an Academic Senate, and its scheme of governance was certainly studied by the Owens Extension Committee.[20] University College was, however, a proprietorial institution until 1869, when private legislation put an end to proprietorial rights, but transformed shareholders into governors with a right to nominate their successors, alongside life governors appointed by Council.[21] Senate was defined in the bye-laws rather than in the College's constitution and was formally advisory. It did not yet have a clearly demarcated responsibility for strictly academic matters; nor was there professorial representation on Council. There was no structured relationship with public authorities, civic or national. The Radical social innovator Henry Solly, a student at the College back in the 1820s, sensed that he now saw a 'noble institution degenerating into a close corporation of co-opted rulers'.[22] In this sense, University College's governance model, although suggestive, was much less advanced than that forged by Owens in 1870.

The Scottish universities, meanwhile, were themselves in a position of flux in this period. The Universities (Scotland) Act of 1858, a fundamental legislative intervention, imposed a large degree of homogeneity on institutions that had previously been very different. It put an end, for instance, to Edinburgh University's subjection to the town council.[23] It even held out the abortive hope of a single examining university for Scotland. Henceforth, the universities were governed according to a tripartite institutional structure. Confusingly, in their case (as, in fact, in Bryce's initial draft for Owens) the Court was the small executive body: seven members, of whom one (the rector, elected by the student body) by tradition did not attend. The Senate (or *senatus academicus*) consisted of the professors, and had a similar role to its counterpart at Manchester, with the important difference that it, rather than the Court, was primarily responsible for financial management; while the General Council consisted of the graduates of the university.[24] This system of governance gave no influence to the city, or to the professional or business communities of the region, except in so far as they could incidentally speak through the graduates in Council. Indeed, in the case of Edinburgh, the Act of 1858 liberated the university from its subordination to municipal opinion. Bryce was very familiar with the Scottish university system, not only because he had studied at Glasgow before the reforms of 1858, but also because his father (another James Bryce), as the founder and long-term secretary of the Glasgow Graduates' Association, had led the movement for, as he put it, 'the infusion of a popular element into the management of our Universities' through the representation of the graduates.[25]

What was distinctive and new about the Owens College scheme was the institutionalisation of the dominant role of lay members in the structures of authority. Here, Bryce's scheme had a clear purpose. Under the terms of John Owens's will, the College since its foundation had been ruled by a body of trustees, somewhat in the manner of an American private college. The trustees were appointed in the first instance by Owens himself, mostly from among his friends in the Manchester business community. His business partner, George Faulkner, was the first chairman of the trustees; Faulkner's successor was Alderman William Neild, a calico printer and latterly a banker, and on his death in 1864, Neild was succeeded by his son Alfred. Pragmatically, it was necessary to the success of the extension movement that it should have the backing of the existing trustees, who had in any case proved, for the most part, both committed to the interests of the College and careful not to step on the toes of the principal and professors. The Extension Committee, too, being chiefly focused on raising subscriptions from the Manchester business community, was dominated by laymen with commercial or professional backgrounds, such as Thomas Ashton and Robert Darbishire. So the explanation for the preponderance of laymen in the governance of the incorporated college lay on the one hand in path dependency, and on the other in the power of money. The Council appointed in 1870 drew substantially on the outgoing trustees: Robert Darbishire, Murray Gladstone (the Prime Minister's cousin) and W. H. Houldsworth were members of both bodies, and Alfred Neild, the last chairman and treasurer of the Trustees, was the first chairman of the Council and treasurer of the College. Some of these – Darbishire above all – had been closely involved in the extension movement, and they were joined on the Council by the leading figures of that movement: Thomas Ashton, Richard Christie and (as a representative of Senate) the Professor of Chemistry, Henry Roscoe, who was, more than anyone, the driving force behind the extension movement.[26]

Still, it was not simply that lay governors were in the ascendant: the question was, which laymen, and how were they chosen? In this respect, the fullest exposition of the thinking that lay behind the new constitution can be found in the remarks made by Thomas Ashton to a subscribers' meeting in December 1869:

> The Committee, in framing the constitution of the College, had endeavoured to establish a governing body which should not be too large to remove the feeling of individual responsibility from each of its members, and yet at the same time sufficiently permanent to prevent the College suffering from any uncertainty of management. The constitution also offered to the public the opportunity of making known its increasing or changing wants, by the admission of a certain number

of nominated members, and also by the introduction of members selected by the Government and by the corporations of Manchester and Salford. The Committee hoped that by those measures they had provided against what seemed to be the natural tendency of all institutions to permit the growth of abuses amongst them.[27]

Or, as the Owens College Extension Act of 1870 – drafted, in the first place, by Robert Darbishire – would put it, there was a need to place higher education in Manchester and its neighbourhood 'under the management of a public body rather than of trustees of private nomination'.[28] The instructions issued to Bryce in 1869 had indeed drawn attention to 'certain inconveniences inherent in the nature of a private trust' and 'the obvious necessity of affording to the contributing public … sufficient guarantees for the right use, the due administration and the effective maintenance of the enlarged institution'; these considerations made it necessary to place the new foundation 'on an assured basis as one homogeneous Public Trust'.[29] The constitution approved in 1870 addressed this issue by establishing a balance between a majority of life governors appointed in the first instance by Act of Parliament and thereafter self-renewing, and a large minority of governors nominated by or from stakeholder bodies: central and local government, local Members of Parliament and former students of the College.

To understand why Ashton and his colleagues on the Extension Committee attached such importance to the distinction between a public and a private trust, we must turn to the wider context of educational reform in the 1860s, in Manchester and beyond; and in the first place to the Schools Inquiry Commission, which was the work that brought Bryce to Manchester in the first place.

James Bryce, the Taunton Commission and 'Representative' Trusts

When he was commissioned to draft the Owens College constitution Bryce was a young man of 31. He had nevertheless established his scholarly reputation very young, with his study of *The Holy Roman Empire*, first published in 1864. He had also taken on his first public office in 1865, as Assistant Commissioner for the Schools Inquiry Commission (the Taunton Commission), appointed in 1864 to investigate those schools – largely the endowed grammar schools – that had been outside the remit of both the Newcastle Commission on the elementary schools and the Clarendon Commission on the great public schools. This was one of the fundamental royal commissions that reshaped British social institutions in the nineteenth century. The first complete investigation of the tangled mess of English secondary schooling, it began the process of subjecting those schools to systematic public control.[30] It identified a subset of the endowed schools that were in a position to compete with the great public schools previously investigated by the Clarendon Commission. As Jonathan Parry writes, its effect was to create the late-Victorian public school system – no trivial legacy.[31] It was also largely responsible for the establishment of secondary schooling for girls.[32]

Bryce was a mere assistant commissioner, charged with the empirical investigation of the schools of Lancashire and, later, of Shropshire, Worcestershire and large parts of Wales. But the modest title should not lead us to underestimate his significance. Detailed work on the ground gave him – and some of his fellow assistants, such as Joshua Fitch – an authority that surpassed that of most of the actual commissioners. Of all the assistants, Bryce was the one who was cited most in the final report. It was he, more than anyone, who pressed on the commissioners key questions about provision for girls' schooling and the proper mode of governance for endowed schools.

Fundamentally, the problem that the Commission was charged with resolving was this: there was no central or local government funding for secondary schools, and at the time there was no political appetite to institute such funding. There were several thousand secondary schools, many of them in possession of endowments, in some cases inadequate but in other cases more than adequate for the number of pupils they currently educated. The perception was that if these resources were conceived as public property in the broadest sense – and charitable endowments were by definition destined for a public purpose – they were sufficient to meet national needs. But their geographical spread was uneven; they were inefficiently managed; and endowed schools were constrained by the terms of the endowment which often prevented them from offering a non-classical education, or from charging even modest fees. This was an obstacle to the extension of the curriculum to embrace 'modern' subjects, notably science and modern languages. Further, endowments were more or less entirely limited to the education of boys, whereas there was a growing sense of the need to make equivalent provision for the education of girls.[33]

An important context here was the highly contested place of historic endowments in Victorian politics.[34] Endowed foundations were at the heart of the fight over institutional reform: municipal corporations, Irish bishoprics, English cathedral chapters, Oxford and Cambridge colleges, public schools, parochial charities and city livery companies: all were subject to public investigation, and all to a greater or lesser degree fought back by challenging the authority of the state to redeploy or redefine the purpose of their endowments. Typically, Conservatives defended what Disraeli called 'the sacredness of Endowments', whereas Gladstone pushed back with the charge that existing institutions gave 'far too much scope for the action of local prejudice and selfish interest as against the public welfare'.[35]

Some Liberals, such as Gladstone's first Chancellor of the Exchequer, Robert Lowe, were trenchantly opposed to the very existence of charitable endowments, and instead looked to market mechanisms to ensure an education system responsive to market mechanisms. Lowe had previously been responsible for instituting 'payment by results' in elementary schools. Other Liberals and Radicals conceived of education as a public good, and were concerned not to eradicate endowments but instead to subject them to public control so that they served the public interest. This was Bryce's position, and in fact he later crossed swords with Lowe in the press on the uses of university endowments.[36] His report found that the system of endowed schools had the advantage of 'publicity', by which he meant that, as opposed to proprietorial schools, the endowment made the school less dependent on parents, but also more accountable to wider 'public opinion'.[37] The English system of management by local bodies of respectable citizens was 'more conformable to the genius of English institutions' than the system of direct state control that was held in continental Europe to be the only way of ensuring the public accountability of schools.[38] But he acknowledged that the reality often fell a long way short of this ideal of accountable local administration. Trustees would sometimes forget the proper conception of trusteeship as 'a delegated authority ... to be exercised for the good and in accordance with the wishes of the people', and instead regard their office as 'a private and personal affair', even 'the hereditary possession of their family or their connexion'. Such 'narrowness and cliqueishness in governing bodies' tended to alienate the local citizens from the school. Bryce noted a general wish in Lancashire towns 'to see some measure adopted whch may give a more distinctly public character to the school, and induce the citizens to feel a real practical interest in all that belongs to it'.[39]

One of the key conclusions in Bryce's report was that governing bodies should be reconstituted through 'the infusion of a representative element', which would have the effect of giving the townspeople 'a more direct and lively interest in the welfare of the school'.[40] This was a particular concern of Bryce's, although Fitch, reporting on Yorkshire, likewise held that 'the constitution of governing bodies' was one reason for the decline in the endowed grammar schools he investigated.[41] Fitch had some especially interesting things to say on this point, observing that members of governing bodies needed two qualities which were rarely combined: 'specific knowledge of the neighbourhood and its wants', and 'a general knowledge of education, and on the principles on which it should be given'. The former would be most likely to be found in 'reputable and intelligent inhabitants of the place'; the latter, by 'men of higher education at a distance, who are free from local prejudices, and who are capable of taking what Comte calls *vues d'ensemble*'. Governing bodies should be so constituted as to allow for an appropriate number of both.[42] But it was Bryce who formulated the concept of the *representative* governance of a trust, a concept which was introduced into English public discourse by the Schools Inquiry Commission and its aftermath.[43]

Bryce was clear that an active governing body, aware of its public responsibilities, was essential to the effective operation of an endowed school. We can get a sense of his concerns from his reports on schools that he thought particularly defective in this regard. Blackburn Free Grammar School could trace its origins to a pre-Reformation grammar school taught by a chantry priest, and had been re-established under Elizabeth I with a permanent income out of the extinguished chantry endowment. Bryce evidently regarded it as inadequate: it had fewer than a hundred pupils on its roll, whereas he judged that the population of Blackburn and surrounding towns was sufficient to sustain a grammar school of three hundred boys or more. It did not send boys on to Oxford or Cambridge. Some of the reasons for its failure were common to much of Lancashire, such as parents' lack of interest in any kind of liberal education, whether classical or modern. But the specific reasons were much more to do with the inadequacy of the governance. There were no fewer than fifty governors, of whom it was rarely possible to get as many as five or six at a meeting; and they were a self-electing body who excluded non-Anglicans, with the result that nonconformists in the town regarded the school as an alien institution to which they would not subscribe, for instance for new buildings. Apart from new and larger buildings, the single most important change needed was 'the reconstitution of the governing body, diminishing its numbers, infusing into it a representative element, and placing it in communication with some central authority which may stimulate and guide its action in raising the character of the school'.[44]

Similarly, he thought that Middleton Grammar School, to the north of Manchester, urgently required 'the establishment of a local governing body who are likely to interest themselves in its welfare', whereas since its foundation in the sixteenth century it had been run by Brasenose College, Oxford, which had been scandalously neglectful.[45] A few miles to the west, Bolton Free Grammar School had a local governing body of twelve, who were required to be freeholders in the parish. They were also required to be Anglicans, however, and it was a self-renewing body. In practice, it was difficult to get a quorum of seven, and decisions were effectively delegated to an Education Committee with a quorum of three. The school, Bryce found, had 'no air of prosperity about it'. He recommended that 'a representative element ought to be infused into the trust, so as to stimulate the action of the board of trustees, and give to the town more interest in the school'.[46]

Bryce did not equate a representative element with the elective principle. In some cases, it is true, he found that elected officials ran schools well. He admired the Lancaster Free Grammar School, whose fifteenth-century founder entrusted it, along with an endowment, to the care of the mayor and corporation. The success of the school, which had 158 pupils, exemplified 'the advantage of making the management of a school really public': it ensured that the local inhabitants took pride in the school because they regarded it as theirs. He noted that the effective management of Lancaster Grammar School did not prove that other town councils would be equally judicious if entrusted with control over schools, but he at least inferred that 'cases like Lancaster show the desirability of infusing a representative element into those boards of trustees, which are at present, like those of so many Lancashire schools, stagnant, exclusive, devoid of public spirit'.[47] It was openness, rather than election, that mattered. By a representative trust, Bryce primarily meant a body of trustees who were broadly accountable to local – and in some cases national – public opinion.[48]

We can see that point when we consider the largest and best-endowed school that Bryce inspected: Manchester Grammar School. It was one of those endowments of sufficient national importance that the Commissioners themselves made formal recommendations in their report.[49] The composition of the body of twelve trustees ('feoffees') had been much contested, and had been substantially reformed in 1849, although they remained a self-renewing body. When Bryce visited, he found them to be 'persons of influence in the city, [who] appear to enjoy its confidence, and although the cares of business do not permit them to give much continuous attention to the school affairs, they seem to take a lively interest in its welfare'. Bryce was, however, critical of the fragmentation of responsibility embodied in the school's constitution, which he found 'somewhat complicated'.[50] The head ('High Master') and the usher were appointed not by the feoffees, but by the President of Corpus Christi College, Oxford, who otherwise had no role in the school; while the Dean of Manchester was *ex officio* visitor, and in conjunction with the High Master he had responsibility for appointing the other teaching staff. In cases of disagreement between the Dean and the High Master, the feoffees acted as umpire. The Commission thought that it was inadvisable to have 'more than two seats of authority' in a school, namely more than the governing body and the head, and recommended that the separate powers of the President of Corpus Christi and the Dean of Manchester should be abolished, although they might be *ex officio* governors.[51] This recommendation was implemented in the scheme drawn up by the Charity Commission in 1875, and implemented in amended form in 1877. The President of Corpus Christi and the Dean of Manchester became *ex officio* governors, along with the mayors of Manchester and Salford; eight representative governors were appointed by the Corporations of Manchester and Salford, by the justices of the peace for Manchester and Salford, the Manchester and Salford School Boards, and the Universities of Oxford and Cambridge. These twelve would be balanced by 'co-optative' governors: initially the twelve existing trustees, who were entitled to serve for life, gradually falling to nine.[52] The reforms thus combined the concentration of authority with a governing body that was capable of holding the High Master to account and was itself answerable to wider public opinion.

Reforming Higher Education: Presbyterian Answers to Manchester Questions

The Taunton Commission was concerned with secondary education, and the Owens reformers with higher education. The connection, however, was intimate. The division between 'higher' and 'secondary' education was not at all clear-cut in the 1860s and 1870s. Indeed, the term 'secondary education' only came into common usage in the 1890s, in the wake of the Royal Commission on Secondary Education, appointed in 1894 under the chairmanship of the Chancellor of the Duchy of Lancaster, none other than James Bryce. In the 1860s, it was by no means unusual to use the term 'higher education' promiscuously with reference to any kind of advanced and non-vocational post-elementary education: the fundamental binary was between 'elementary' and 'higher' education.[53] That was the sense in which campaigners for the 'higher education of women' used the term: they were interested both in institutions like Girton College in Cambridge and Bedford College in London, and in the schools of what became the Girls' Public Day School Company (later Trust). Indeed, in the late 1840s, Bedford College and F. D. Maurice's Queen's College – both pioneers – had looked like similar kinds of project. Yet Bedford College, initially more like what we would think of as a secondary school, subsequently became a college of the University of London, and eventually merged with

Royal Holloway; while Queen's College, which had had aspirations to provide something resembling a university education, settled down to become a private day school for girls aged eleven to eighteen.[54]

Bryce certainly saw Owens College as falling under his remit: he did not inspect the College or examine its students as he did with boys' grammar schools and the like, but he certainly expressed trenchant views as to its place in the educational ecology of Manchester. He thought that Owens should have many more students than it did, and he judged its slow take-off as being intimately connected with the inadequate state of 'secondary' schooling for boys in Manchester and its hinterland. He also considered that the existence of a thriving university college, of the kind Owens had the potential to become, would act as a stimulus to the educational ambitions of schoolboys and their parents. He proceeded to set out in his report what was, in effect, a prospectus for the extension movement. The College was hindered by inadequate buildings in an obscure part of the city, which meant that it was largely unknown, and unable to forge a bond with the Manchester public. It needed greater visibility, as well as space for expansion.[55] The College's future depended on better buildings in a more imposing location, with student lodgings nearby, and on a greater willingness on the part of the business community to recognise the 'value of a scientific and literary culture'.[56]

Bryce's involvement with Owens College grew directly out of his investigations for the Taunton Commission. Among his enormous collection of papers in the Bodleian Library are some of the notebooks he kept in his work as an Assistant Commissioner. His pencil-written notes are often barely legible, but they merit close study. We find some detailed notes from his interview with Joseph Greenwood, Principal of Owens College in March 1866; these are followed immediately by an outline of a course of lectures on jurisprudence.[57] He was not lecturing on the subject anywhere at this time; indeed, he was not called to the bar until June 1867. Whether or not Greenwood had already broached the subject of Bryce's lecturing for Owens College, the possibility was certainly in Bryce's mind, and in fact the more elaborate notes he sketched somewhat later in the same notebook correspond closely to the course of seven lectures he gave at Owens in 1871–72.[58]

So far, we have seen that the reform of Owens College was fundamentally about the transformation of a close trust into a properly public form of governance that would enable the College to command public confidence – precisely the kind of transformation that Bryce had advocated for the endowed schools in his report for the Taunton Commission. The concept of the 'representative government' of a trust – meaning the inclusion on the governing body of a number (usually a minority) of trustees nominated by what might now be called stakeholder bodies – was one that he formulated in his report, and that subsequently became a familiar feature of the governance arrangements of endowed schools, as they were remodelled in the wake of the Taunton Commission's report by the Endowed Schools Commissioners and subsequently by the Charity Commissioners. The Owens College constitution of 1870–71 may well have been the first such scheme, and the Owens College governors told the Charity Commissioners that this form of government by a 'body of a public and widely representative character' made the College a suitable recipient of some of the accumulated funds of the Hulme Trust.[59] The evidence does not enable us to be sure how far it was Bryce and how far it was the Owens College reformers who were the innovators here. Probably, it was the encounter between him and them that mattered. The instructions issued to Bryce by the constitution committee in 1869 were clear about the kind of constitution they wanted, and in particular about the distinction between public and private forms of governance; but by that time they were certainly familiar with Bryce's report for the Schools Inquiry Commission, published in 1868, which expounded that very distinction. Whether Bryce influenced the Manchester reformers, or they influenced him, or both, is not centrally important. What matters is that the reform of Owens College should be understood in the wider context of the reform of educational endowments and their proper governance in a liberal age.

The Owens College reformers were receptive to the case for ensuring the accountability of educational trusts to public opinion, because this was a central issue in Manchester politics of the time. While many parts of the country saw local contests over the control of educational and other kinds of charitable endowments, the governance of educational endowments was a notably contested question in Manchester in the middle of the nineteenth century. The city was the home of three important educational charities: Chetham's Hospital, Manchester Grammar School and William Hulme's Charity. The three bodies of trustees or 'feoffees' had thickly overlapping memberships, and were dominated by the Anglican gentry of the surrounding area, such as the Tatton branch of the Egerton family. The connections were strongest between the Hulme trustees and the feoffees of the Grammar School, especially prior to the latter's reform in 1849. Three of the ten Hulme trustees in 1848 were Egertons or Tattons; and of these ten, six were current or recent feoffees of Manchester Grammar School.[60] As late as 1877, all twelve Hulme trustees were Anglican, and the sole Liberal was a godson of King George IV. The trustees included Lord Egerton of Tatton, Egerton's son and heir, his first cousin, and a member of a distant branch of the Egerton family. Only one trustee, William Henry Houldsworth, could be said to represent new money.[61] This tight-knit group controlled resources that Liberal reformers identified as potentially capable of helping to fund a fuller system of secondary and higher education in the city.

Manchester had a politically conscious professional and mercantile middle class, with strong links to religious nonconformity. They resented the dominance of a social elite, overwhelmingly Anglican and Tory, who mostly lived at some distance from the city.[62] The control of charitable trusts, and especially educational trusts, was therefore politically charged, and there were prolonged contests over the control and reform of these three trusts, especially in the wake of the Charitable Trusts Act of 1853, which established the Charity Commission on a permanent basis.[63] A leading figure in pressing for public control was the solicitor Alexander Kay, a veteran of Cobden's campaign for Manchester's incorporation as a borough that came to fruition in 1838. Kay was the fourth mayor of Manchester, and (like several early mayors) a member of the Cross Street Unitarian congregation.[64] It was Kay who, in 1847, successfully proposed that the Council should establish a Charitable Trusts Committee 'to enquire into all charities within the borough of Manchester, and to report thereon from time to time, and upon all matters relating thereto, as they shall think necessary or desirable'; and his own public letter to the mayor in May 1854, and his paper to the Manchester Statistical Society in January 1855, prompted the committee to take up the issue.[65] Also in 1855, the librarian Edward Edwards – the first chief librarian of the Manchester Free Library, and 'a man of decided views and quick temper' – published a vigorous critique of the misuse of Manchester's educational endowments, including all these three foundations. Kay and Edwards both anticipated the thrust of Bryce's report. Thus, Edwards urged the need for 'the constant PUBLICITY of the accounts and of the proceedings of those who govern' charitable and educational trusts, and maintained that 'unless public opinion be brought to bear thoroughly and persistently on Trustees and Feoffees, even the improvements that may come to be effected … will prove incomplete and transitory'.[66]

Significantly, when Henry Roscoe first approached his fellow Unitarian Thomas Ashton for assistance with the extension of Owens College, Ashton is said to have objected 'that the Governors of the private Trust were strong Churchmen and mainly Tories, with whom he had little sympathy'.[67] He was wrong, in fact, about the trustees of Owens College, as he would go on to discover; among them were Cobden and several of his allies, including Kay (who died in 1863) and several other Cross Street Unitarians, such as James Heywood and John Benjamin Smith.[68] But the fact that Ashton had this perception was certainly due to the long-standing battles in which he and others were engaged over the Hulme and Manchester Grammar School trusts. These were long and complex contests, which, for the reformers, fundamentally turned on the question of how to wrest control of these trusts from the exclusive control of a small group of predominantly Tory and Anglican gentry families, and how to find a way of ensuring their accountability to public opinion. In April 1871, just as the extension of Owens College was coming to fruition, 'a large and influential meeting' was held in the Manchester Town Hall to press for the reform of Hulme's Charity. It was striking just how prominent the Owens College lay governors were in this movement, and in particular the protagonists of the extension movement. The committee appointed to devise schemes of reform included Thomas Ashton, Charles Beyer, Richard Christie, Robert Darbishire, Sir William Fairbairn, Joseph Greenwood, Oliver Heywood, Edward Langworthy, Alfred Neild, Sir Joseph Whitworth and a good number of other Owens College names.[69]

Ashton himself, a governor of Manchester Grammar School from 1868, led this campaign and was eventually appointed a governor of Hulme's Charity too in 1881, serving successively as vice-chairman and then as chairman. Prior to his appointment as a governor of the charity, he led the opposition to the oligarchic character of its governance: 'the effect of the scheme as it stands', he complained of the draft scheme of 1880, 'will therefore be to place to a very great extent the future control of middle-class education in Manchester and its neighbourhood in the hands of a body self-elected, consisting at present wholly of members of one religious denomination, irresponsible to the public, possibly non-resident in the district and thus uncontrolled by its public opinion and ignorant of its needs'.[70] Having secured a more representative scheme, he became the central figure in the reconstruction of Hulme's Charity, one of the principal beneficiaries of which was Owens College, for Liberal opinion in Manchester (including Kay in his paper to the Statistical Society) had long held that the funds of 'this perverted charity' could transform Owens College into a Manchester university.[71] Under Ashton's leadership, the charity's resources were also redeployed to support new initiatives such as the Manchester High School for Girls (established 1874), and the High School's founders were clear that they should impart to its governing body 'a thoroughly public character by including in it representatives to be chosen by various public bodies', including representatives of Owens College, the School Boards of Manchester and Salford, and the Charity Commissioners or the Privy Council's Education Department.[72] Ashton's family developed close connections with the school, and no fewer than three of his six daughters served as governors. The first to do so was his second daughter, Marion, who was one of the first representative governors appointed by Hulme's Charity in 1884. She served until 1889, when she married James Bryce, two decades after her father had invited him to draw up the scheme of governance for Owens College.[73]

In his alertness to the significance of the distinction between a private trust and a public institution, Bryce was an important figure, but one who stood close to the mainstream of advanced Liberal thinking in the Gladstonian era.[74] In preparing his report on Lancashire schools, he was in close dialogue with a Manchester public opinion that was very familiar with the problem of the appropriate management of charitable endowments to ensure conformity with public purposes. But in considering the problem of the relationship between the professoriate and laymen in the governance of Owens College, Bryce added something distinctive to the mix. His vision was of a college in which laymen were numerically preponderant both on the Court of Governors and on Council, so as to guard against the danger that academics would run the College in their own group interest rather than serving the wider public interest. At the same time, these laymen would acknowledge that the College could prosper only if it could recruit, develop and retain distinguished scholars and scientists, and to do that it must give them free rein in purely academic matters. There could be institutional safeguards, notably in allowing Senate full authority over the curriculum, but since control of the purse strings in the end affected all activities in the College, it also required qualities of wisdom, prudence and moderation among the lay governors. Where did this vision come from? Bryce was reared in Scots-Ulster Presbyterianism: in particular, in the secessionist strand of Presbyterianism that rejected the idea of church establishment and took questions of church organisation very seriously indeed. There is a striking affinity between the academic polity that Bryce instituted at Owens College and the ecclesiastical polity of the Presbyterian churches. Bryce was familiar with this polity from boyhood, and he understood it to be republican and not democratic.[75] In particular, the distinction between ruling elders (laymen) and teaching elders (clergy) was fundamental, as was the imperative that the ruling elders, although supreme in their own domain, should not encroach on the prerogatives of the clergy. That is the most likely source for Bryce's understanding of the proper relationship between lay governors and academics in a well-ordered modern university, and it underpinned the constitution that he prepared for Owens College.

Conclusion

This article has shown that the central feature of the Owens College extension was its reconstitution of the College as a public foundation, as distinct from a close trust. That process implied a fundamental reconstruction of the relationship between the College and the city. The new governance model established at Owens College in the 1870 constitution became normative for civic colleges and universities in England. In his history of the post-war University of Manchester, Brian Pullan writes that the university of that period was still governed by the charter of 1903, a document that 'seemed to echo the mixed constitution of a republic in Renaissance Italy or the Holy Roman Empire, for it aimed at combining the virtues of government by the One, the Few and the Many'.[76] Pullan – himself best known as a historian of Renaissance Venice – might have added that that charter was itself modelled on the constitution of 1870–71, and that that constitution was drafted by a man who was, at the time, best known as a historian of the Holy Roman Empire. That said, it is unlikely that the Holy Roman Empire was much of an inspiration for Bryce when he drafted the constitution for Owens College. Instead, that constitution owed much more to the political struggles of early and mid-Victorian Manchester.

When, in 2004, the Victoria University merged with UMIST to create a formally new institution, The University of Manchester (with an idiosyncratic capital 'T'), no statute or ordinance or regulation was treated as sacrosanct, and the intention was to design a new university from first principles (although those first principles were remarkably similar to the received wisdom in the corporate world of 2004). That was the moment when the structures first devised in 1869–71 were set aside. Lay governors survived, but the notion of the 'representative' governor, and hence the nexus that bound the university to its stakeholders, disappeared, except for a solitary governor nominated by the Alumni Association. That change was mirrored in changes in the governance of other civic universities. Lay members of governing bodies are nearly always appointed, in effect, by co-option, usually through a Nominations Committee or similar: as it happens, the same process as that used in business for the appointment of non-executive directors. Critics charge that this system creates homogeneous governing bodies, as governors fill vacancies with governors like themselves.[77] This is much the same sort of criticism as Bryce and Darbishire and Ashton levelled at 'close trusts' in the Victorian period.

Notes

1. This paper draws in part on work undertaken during my tenure of a Major Research Fellowship MRF-2019-062, awarded by the Leverhulme Trust for the period 2020–23. I thank the Trust for its munificent support, the main outcome of which, a major study of James Bryce, is forthcoming from Princeton University Press. The article draws on some material used in my chapter, 'James Bryce's Manchester: The Politics of the Remaking of Owens College, 1865–75', in Stuart Jones (ed.), *Manchester Minds: A University History of Ideas* (Manchester: Manchester University Press, 2024), which approaches the same subject from a different angle.
2. Eric Ives, Diane Drummond and Leonard Schwarz, *The First Civic University: Birmingham 1880–1980* (Birmingham: University of Birmingham Press, 2000), pp. 131–3.
3. William Whyte, *Redbrick: A Social and Architectural History of Britain's Civic Universities* (Oxford: Oxford University Press, 2015), pp. 136, 190.
4. B. W. Clapp, *John Owens, Manchester Merchant* (Manchester: Manchester University Press, 1965), p. 173.
5. The only study is the article-length one by W. H. Chaloner, *The Movement for the Extension of Owens College, Manchester, 1863–73* (Manchester: Manchester University Press, 1973).
6. W. R. Ward, *Victorian Oxford* (London: Frank Cass, 1965), p. 159; Graeme C. Moodie and Rowland Eustace, *Power and Authority in British Universities* (Montreal: Queen's University Press, 1974), p. 29.
7. Mabel Tylecote, *The Education of Women at Manchester University, 1883 to 1933* (Manchester: Manchester University Press, 1941), pp. 1–16. A Manchester and Salford College for Women was established in 1877, not formally connected with Owens College, but drawing heavily on the College's teaching staff.
8. Edward Fiddes, *Chapters in the History of Owens College and of Manchester University 1851–1914* (Manchester: Manchester University Press, 1937), p. 181; Joseph Thompson, *The Owens College: Its Foundation and Growth; and its Connection with the Victoria University, Manchester* (Manchester: Cornish, 1886), pp. 633–49.
9. Chaloner, *The Movement for the Extension of Owens College*.
10. 'Owens College's Constitution. A Pattern for Other Modern Universities', *Manchester Guardian* (24 May 1951), p. 3.
11. I have made the case for historians to take university constitutions seriously in H. S. Jones, 'Higher Learning and Authorities', in Heather Ellis and Tamson Pietsch (eds), *A Cultural History of Higher Learning in the Age of Industry* (London: Bloomsbury, forthcoming).
12. Chaloner (*The Movement for the Extension of Owens College*, p. 15) says that Bryce was at this time Regius Professor of Civil Law at Oxford, but in fact he was not appointed to that chair until May 1870, a year after the constitution had been drafted and while the first Owens College Bill was going through Parliament. He held the Regius Professorship, which was a non-resident chair, concurrently with the Professorship of Jurisprudence at Owens College, which was also a part-time position.

13 The bulk of the material is in Manchester, University of Manchester Archives, OCA 7/2/48; but Bryce's manuscript draft is Oxford, Bodleian Library, MS Bryce 162, fos 160r–167r. To the best of my knowledge, the latter document – which is out of place, being filed in a box comprising Bryce's educational correspondence in the period 1897–1907 – has not previously been used.

14 The misnamed 'Robbins universities' of the 1960s departed somewhat from this model, since they gave less power to the lay governors, who were still, however, in the majority on Council: see A. H. Halsey and M. A. Trow, *The British Academics* (Cambridge, MA: Harvard University Press, 1971), pp. 108–10.

15 James Bryce, *The American Commonwealth*, 1 (London: Macmillan, 1888), pp. 561–2. Bryce visited the United States for the first time in 1870, after he had drafted the Owens College constitution and before taking up his duties as Professor of Jurisprudence. It is therefore unlikely that the American constitution was a direct influence on his thinking about the Owens College constitution.

16 Up to the 1870s at least, turnover in fellowships was rapid and turnover in headships was slow (the reverse of the situation in the twenty-first century). That tended to reinforce the power of heads as opposed to fellows.

17 On Cambridge, see Peter Searby, *A History of the University of Cambridge, volume 3: 1750–1870* (Cambridge: Cambridge University Press, 1997), pp. 507–44.

18 The University of London had a Senate and (from 1858) an incorporated Convocation of graduates. But it was anomalous in almost every way, being effectively no more than an examining board, with no professors or students of its own. It was, in addition, funded by central government and subject to close central government control: see F. M. G. Willson, *Our Minerva: The Men and Politics of the University of London, 1836–1858* (London: Athlone, 1995), especially pp. 46–58. It had a weak connection with London, since it examined candidates whatever their place of residence or study. Bryce and others considered the name 'university' a misnomer.

19 A. J. Scott, a Glasgow graduate, was a professor of English Language and Literature at University College prior to his appointment at Owens, while his successor, J. G. Greenwood, was a graduate of University College.

20 Manchester, University of Manchester Archives, OCA/7/2/48 ('Manchester and Owens College. Instructions to Mr Bryce').

21 Negley B. Harte and John North, *The World of University College London, 1828–1978* (London: University College, London, 1978), p. 71; H. Hale Bellot, *University College London, 1826–1926* (London: University of London Press, 1929), pp. 305–7.

22 Henry Solly, *'These Eighty Years', or, The Story of an Unfinished Life*, 2 (London: Simpkin & Marshall, 1893), p. 493.

23 Robert Anderson and Stuart Wallace, 'The Universities and National Identity in the Long Nineteenth Century, c.1830–1914', in Robert Anderson, Mark Freeman and Lindsay Paterson (eds), *The Edinburgh History of Education in Scotland* (Edinburgh: Edinburgh University Press, 2015), pp. 272–4; Robert D. Anderson, 'The Age of Reform', in Robert D. Anderson, Michael Lynch and Nicholas Phillipson (eds), *The University of Edinburgh: An Illustrated History* (Edinburgh: Edinburgh University

Press, 2003), pp. 119–22; Laurance James Saunders, *Scottish Democracy, 1815–1840* (Edinburgh: Oliver and Boyd, 1950), pp. 313–28.

24 Michael Moss, J. Forbes Munro and Richard H. Trainor (eds), *University, City and State: The University of Glasgow since 1870* (Edinburgh: Edinburgh University Press, 2000), p. 27.

25 'The Glasgow Graduates' Association, closing meeting. Presentation to Dr James Bryce', *Glasgow Herald* (4 June 1862), p. 6.

26 The authoritative account of Roscoe's role is now Peter J. T. Morris and Peter Reed, *Henry Enfield Roscoe: The Campaigning Chemist* (New York: Oxford University Press, 2024), pp. 103–28.

27 'Owens College Extension', *Manchester Guardian* (4 December 1869), p. 5.

28 Owens Extension College (Manchester) Act 1870 UK Private and Personal Acts (33 & 34 Victoria c. 2). That Darbishire drafted the bill is clear from his correspondence with his son: Lexington, KY, University of Kentucky Special Collections, Darbishire family papers, Box 1, Folder 14 (R. D. Darbishire to Godfrey Darbishire, 5 December 1869).

29 Manchester, University of Manchester Archives, OCA/7/2/48 ('Manchester and Owens College. Instructions to Mr Bryce to prepare first Sketch of a Constitution').

30 The fullest study is David Ian Allsobrook, *Schools for the Shires: The Reform of Middle-Class Education in Mid-Victorian England* (Manchester: Manchester University Press, 1986).

31 Jonathan Parry, The *Rise and Fall of Liberal Government in Victorian Britain* (London: Yale University Press, 1993), p. 181.

32 On the Taunton Commission's role in making provision for girls' education, the standard study is Sheila Fletcher, *Feminists and Bureaucrats: A Study in the Development of Girls' Education in the Nineteenth Century* (Cambridge: Cambridge University Press, 1980).

33 H. S. Jones, 'Gladstonian Liberalism, Public Service and Private Interests: Reforming Endowments', in Ian Cawood and Tom Crook (eds), *The Many Lives of Corruption: The Reform of Public Life in Modern Britain, c.1750–1950* (Manchester: Manchester University Press, 2022), p. 205.

34 On the electoral stakes, especially in London, see Lawrence Goldman, 'The Defection of the Middle Class: The Endowed Schools Act, the Liberal Party, and the 1874 Election', in Peter Ghosh and Lawrence Goldman (eds), *Politics and Culture in Victorian Britain: Essays in Memory of Colin Matthew* (Oxford: Oxford University Press, 2006), pp. 118–35. The standard study of the larger problem remains David Owen, *English Philanthropy 1660–1960* (Cambridge, MA: Belknap, 1964).

35 Jones, 'Gladstonian Liberalism', pp. 200–19.

36 Robert Lowe, *Middle Class Education: Endowment or Free Trade?* (London: Bush, 1868); [James Bryce], 'The Worth of Educational Endowments', *Macmillan's Magazine*, 19 (1868–69), pp. 517–24.

37 The centrality of the notion of 'publicity', in all its ramifications, to nineteenth-century Liberal politics is analysed by Patrick Joyce, *The Rule of Freedom: Liberalism and the Modern City* (London: Verso, 2003), pp. 51–69, and James Thompson, *British Political*

Culture and the Idea of 'Public Opinion', 1867–1914 (Cambridge: Cambridge University Press, 2013), pp. 136–82.

38 Royal Commission to Inquire into Education in Schools in England and Wales (Schools Inquiry Commission) PP 1867–8 [3966] IX: 440 (henceforth cited in the form SIC 3966-V, 440).

39 SIC 3966-IX, 442.

40 SIC 3966-IX, 531, 764.

41 SIC 3966-IX, 165.

42 SIC 3966-IX, 120.

43 The term 'representative governor' (in this sense) does not appear in the Google Books corpus before the 1860s. From the 1870s, it becomes common in the context of the constitutions of remodelled governing bodies.

44 SIC 3966-XVII, 170–6; quotation at 173.

45 SIC 3966-XVII, 336–42.

46 SIC 3966-XVII, 182–8.

47 SIC 3966-XVII, 286.

48 By no means all nonconformists were content with this outcome: for a dissident, see Vigilans, *Nonconformists and their Rights as Citizens, Especially in Relation to the Endowed Schools Act. With a Sketch of the Old Dissent* (London: Elliot Stock, 1873), p. 63: 'the title of "Representative" applied to some of the governors is misleading. A Representative Governor should surely represent the people for whom the benefits of the endowment are intended.'

49 The report, formally in the name of the Commissioners themselves, can be treated as Bryce's, as it was in contemporary reports, e.g. 'School Inquiry Commission', *Manchester Guardian* (5 March 1868), p. 3.

50 SIC 3966-XVII, 314.

51 SIC 3966-I, 525.

52 'Manchester Grammar School New Scheme', *Manchester Guardian* (4 August 1875), p. 5; 'The Grammar School Scheme', *Manchester Times* (27 May 1876), p. 7; 'Manchester Grammar School', *Manchester Guardian* (14 May 1877), p. 5.

53 For instance, *National Education and the Church of Scotland* (Edinburgh: Edmonston & Douglas, 1868), p. 9.

54 On Bedford College, see Janet Howarth, 'Introduction' to Emily Davies, *The Higher Education of Women* (London: Hambledon, 1988), p. xxvii.

55 Bryce certainly made a rhetorical connection in his report between darkness and cliquish government, and between light and public accountability. On this broader theme in nineteenth-century liberalism, the key study is Chris Otter, *The Victorian Eye: A Political History of Light and Vision in Britain, 1800–1910* (Chicago: University of Chicago Press, 2008).

56 SIC 3966-IX, 721.

57 The interview with Greenwood is noted in Oxford, Bodleian Library, MS Bryce 347, fos 3v–5r; the notes headed 'Jurisprudence – Ist Course – Outline' are at fos 6r–7r. Internal evidence from this volume of notes allows us to date the interview to March 1866.

58 The lecture notes are in *ibid.*, fos 44v–87r, under the heading 'Jurisprudence – First Course'. The content of the lectures he gave at Owens in 1871–72 can be inferred from the examination paper printed in the following year's calendar: *The Owens College, Manchester: Calendar for the Session 1872–3* (Manchester: Sowler, 1872) (Manchester, University of Manchester Archive, OCA/4).

59 Manchester, Chetham's Library, Hulme/3/1/3/7 (Alfred Neild to Charity Commissioners, 6 December 1875). Like many endowments, the Trust's income had grown more rapidly than the expenditure stipulated in the founder's will.

60 This sentence is based on the list of the Hulme trustees in Manchester, Manchester Central Library, Council Minutes, Charitable Trusts Committee Minute Book No. 1, p. 337, and lists of the feoffees of the Grammar School in Alfred A. Mumford, *The Manchester Grammar School, 1515–1915: A Regional Study of the Advancement of Learning in Manchester since the Reformation* (London: Longmans, Green, 1919), appendix 9, and in W. R. Whatton's 1834 history, in *The Foundations of Manchester: Comprising the College and Collegiate Church, the Free Grammar School, and Chetham's Hospital*, 3 (Manchester: Agnew, 1848) p. 102.

61 See the list of Hulme trustees in *Manchester Courier and Lancashire General Advertiser* (18 May 1877), p. 6 (Manchester, Chetham's Library, Hulme/3/1/3/7).

62 On the significance of the desertion of the city by gentry families since the early eighteenth century, see V. A. C. Gatrell, 'The Commercial Middle Class in Manchester, c.1820–1857' (PhD thesis, University of Cambridge, 1971), pp. 140–2.

63 'Association for the Reform of Educational Endowments', *Manchester Courier and Lancashire General Advertiser* (7 February 1857), p. 10. We lack a connected study of the reform of these institutions, but there is a luminous study of Manchester Grammar School by R. F. I. Bunn, 'The History of the School', in J. A. Graham and B. A. Phythian, *The Manchester Grammar School, 1515–1965*, 1 (Manchester: Manchester University Press, 1965), and a lively and detailed older history by Mumford, *The Manchester Grammar School*. On the Hulme Trust, the best study is I. B. Fallows, *William Hulme and his Trust* (Chichester: Phillimore, 2008).

64 Shena D. Simon, *A Century of City Government: Manchester 1838–1938* (London: George Allen & Unwin, 1938), pp. 84, 93.

65 Thompson, *Owens College*, 90.

66 Edward Edwards, *Manchester Worthies and their Foundations; or, Six Chapters of Local History; With an Epilogue, By Way of Moral* (Manchester: Galt, 1855), p. 80.

67 Henry Enfield Roscoe, *The Life and Experiences of Henry Enfield Roscoe, D.C.L., LL.D., F.R.S.* (London: Macmillan, 1906), p. 111. The struggle over the Hulme Trust was very much still in progress at this time.

68 The trustees are listed in Thompson, *Owens College*, p. 31.

69 *Manchester Weekly Times* (15 April 1871), p. 3 (Manchester, Chetham's Library Hulme/4/1/3/4).

70 Manchester, Chetham's Library, Hulme/2/1/9 (Trustees' Meetings Minutes, memorial entitled 'Hulme's Charity', drafted by Thomas Ashton).

71 'Owens College', *Manchester Times* (1 July 1854), p. 4; also 'Hulme's Charity', *Manchester Guardian* (10 December 1868), p. 4. One suggestion was the creation of

a 'Hulme's College' which, together with Owens, would form the nucleus of a collegiate university: for instance, Alexander Kay, *Hulme's Charity. A Letter to Benjamin Nicholls, Esq., Mayor of Manchester, on the Past Management of this Charity, with Suggestions for the Future Application of its Large Surplus Income* (London: Longman, Brown, Green, and Longmans, 1854), pp. 32–4.

72 Manchester, Chetham's Library, Hulme/3/1/3/7 (Memorial of the Managing Committee of the Manchester High School for Girls to the Charity Commission).

73 The other two sisters were Charlotte (Mrs E. T. Broadhurst, later Lady Broadhurst) and Margaret, the famous Manchester suffragist and peace campaigner, and the first woman to sit on Manchester City Council. Intriguingly, all three at different times represented the Hulme Trust on the governing body See William J. Smith, 'Manchester High School for Girls: The Pioneering Years, 1874–1924' (PhD thesis, University of Manchester, 2004), pp. 109–10; 'An Educational Jubilee: Fifty Years at the High School. Manchester Pioneers of 1874', *Manchester Guardian* (10 January 1924), p. 11.

74 On this point, see Jones, 'Gladstonian Liberalism', pp. 200–19.

75 He called Calvin 'more than anyone else the modern founder of a republican system in the Church', while also stressing that he was anything but a Liberal: see 'James Bryce on John Calvin', *New York Observer and Chronicle* (20 May 1909), p. 627.

76 Brian Pullan with Michele Abendstern, *A History of the University of Manchester, 1951–73* (Manchester: Manchester University Press, 2000), p. 6.

77 Steven Jones and Diane Harris, *University Governance: Views from the Inside* (Council for the Defence of British Universities, 2024), https://cdbu.org.uk/wp-content/uploads/2024/01/CDBU-University-Governance-Report-FINAL.pdf [accessed 24 January 2024].

Lancashire Trade, University Work: The University of Manchester and the Regional Economy, c.1930–39[1]

CHRIS GODDEN, UNIVERSITY OF MANCHESTER

Abstract

This article explores some overlooked aspects of the University of Manchester's efforts in the 1930s to support Lancashire's industry and commerce. Two examples are considered: 'realistic economic research' conducted by the Economics Research Section into Lancashire's post-war economic problems, and the reintroduction of Chinese studies aimed at supporting Lancashire cotton merchants. While the successes of both endeavours were limited, the article concludes by briefly considering the legacy of such efforts on the university's research philosophy, particularly through the introduction of the Simon Fund in 1944.

Keywords: Manchester; Lancashire; applied economics; Economic Research Section; Chinese Studies; Simon Fund

The civic universities that came into being as independent institutions at the start of the twentieth century had, from the outset, an ambivalent relationship with their local economies. They regarded themselves as serving and accountable to their cities, but they were expected to dignify their cities rather than be subservient to the needs of the economy. As David Jones has suggested, efforts by the civic universities to forge close links with their cities and surrounding areas involved a mixture of commercial motives and burgeoning civic pride.[2] It is evident that different factors influenced these efforts in different cities and regions. For example, while some universities, such as Liverpool, showed little concern for higher education's connections with local industry, others, notably Birmingham and Manchester, were keenly aware of the realities of regional commercial activity.[3] By the beginning of the twentieth century, the significance of the University of Manchester to its local community – to the 'lives and activities of Lancashire men and women' – reflected the importance of its teaching and research given its location within a globally commercial city and its connections to Lancashire's cotton industry.[4] There is no question that the teaching of particular subjects – such as economics and modern languages, both long part of the University of Manchester's evening class tradition – was heavily linked to the city's commercial and industrial needs.[5]

This article is firmly built around this local context, and explores two examples of the University of Manchester's work, linked (in different ways) with Lancashire industry and commerce in the 1930s. These examples must be understood against the backdrop of economic and social dislocation that Lancashire had faced during the inter-war period – the emergence and persistence of high levels of regional unemployment linked with the loss of once-secure export markets for Lancashire cotton goods.[6] This 'Lancashire focus' serves as the lens through which these aspects of the University's work – one linked with applied economic research, the other with language training – should be viewed, both illustrating efforts by the University to support, and expand connections with, the regional economy.

The first section of the article considers the work of the Economic Research Section, a regional investigation section of the University of Manchester's Faculty of Commerce and Administration. Established in the early 1930s, its role was to investigate the economic and social impact of industrial depression in the Lancashire region. By the mid-1930s, the Research Section was recognised nationally as an integral feature of the University's work, with its research focused on understanding and attempting to solve regional economic problems.[7] Its publications during this period included *An Industrial Survey of the Lancashire Area* (1932), *Juvenile Unemployment* (1933), *Wages and Labour in the Lancashire Cotton Spinning Industry* (1935), and *Re-adjustment in Lancashire* (1936).[8] Despite conducting significant investigations into local economic conditions, the Economic Research Section remains a largely forgotten aspect of Manchester's research culture in the early twentieth century. Even Keith Tribe's study of the Faculty of Commerce and Administration failed to evaluate the Section's activities.[9] This article seeks to briefly address this. Its second section shifts the focus to cover the efforts to support a revival in the teaching of Chinese studies. Modern languages had long been represented at the University of Manchester and again, this provision was largely connected to the commercial needs of the region.[10] By the early 1930s, external funding enabled the University to establish a new academic post – a reader in Chinese Language and Social Economy – intended to serve as a link between the University and Manchester's Chamber of Commerce.

In their account of the University during the inter-war period, Alex Robertson and Colin Lees briefly mentioned the teaching of Russian, Spanish and Italian, but made no reference to Chinese. Again, this article provides an opportunity to correct this omission by briefly covering a forgotten aspect of the University's modern language provision (and the links with Lancashire commerce) in the 1930s. The final section draws some themes together, recognising the continuity and opportunities that, through the research it produced and the people it trained, underpinned the University of Manchester's attempts to support the commercial and professional life of the region. This section also briefly considers the possible legacy of this work (particularly the research philosophy that supported the Economic Research Section) in the activities of the University's Simon Fund, established by Lord Ernest Simon in 1944 to encourage research in the social sciences.

Manchester's Economic Research Section

In the late nineteenth and early twentieth centuries, the commercial character of many industrial cities (such as Manchester and Birmingham) meant that local universities were fully aware of the technical and labour requirements of industry. For example, the curriculum programme at Birmingham's Faculty of Commerce (established under Sir William Ashley), itself a reaction to Alfred Marshall's theory-oriented Economics Tripos at Cambridge, consisted of classes in accounting, commerce, applied science and business techniques, languages and history.[11] This was very similar to Manchester's Faculty of Commerce, where students were taught a curriculum consisting of political economy, commerce, modern languages, geography, history, commercial law and accounting.[12] Yet while the University of Birmingham has the distinction of having established the first Faculty of Commerce in Britain in 1902, the successes of Manchester's Faculty of Commerce and Administration (established in 1903) have been much more widely recognised. Keith Tribe has demolished the Birmingham story: while Birmingham has received significant attention (given its position as the first Faculty of Commerce), Manchester's commerce degree was, Tribe argues, much stronger than Birmingham's, and by the 1920s student numbers at Manchester meant that it was awarding commerce degrees at three to four times Birmingham's rate. Even Liverpool, which did not have a particularly strong economics department in the 1920s and 1930s, was performing much better than Birmingham.[13]

Manchester's Faculty of Commerce has been identified as a symbol of much that was progressive and desirable in a university during the inter-war period.[14] A key feature of this success – again, contrary to the work undertaken at Birmingham and, to an extent, also at Liverpool – was the faculty's focus on regional economic issues. This work had been properly started under Professor Sydney Chapman (Professor of Political Economy, 1901–08),[15] who had established links with industry and commerce in Lancashire and who, with Harry Mainwaring Hallsworth, had undertaken investigations into the specialised economic/commercial character of the region.[16] This approach was further expanded in 1927, when Henry Clay was appointed to a new chair in social economics, made possible through the University's receipt, from an anonymous donor, of £1,000 a year for five years.[17] Robertson and Lees have identifed this anonymous donor as Ernest Simon, the industrialist, Liberal politician and former Lord Mayor of Manchester, who was already an important lay figure in the University's governance.[18] The new post was focused on the investigation of Britain's post-war economic and social problems. This approach can be seen in two of the books that Clay published while occupying the position: *The Post-War Unemployment Problem* (1928) and *The Problem of Industrial Relations* (1929).[19] Chapman and Hallsworth's earlier work on the Lancashire cotton industry was followed by George Daniels, whose historical-descriptive accounts of the industry's development was later expanded (with the assistance of John Jewkes, of whom more below) into a detailed examination of the industry's post-war difficulties.[20] Daniels's early work had also been influenced by George Unwin, who had been appointed to Britain's first Chair in Economic History at Manchester in 1910.[21] Yet it was from Chapman and Daniels that a particular approach to economic research was adopted at Manchester in the early twentieth century. In his book, *Portrait of a University* (1951), published to commemorate the centenary of the foundation of Owens College, Henry Buckley Charlton devoted some space to Daniels, his character, and his contributions to the University. It is worth quoting Charlton at length (italics mine for emphasis):

> [Daniels] was by nature that sort of born realist who can afford to treat himself to romantic notions. He never lost his grip on the immediate necessities of the moment. *He never forgot how close to Manchester's public interest his own branch of study lay.* At his instigation, the Faculty of Commerce developed, and then by establishing a professorship in the subject, canonised *the pursuit of what can only be called realistic economic research, that is, the study of conditions in society and in industry as they now are*, and an attempt to use such enquiries either to strengthen or to modify accepted academic dogma in those regions of thought.[22]

Following a similar line, Sydney Chapman's unpublished autobiography provides insights into his approach to realistic economic investigations and his commitment to the study of the Lancashire cotton industry, stating as he does that his 'realism was primarily derived from Lancashire'.[23] It is significant that Charlton's book, which aimed not to narrate the University's history but to evoke its distinctive ethos, should comment on the 'realistic' research approach undertaken by Manchester's Faculty of Commerce. Although forgotten now, it was this approach to 'realistic economic research' that defined Manchester economics in the early twentieth century, with its focus on research closely connected to the study of real-world economic conditions and complexities, 'of conditions in society and in industry as they now are', in the Lancashire region. Charlton also wrote that Manchester's Faculty of Commerce and Administration has been 'one of the strongest life-lines binding [the university] to the region', and that it had 'seized on every opportunity to apply itself to the problems of its area'.[24] The strength of these connections and commitments – to the investigations of actual economic and social conditions, and the broader picture of a regional economic system facing the shrinking of old, staple industries and the resulting persistent unemployment – eventually led to the creation of the Economic Research Section.

Initially established to support an industrial survey of North Lancashire and West Cumberland in 1931, Manchester's Economic Research Section had the distinction of being the first applied economic research organisation associated with any British university.[25] It was not until 1935 that the Rockefeller Foundation provided finance for the creation of the Oxford Institute of Statistics, while the Department of Applied Economics in Cambridge was not founded until after the Second World War.[26] A driving force behind the Ecosnmic Research Section throughout the 1930s was John Jewkes. One-time assistant secretary to the Manchester Chamber of Commerce, Jewkes had been appointed Lecturer in Commerce at the University in 1927, later being made supervisor of the Economic

Research Section. In confirming Jewkes's appointment as Professor of Social Economics in 1936 (the professorship mentioned in the quote from Charlton), it was noted that the post had 'a special interest in the line of realistic research with which the Economics Research Section is concerned'.[27] It is perfectly clear that this nomenclature – Social Economics – was a professional title used by Manchester in this period to define this specific line of 'realistic research' that was closely linked to Lancashire's post-war economic situation.

The Economic Research Section's first project – the industrial survey of North Lancashire and West Cumberland – concentrated on the problem of surplus labour across the region (with a remarkably wide coverage, including population trends, technical change in the cotton industry, local government, coal mining, and the engineering trades), and the prospects for its absorption into either existing or new industries.[28] This was followed, in 1933, by a separate survey of the industrial belt of Cumberland (Carlisle excluded) and Furness which similarly offered, as one contemporary reviewed noted, 'a picture of industrial decay, of pools of surplus labour, of almost derelict towns and villages, and of a hazardous economic future'.[29] The focus here was with the local distribution of unemployment, and the numerous problems facing the post-war iron and steel industry, including the associated industries of coal mining, iron-ore making and coke making, and shipbuilding industries. The same year saw the Research Section publish a study on juvenile unemployment in the industrial north,[30] highlighting the deep economic and social problems arising from the hopeless post-war disorganisation of the juvenile labour market.[31] Two years later came a detailed investigation into the wage structure of the cotton industry, which demonstrated how rising labour costs before the First World War had been intensified by post-war difficulties and increased foreign competition,[32] as well as a study of unemployment insurance statistics across several British industries, including motor manufacture, building and agriculture.[33] A final industrial survey in 1936, a sequel to the original study initiated by the Board of Trade, examined the continuing problems of unemployment in the whole of Lancashire south of Lancaster (excluding Merseyside) and the adjoining industrial fringes of Cheshire and Derbyshire.[34] This book – *Re-adjustment in Lancashire* – was described by one American critic as 'one of the best of the several excellent regional studies resulting from the post-war depression in England', and as 'an admirable case study in realistic economics'.[35]

Regional economic studies of this kind were, of course, not unique to Manchester during this period. A Birmingham comparison is once again useful here. In the mid-1920s, the owners of the confectionery company, Cadbury Brothers, commissioned Birmingham's Faculty of Commerce to undertake a survey of the industrial development of the West Midlands. This survey was completed by the economist George Cyril Allen, and published as *The Industrial Development of Birmingham and the Black Country* in 1929.[36] This study compares favourably with the Economic Research Section's studies of the Lancashire region (especially in discussing post-war economic difficulties), yet Allen's publication was the exception in Birmingham's otherwise notable failure to produce any in-depth studies of the region's economic and social conditions.[37] Another example would be *The Social Survey of Merseyside*, published by the University of Liverpool in three volumes in 1934, which dealt with the social and economic structure of Merseyside including housing, poverty and unemployment.[38] Undertaken between 1929 and 1932, the Merseyside study (supported by a grant from the Rockefeller Foundation) had been conducted by the University of Liverpool's School of Social Sciences and Administration, under the direction of David Caradog-Jones. Liverpool's continued work in this area through the 1930s was clearly more significant than Birmingham's limited approach, to the point that the University of Liverpool Press established the 'New Merseyside Series' to publish research by the Statistics Division of the School of Social Sciences, including *The Future of Merseyside: Town and Country Planning Schemes* by W. G. Holford and W. A. Eden (1937), and *Trade Revival in a Depressed Area* by Caradog-Jones (1937).[39]

Yet it was Manchester's Economic Research Section that became the best known of such economic/social research endeavours at that time, with its various studies of Lancashire industrial life – ranging from an examination of juvenile unemployment to a study of wages in the Lancashire cotton-weaving industry – defining a uniquely 'Manchester' approach to economic research. At a meeting of the Manchester University Economics and Commerce Society in January 1935, Professor Noel Hall, then Head of the Department of Economics at University College London, commended the Economic Research Section for its enormous success as a recognised centre for the study of regional economic problems. Hall also specifically highlighted Manchester's Economic Research Section as Britain's most effective laboratory for the study of 'dynamic and realistic economic problems'.[40]

A review of the Economic Research Section's publications allows us to appreciate the main characteristics of their approach to economic/social research. First, there were a set of foundational ideas built around a long-standing, close awareness of the historical, institutional and structural elements of the Lancashire economy, and the contexts in which economic activity occurred. The collapse of trade and employment after the First World War was more pronounced in Lancashire than in the country as a whole, and the University's research into Lancashire's industrial situation reflected a genuine familiarity with the region's industries, its workforce and the myriad problems arising from post-war industrial decline. When reviewing some of the Economic Research Section's works in the late 1930s, one commentator even suggested a line of continuity dating back to the nineteenth century: 'since the days of Stanley Jevons, the Economics Department of the University of Manchester has rendered valuable service to society in Lancashire and beyond by its continuous research into current economic problems and the resultant stream of wise counsel upon matters of immediate policy'.[41]

Second, we can identify the influence of leading figures in the 1930s (most notably Daniels and Jewkes) who shared a common view about Lancashire's economic position, and who supported a research culture linked to the study of applied economic problems. In terms of a community of scholars delivering this programme of research, the Economic Research Section gave employment to several young economists and research students throughout the 1930s. Linked with this, much of the Research Section's work was supported (similarly to Liverpool's survey of Merseyside) by funding from the Rockefeller Foundation, a major source of funds for the development of the social sciences in Britain during this period. The Research Section received a total of $8,000 from the Rockefeller Foundation between 1933 and 1934, followed by a five-year terminating plan (totalling $30,000) covering the period September 1935 to August 1940.[42]

Third, we can see a particular methodological approach that favoured statistical investigation as a means of revealing contemporary economic conditions and relationships, over the application of economic theory (for example, analysing unemployment by area, occupation, sex, age and marital status), and linking all of these with the changed international pattern of post-war trade. In their study of the history of applied economics, Roger Backhouse and Jeff Biddle outlined the ambiguities associated with the term 'applied economics' and the various sets of activities that it could encompass. For example, one approach to applied economics involved the application of an economic toolkit centred around a core body of economic theory. Backhouse and Biddle also (briefly) identifed another approach, which they described as being of a 'more inductive, less formal level, not applying economic theory in any recognisable way'.[43] They did not reference the Economic Research Section, yet this 'more inductive, less formal' model certainly fits with the form of 'realistic economics' undertaken in Manchester in the 1930s. Put simply, the approach adopted by the Economic Research Section was not concerned with matters of theory, but rather with the scientific approach of observation and inference centred around the investigation of social and industrial conditions operating in Lancashire at that time.

The three characteristics outlined here are perfectly captured in comments by the economist Ronald Tress (Master of Birkbeck College, University of London, 1968–77) when recollecting his association with the Economic Research Section in the 1930s. In an interview with Keith Tribe in 1995, Tress recalled the events and discussions that surrounded his appointment to a one-year fellowship at Manchester, based in the Research Section, in the late 1930s:

> There was an advertisement for studentships ... Manchester was advertised ... and since I was living seven miles west of Chester I submitted an application, about the application of monopolistic competition to the cotton industry! ... Anyway, I got summoned for an interview ... George Daniels, who was an old type of economist, he took the line that ' We know something about the cotton industry up here to know!', or Lancashire words to that effect. But he left it to John Jewkes and Harry Campion to take me off, and they said, 'Well, now, look, forget all that about monopolistic competition. There is a study we want to do about unemployment and depressed areas, and if you are willing to take that on it's yours.' So I did.[44]

In summarising the characteristics of Manchester's approach to realistic economic research, we can add a fourth characteristic. The projects undertaken by the Economic Research Section were not merely intended to sketch out prevailing economic and social conditions; an underlying desire was that the revelation of facts would indicate lines of possible action and reform. Empirical studies of social and economic problems enabled economists at the Economic Research Section to articulate a long-run economic and social policy prescription around a broad programme of state intervention (a national system of industrial planning) aimed at encouraging coordinated local authority responses (around finance, public works and social services) and supporting measures to prevent the further dislocation of the labour market.[45] For example, investigations into the cotton spinning industry set out remedies linked to better organisation of the labour market, more flexible staffing, and the fixing of a minimum wage for some employees. Similarly, the failure to deal with the problem of juvenile unemployment militated against the region's recovery, and it was recognised that ongoing technical change in the cotton industry would, at least in the short run increase the dislocation of the juvenile labour market. It was proposed that the supply of labour coming on to the market be restricted by raising the school-leaving age to fifteen.[46]

There can be no question that Manchester established a creative centre for regional economic analysis in the 1930s. So why have Manchester's efforts in this area been forgotten today? A few reasons stand out. First, the Economic Research Section may have sought to promote a new outlook for Lancashire in the 1930s by offering policy guidance aimed at assisting economic recovery, but its influence was limited, and its policy advice was not adopted. Second, we must recognise the gradual loss of some of the key figures in this story: Sydney Chapman – who can be seen as a pioneer of the 'realistic economic research' method in the early twentieth century – left Manchester in 1918 to join the Board of Trade, later becoming the Government's Chief Economic Adviser; Henry Clay left Manchester in 1930 (just before the creation of the Economic Research Section) to become economic adviser at the Bank of England, and later Warden of Nuffield College; John Jewkes (later to become a staunch opponent of economic planning) left Manchester in 1948 to become Professor of Economic Organisation at Oxford; and perhaps most crucially, George Daniels died in 1937. Finally, the Economic Research Section's approach to economic/social research highlights the ephemeral qualities of their work. Their research was focused on the contemporary world and so, by definition, dealt with ephemeral phenomena. In their study of applied economics within the history of economic thought, Backhouse and Biddle summarised this issue perfectly: 'the common, often implicit, justification for the neglect of applied economics is that it deals with issues that are by their nature ephemeral and therefore of less intrinsic interest today than theoretical ones'.[47]

Another way of putting this, succinctly summarised by Martin Bulmer, is simply to say that 'empirical social research does not wear well with time'.[48] The University of Manchester's commitment in the 1930s to investigating the problems facing Lancashire's weaving towns, the juvenile labour market and unemployment in depressed areas reflected a pressing need to study those matters at that moment in time. There could be no reliance on the automatic appearance of newer industries, and so empirical research was undertaken with the clear intention of providing a basis for constructive action. Yet economic/social research undertaken under those conditions, uninformed by general ideas, or failing to integrate research and theory as part of its overall programme, can be seen to constitute a rather sterile form of activity, one that inevitably dates leaving little (if any) lasting impact. The primacy given by historians to inter-war economic theory, and hence to institutions such as the University of Cambridge and the London School of Economics, has inevitably led to Manchester's absence from intellectual and sociological histories of twentieth-century economics.[49] An excellent example of this state of affairs can be found in Fiorenza Belussi and Katia Caldari's study of the rise and decline of Lancashire's 'industrial district', as presented in the writings of British economists.[50] None of the publications by the Economic Research Section covering Lancashire's industrial problems are examined, or even referenced, and Belussi and Caldari's study is limited to work by three economists: Sydney Chapman (inevitably covering his publications on Lancashire from before the outbreak of the First World War), Alfred Marshall and John Maynard Keynes.

Chinese Language and Social Economy

When the Department of Chinese was formed in 1901, the University of Manchester was clear that neither the funding situation, nor the work available, could justify a full-time professor. Edward Harper Parker, the first head of the Department, certainly had sufficient enthusiasm for his subject to take up a part-time appointment, and for over twenty-five years he served as both Professor of Chinese at Manchester and Reader in Chinese at Liverpool University.[51] Throughout his time at Manchester, Parker taught very few students.[52] Following his death in 1926, the post was not renewed, and Manchester fell behind several British universities in the teaching of Chinese. In the early 1930s, however, money from the Boxer Indemnity Fund was placed at the disposal of the Universities' China Committee in London to encourage the teaching of the Chinese at four British Universities – Oxford, Cambridge, London and Manchester – through the endowment of professorships and readerships. Each position would have a specific focus, to avoid the duplication of work: Oxford's would focus on religion and philosophy, Cambridge's on history, London's on art and archaeology, and Manchester's on economics and commerce.

Manchester's grant was comparatively small, and the University concluded that it could only offer a lectureship or readership at a stipend of £600. Nevertheless, through this funding Manchester was able to make an appointment to revive the Department of Chinese. The focus of this new role – on Chinese economics and commerce – was clear from the outset, and in April 1933, Professor Walter Moberly wrote to Professor Jerome Greene at University College, Aberystwyth, asking for advice on a suitable candidate: 'the University is looking to get a man with a good knowledge of the economic situation in China, who will make contacts readily and act as a sort of informal liaison officer between students, the University, and that section of the Manchester business community which is interested in China'.[53]

Moberly's letter went on to state that some instruction in Chinese language should be offered, although the University did not regard this as the most important part of the role.

Moberly's search for candidates led to the suggestion of Dr Franklin Ho (a former student of Irving Fisher's at Yale), a noted expert on Chinese banking and trade.[54] Another suggestion was John Bernard Tayler, Professor of Economics at Menching University, Industrial Secretary to the National Christian Council of China in 1931, and author of the book, *Farm and Factory in China* (1928).[55] The third name suggested was Edgar Walter Mead, a former British consular official in China who had twenty years' experience as assistant secretary in the British Legation in Peking and chief inspector in the Chinese Salt Administration.[56] Mead had returned to Britain in 1929, and had expressed an interest in taking up an academic post: he had unsuccessfully applied, in 1930, for the post of professor of Chinese in the School of Oriental Studies at London University, which eventually went to Sir Reginald Johnson.[57]

The University consulted Gilbert Hubbard, former First Secretary to His Majesty's legation in Peking (Beijing) and author of several books on British policy in the Far East, who offered his thoughts on the three suggested names. While acknowledging Ho as the pick of American-trained Chinese economists, Hubbard expressed doubt as to the practicalities of his academic training ('its concentration on tables, schedules, essays, etc. – often rather remote from the facts'). Similarly, Tayler was noted as having specialist knowledge of Chinese rural problems, but little in the way of practical knowledge of trading conditions or China's merchant community.[58] Of Mead, Hubbard offered the following assessment:

> He is a person of distinctly attractive character who should get on well with English students and Manchester business men ... He would be an amateur as far as Chinese Economics and Commerce are concerned, but would, I should say ... easily acquire for himself the necessary knowledge (though, of course, a real grasp of the technique and difficulties of foreign trade in China can hardly be found in anyone other than a merchant with practical experience).[59]

In May 1933, the *Manchester Guardian* reported the University's plans to revive the study of Chinese through the Universities' China Committee funds, expressing the hope that the University would secure the services of someone 'intimately acquainted with the present position of commerce and industry in China'.[60] Two months later came the full announcement of Mead's appointment, as well as the hope that this would successfully bring 'into closer contact with the University the business interests of the city and the Chamber of Commerce which are associated with China'.[61] At the beginning of the following academic year, the University reported the revival in the Department of Chinese through Mead's appointment as Reader in Chinese Language and Social Economy, later more often referred to simply as Reader in Chinese Language and Commerce.[62]

The nomenclature here is again interesting (not to say unusual) and, in the absence of evidence from the University's archives, offers an opportunity for speculation. The different versions of Mead's title – Reader in Chinese Language and Social Economy, later becoming Reader in Chinese Language and Commerce – linked his role (and the Boxer Indemnity Fund endowment) with the activities of the Faculty of Commerce and Administration. But was the original 'Social Economy' part of his title intended to signify a link (however ill-defined) to Manchester's pre-existing approach to 'realistic economic research'? There had certainly been contemporary speculation of a link to this aspect of Manchester's research culture. As noted, the *Manchester Guardian* suggested in May 1933 that the holder of the new post should be an expert who would undertake investigations into the economic situation in China. As far as can be established, no such research was ever undertaken by Mead, and so we are again left to speculate as to what such a project, had it been devised and undertaken, may have entailed. We would certainly expect it to have linked with the Economic Research Section's work, possibly dealing with the outlook for the Lancashire cotton industry based on economic/political conditions in China.[63] Might the expectation have been for Mead to undertake an investigation into the industrialisation of the Far East, and the comparative costs of labour/production between East and West?

Over the next few years, Mead was active in delivering lectures in and around Manchester on various Chinese topics. These included lectures on 'Foreign Trade in China' to the Manchester Chamber of Commerce;[64] a series of lectures covering the geographical and commercial importance of Chinese cities, for the Department of Geography;[65] lectures at Manchester's Central Library on 'The Problems Confronting China', arranged jointly by the University's Extramural Department and the Manchester Geographical Society; and an introductory course on 'Religion in China' for students studying Comparative Religions.[66] Mead also assisted the Manchester Chamber of Commerce in establishing the Anglo-Chinese Society of Manchester, which was intended to promote social gatherings between Chinese residents in the city and other members of Manchester's community.[67] Much of this work reflected the view that some familiarity with China's history, institutions, geography, trade and finance (in addition to some basic instruction in Chinese language) was essential to smooth the path of commerce between Lancashire and China.[68] A brief comparison can be made here to an earlier attempt by the University to promote languages provision to the Manchester business community. In 1919, Michael V. Trofimov (1884–1949) had been appointed to the newly instituted Sir William Mather Chair of Russian,[69] a position that, as with Mead's appointment in 1933, reflected a belief in the importance of language education (in this case elementary courses in Russian) to Manchester's commercial prosperity.[70]

The position of reader in Chinese Language and Social Economy came to an end with the outbreak of the Second World War. Mead left the University in October 1939 to take over as director of the Far Eastern Section of the Royal Institute of International Affairs (then stationed at Balliol College, Oxford) for the duration of the war.[71] He died in Oxford in January 1941. His obituary in the *Manchester Guardian* made no reference to the original intentions behind his appointment to the readership in 1933, emphasising instead his role as unofficial advisor to students (particularly those from the Far East), his interest in matters relating to student well-being, and his active role as a member of the University's Appointment Board: 'he was instrumental in increasing to a larger extent the closer connection between the Appointments Board and the employers in industry and commerce'.[72] The Manchester University Appointments Board, an early version of what would today be described as the Careers Service, was created in 1934 against the background of rising graduate unemployment. Originally chaired by Frederick Marquis (Chapman's former collaborator, later Lord Woolton), the Board had representatives of the University, students' union, and the local business community, and was tasked with helping to ensure greater cooperation between employers and the University in providing work for graduates. Importance was attached to appealing for the active cooperation of the trade and commerce of the city through the medium of the Chamber of Commerce, a body with which Mead had been closely associated since his arrival in Manchester.[73]

How are we to judge Mead's role? A possible comparison that springs to mind here would be another Edgar – in this case, Professor Edgar Allison Peers, who had been appointed Gilmour Professor of Spanish at the University of Liverpool in 1922. Allison Peers was a language teacher and prolific writer, who established the Liverpool Society of Spanish Studies, the Liverpool Summer School of Spanish (held in Santander for many years), and the *Bulletin of Hispanic Studies.*[74] Mead and Allison Peers were contemporaries teaching and promoting their respective languages, although some obvious differences can be noted. Allison Peers was a recognised authority on Spanish thought and literature, for example, while Mead was not an expert on Chinese economics and commerce, and his publications consisted of summaries of leading articles in the Chinese press for the Royal Institute of International Affairs (between July 1935 and June 1937) and numerous reviews of books on China for the *Manchester Guardian.*[75] Furthermore, Allison Peers was hugely successful in establishing the University of Liverpool's position as a centre for modern Hispanic studies. In sharp contrast, the (revived) Department of Chinese at Manchester under Mead never became a centre for Chinese language or the study of Chinese commercial problems. Mead's course on Chinese language, modern history and institutions recruited its maximum intake of four students in 1936;[76] for all other years, it continued with only a single student.[77] The University's records show that, despite his work being promoted by the Chamber of Commerce, the depression affecting Manchester trade with China in the 1930s ultimately made it very difficult to attract students.[78]

Yet is it not too easy a game to identify glaring differences between the academic careers and successes of these two Edgars? Allison Peers's academic career extended for over thirty years, while Mead's was less than a decade. I would argue that an understanding of Mead's work at Manchester is not assisted by comparison with an established academic of the status of Allison Peers. Instead, it requires an appreciation of the *non-academic* aspects of Mead's role, which had been a key part of Moberly's original request for suitable candidates – that the reader in Chinese

Language and Social Economy would serve as a liaison officer between the University and the business community interested in China. Building on this, we can better appreciate the nature of Mead's role by the late 1930s, with his work eventually becoming that of a liaison between the University and the wider business community in supporting the future careers of its graduates.[79]

Conclusion

The aim of this article was to consider how these two examples of the University of Manchester's work in the 1930s linked, albeit in different ways, with Lancashire industry and commerce. By way of conclusion, let us consider the following points. First, and perhaps most obviously, we can see the extent to which the University was dependent on external funding to support such kinds of activities; for the Economic Research Section this involved funding from the Rockefeller Trust, and for the Department of Chinese from the Boxer Indemnity Fund.

Second, both examples illustrate the ways the University utilised this funding to build on pre-existing ideas and approaches. Building on efforts to link language provision with Manchester's commercial interests (for example, following the example of the creation of the chair in Russian studies after the First World War), the re-introduction of Chinese Studies in the 1930s reflected a view that the study of Chinese language, together with aspects of Chinese history and the relationships between China and the rest of the world, was essential for instructing Lancashire cotton merchants.[80] Yet it was Mead's success in making connections with local industry and businesses (something particularly noted following his death) that ultimately supported the regional employment prospects of the University's graduates through his activities with the Appointments Board.[81]

Turning to the Economic Research Section, it must be remembered that the various industrial studies undertaken throughout the 1930s were not unique to Manchester, as similar efforts at Liverpool, and to a much lesser extent at Birmingham, illustrate. There was something distinct about the extent of the work undertaken at Manchester, however, which drew on an established approach and tradition that was closely connected to the Lancashire economy. Set against the backdrop of Lancashire's severe economic problems after the First World War, this established approach ('realistic economic research') led to the creation, and later national recognition, of Manchester's Economic Research Section. Policy proposals flowed from this work, and we can see how members of the Economic Research Section proposed responses to the specific conditions prevailing in Lancashire at that time: the region's economic recovery, they argued, could only be achieved by a more planned industrial structure, and remedial action lay with the State and local authorities. However, these proposals did not lead to any policy responses from either local or central government.

These two examples are forgotten aspects of the University's history from the 1930s. Yet it would be wrong to conclude that the ideas underpinning such efforts – specifically, Manchester's approach to 'realistic economic research' – fully vanished with the outbreak of the Second World War. It is commonly argued that the civic universities lost much of their distinctive mission in the post-war period. I would argue that the principles that supported a particular Manchester approach to applied economic and social research were reinforced and significantly expanded by the establishment of the University of Manchester's Simon Fund, launched in 1944 with a major donation from Sir Ernest Simon, who was by then chairman of the University's Council.[82] The purpose of this fund was, and continues to be, to support fellowships and visiting professorships at Manchester in the social sciences, and its introduction in the 1940s reflected Simon's belief in the importance of applied social research. His decision to establish the fund was no doubt informed by the University's arguably haphazard efforts undertaken in this direction during the inter-war period, and it is worth remembering here that Simon had funded Henry Clay's appointment to a chair in social economics back in the mid-1920s. The one key difference by the 1940s was that Simon was not primarily concerned with local matters, but instead had a wider vision involving the importance of supporting post-war democracy through the wider understanding of political, social, economic and industrial affairs.[83] Over the past eighty years, the Simon Fund has had a profound and positive impact on both the University and the wider academic world, although it is fair to add that its work has been less focused on applied social research than Simon himself had hoped. It is worth noting here that some of Simon's philosophy likely developed from the earlier efforts (some well thought out, some less so) that he had witnessed the University undertake in the 1930s.

Despite some obvious failures and limitations – the teaching of Chinese under Mead performed little better than it had under Parker, and the output of the Economic Research Section had no significant impact on inter-war policy to address unemployment – the two initiatives considered here nevertheless attest to the innovative work undertaken by the University in the 1930s. Here, the University's work was centred on contributions it wanted to make to the economic and professional life of the city and the region, both through its research activities and the students it trained. Nor should we ignore the fact that this approach remains a key consideration of the University of Manchester into the twenty-first century. This work is now undertaken through different activities and on a significantly greater scale, with the University working with businesses and other partners to develop new initiatives and joint projects that respond to industry needs. All of this is anchored to a view, which has taken different forms at different times, of the institution's contributions to the social and economic well-being of the region.

Notes

1 This article draws on substantially revised material originally included in seminars for a post-graduate history module ('From Cottonopolis to Metropolis: Manchester Communities and Institutions') that I have delivered at the University of Manchester for several years; a lecture ('Chinese Studies and Manchester Trade: The Work of Edgar Mead as Reader of Chinese Language and Social Economy, 1933–1941') delivered as

part of the Confucius Institute Free Public Talks Series in April 2013; and a workshop held at the John Rylands Library in May 2023. I would also like to thank Stuart Jones and two anonymous reviewers for their extremely helpful comments on earlier drafts.

2 David R. Jones, *The Origins of Civic Universities: Manchester, Leeds and Liverpool* (London: Routledge, 1988), p. 51.
3 Howard Wach, 'Culture and the Middle Classes: Popular Knowledge in Industrial Manchester', *Journal of British Studies*, 27 (1988), 375–6.
4 John Coatman, 'The Significance of a Lancashire University to the Community', *Journal of the University of Manchester*, 1 (1938), 20–34.
5 Alex B. Robertson and Colin Lees, 'The University of Manchester, 1918–50: New Approaches and Changing Perspectives', *Bulletin of the John Rylands Library*, 84 (2002), 351–2.
6 In 1912, Britain exported 6,913 million square yards of cotton textiles; this had declined to 2,472 million square yards by 1930, and 1,494 million square yards by 1938: Derek H. Aldcroft, *The Inter-War Economy: Britain, 1919–1939* (London: B. T. Batsford, 1970), p. 156.
7 University of Manchester, *Report of the Council to the Court of Governors* (November 1936), p. 17. Copies of these reports are in the University of Manchester Archives in the sequence UOP/2/1/.
8 Economics Research Section, *An Industrial Survey of the Lancashire Area (excluding Merseyside)* (London: H.M. Stationery Office, 1932); John Jewkes and Allan Winterbottom, *Juvenile Unemployment* (London: George Allen & Unwin, 1933); John Jewkes and E. M. Gray, *Wages and Labour in the Lancashire Cotton Spinning Industry* (Manchester: Manchester University Press, 1935); Economics Research Section, *Re-adjustment in Lancashire* (Manchester: Manchester University Press, 1936).
9 Keith Tribe, 'The Faculty of Commerce and Manchester Economics, 1903–44', *Manchester School*, 71 (2003), 704.
10 Robertson and Lees, 'The University of Manchester', 346.
11 See Alon Kadish, 'The Foundations of Birmingham's Faculty of Commerce as a Statement on the Nature of Economics', *Manchester School*, 59 (1991), 160–72; Eric Ives, Diane Drummond and Leonard Schwarz, *The First Civic University: Birmingham, 1880–1980: An Introductory History* (Birmingham: University of Birmingham Press, 2000), pp. 147–8; Keith Tribe, *Constructing Economic Science: The Invention of the Discipline, 1850–1950* (Oxford: Oxford University Press, 2022), pp. 252–65.
12 George W. Daniels, 'Economic and Commercial Studies in the Owens College and the University', *Manchester School*, 1 (1930), 7.
13 Tribe, Constructing Economic Science, pp. 265–88.
14 Robertson and Lees, 'The University of Manchester', 351.
15 See, for example, Sydney J. Chapman, *The Lancashire Cotton Industry: A Study in Economic Development* (Manchester: Manchester University Press, 1904); Sydney J. Chapman, *The Cotton Industry and Trade* (London: Methuen, 1905); and Sydney J. Chapman and F. J. Marquis, 'The Recruiting of the Employing Classes from the Ranks of the Wage Earners in the Cotton Industry', *Journal of the Royal Statistical Society*, 75 (1912), 293–313.

16 The results of this research, a series of articles in the *Manchester Guardian* in February and March 1909 entitled 'Unemployment, with Some Special Reference to Lancashire' (and co-authored with Chapman), remained Hallsworth's main publications throughout his academic career.

17 'Gift to the University of Manchester – Chair of Social Economics', *Manchester Guardian* (30 April 1927), p. 15.

18 Robertson and Lees, 'The University of Manchester', 352; see also H. S. Jones and Chris Godden, 'Burghers and Citizens: the Simons and the University of Manchester', in John Ayshford, Martin Dodge, H. S. Jones, Diana Leitch and Janet Wolff (eds), *The Simons of Manchester: How One Family Shaped a City and a Nation* (Manchester: Manchester University Press, 2024), pp. 251–73.

19 Henry Clay, *The Post-War Unemployment Problem* (London: Macmillan, 1928); Henry Clay, *The Problem of Industrial Relations and Other Lectures* (London: Macmillan, 1929).

20 See, for example, George W. Daniels, *The Early English Cotton Industry, with Some Unpublished Letters of Samuel Crompton* (Manchester: Manchester University Press, 1920); George W. Daniels and John Jewkes, 'The Crisis in the Lancashire Cotton Industry', *Economic Journal*, 37 (1927), 33–46; George W. Daniels and John Jewkes, 'The Post-War Depression in the Lancashire Cotton Industry', *Journal of the Royal Statistical Society*, 91 (1928), 153–206; George W. Daniels, 'Overseas Trade of the United Kingdom in Recent Years as Compared with 1913', *Manchester School*, 2 (1931), 1–9; G. W. Daniels, 'The Present Economic Situation', *Manchester School*, 2 (1931), 65–76. See also John Jewkes, 'The Depression in the Lancashire Cotton Industry', *The Highway*, 21 (1929), 95–100.

21 George W. Daniels, *George Unwin: A Memorial Lecture* (Manchester: Manchester University Press, 1926).

22 H. B. Charlton, *Portrait of a University, 1851–1951: To Commemorate the Centenary of Manchester University* (Manchester: Manchester University Press, 1951), p. 113.

23 Manchester, John Rylands Library, GB 133 Eng. MS 1318 (Sydney Chapman, *Some Memories and Reflections* (unpublished, 1940s), p. 77).

24 Charlton, *Portrait of a University*, p. 113.

25 *Report of the Council* (November 1932), pp. 17, 59; *Report of the Council* (November 1932), pp. 17, 59; UoMA, VCA/7/360 (Department of Economics, 1927–1944); 'Social Economics in the University of Manchester', *Nature* (11 July 1936), p. 68.

26 For details about the Oxford Institute of Statistics, see Norman Chester, *Economics, Politics and Social Studies in Oxford, 1900–85* (Basingstoke: Macmillan, 1986), pp. 55–7; Jan Toporowski, 'The Oxford Institute of Statistics, 1935–1962', in Robert A. Cord (ed.), *The Palgrave Companion to Oxford Economics* (Cham: Palgrave Macmillan, 2021), pp. 147–59.

27 *Report of the Council* (November 1936), pp. 7, 17. See also details in 'Manchester University: Economics Chair for Mr Jewkes', *Manchester Guardian* (11 June 1936), p. 13.

28 Board of Trade, *An Industrial Survey of the Lancashire Area (excluding Merseyside),* (London: HM Stationery Office, 1932); H. W. O., 'Review – An Industrial Survey of

the Lancashire Area (excluding Merseyside), An Industrial Survey of the North-East Coast Area, An Industrial Survey of Merseyside', *Geography*, 18 (1933), 328; 'Industrial Surveys and Employment Problems', *Nature* (3 December 1932), pp. 825–7.

29 John Jewkes and Allan Winterbottom, *An Industrial Survey of Cumberland and Furness* (Manchester: Manchester University Press, 1933); 'Cumberland and Furness – Industrial Decline: A Depressed Area's Problems', *Manchester Guardian* (12 May 1933), p. 9.

30 John Jewkes and Allan Winterbottom, *Juvenile Unemployment* (London: George Allen & Unwin, 1933). See also John Jewkes and Allan Winterbottom, 'Unrecorded Unemployment in the Cotton Industry', *Economic Journal*, 41 (1931), 639–46; Allan Winterbottom, 'An Enquiry into the Employment of Juveniles in Lancashire', *Manchester School*, 3 (1932), 29–46; John Jewkes, 'Unemployment Among Juveniles: Lancashire Inquiry – Labour Problem of the Future: Some Remedies', *Manchester Guardian* (1 June 1933), p. 9; 'Social Surveys and Juvenile Unemployment', *Nature* (18 November 1933), pp. 761–3.

31 In the case of juvenile unemployment, Jewkes admitted that the Research Section had discovered little that was not already known, but had been able to work out a scientific and quantitative statement of its various elements: 'The Juvenile Unemployed', *Manchester Guardian* (5 February 1934), p. 16.

32 John Jewkes and E. M. Gray, *Wages and Labour in the Lancashire Cotton Spinning Industry* (Manchester: Manchester University Press, 1935); 'Cotton, Wages and Labour: The University's Inquiry', *Manchester Guardian* (20 September 1935), p. 9; Barnard Ellinger, 'Review – Wages and Labour in Cotton Spinning', *International Affairs*, 15 (1936), 294–5. See also T. D. Barlow 'Surplus Capacity in the Lancashire Cotton Industry', *Manchester School*, 6 (1935), 32–6.

33 See, for example, Christopher Saunders, 'The Importance of Seasonal Variations in Employment in the United Kingdom', *Economic Journal*, 45 (1935), 269–79; C. T. Saunders, *Seasonal Variations in Employment* (London: Longmans, Green & Co., 1936); 'The Seasonal Trade – Fluctuations of Industry: A Neglected Problem', *Manchester Guardian* (2 April 1936), p. 11.

34 Economic Research Section, *Re-adjustment in Lancashire* (Manchester: Manchester University Press, 1936). The book is presented on the title page as the work of the Economic Research Section; the authors named in a prefatory note by Jewkes were Mr. S. R. Dennison, Mr. W. V. L. Magraw, Mr. D. N. Chester and Mr. C. T. Saunders. See also 'Lancashire Industry: The New Survey – Report to be Reading in a Year', *Manchester Guardian* (19 June 1935), p. 8; 'The Depressed Areas and New Industries', *Manchester Guardian* (16 September 1936), p. 4; 'Location of Industries', *Nature* (6 February 1937), pp. 211–3.

35 Ben W. Lewis, 'Review – Re-adjustment in Lancashire', *Journal of Political Economy*, 46 (1938), 269–70.

36 George C. Allen, The Industrial Development of Birmingham and the Black Country, 1860–1927 (London: George Allen & Unwin, 1929).

37 Ives *et al.*, *The First Civic University*, p. 208.

38 David Caradog Jones (ed.) *The Social Survey of Merseyside*, 3 vols (Liverpool: Liverpool University Press, 1934).
39 See, for example, 'Social Science at Liverpool', *Nature* (28 January 1939), p. 171.
40 'Social Planning: Economic Science Out of Step', *Manchester Guardian* (26 January 1935), p. 15. Three years later, Hall became the first director of the National Institute of Economic and Social Research, established with funding from, among others, the Rockefeller Foundation, the Pilgrim Trust and the Leverhulme Trust.
41 Arnold Plant, 'Review – Wages and Labour in the Lancashire Cotton Spinning Industry', *Economica*, 4 (1937), 110–11.
42 *Report of the Council* (November 1933), p. 11; *Report of the Council* (November 1934), p. 11; *Report of the Council* (November 1935), p. 13. The Lancashire Development Industrial Council also provided £500 to support research into the economic position of Lancashire.
43 Roger E. Backhouse and Jeff Biddle, 'The Concept of Applied Economics: A History of Ambiguity and Multiple Meanings', *History of Political Economy*, 32, Supplement 1 (2000), 8.
44 Keith Tribe (ed.), Economic Careers: Economics and Economists in Britain, 1930–1970 (London: Routledge, 1997), p. 113.
45 Henry W. Macrosty, 'Review – *An Industrial Survey of Cumberland and Furness*', *Economic Journal*, 43 (1933), 692–4; 'The Future of Lancashire: Planning for New Industries – University Survey's Suggestion to the Government', *Manchester Guardian* (9 August 1932), p. 12; 'An Industrial Survey', *Manchester Guardian* (19 June 1935), p. 10; 'Research and Teaching in Universities', *Nature* (22 August 1936), p. 303. The inevitable limitations of some initiatives and interventions were also recognised. In the case of Cumberland and Furness, the commercial potential for the hydrogenation of coal (the production of oil from coal) was viewed as doubtful, the use of coke-oven gas for municipal purposes deemed impractical, and the proposed development of Cumberland as a holiday centre could not offer a guaranteed solution for absorbing surplus labour.
46 This was a step which the government had, at that time, decided not to make mandatory, but had instead left to the discretion of local education authorities. See, for example, 'Unemployed Boys and Girls: The School-Leaving Age', *Manchester Guardian* (12 May 1933), p. 13, and 'Juvenile Unemployment', *Manchester Guardian* (5 September 1933), p. 8.
47 Backhouse and Biddle, 'The Concept of Applied Economics', 13.
48 Martin Bulmer, *The Chicago School of Sociology: Institutions, Diversity, and the Rise of Sociological Research* (Chicago: University of Chicago Press, 1984), p. 5.
49 See, for example, G. L. S. Shackle, *The Years of High Theory: Invention and Tradition in Economic Thought, 1926–1939* (Cambridge: Cambridge University Press, 1967); David E. W. Laidler, *Fabricating the Keynesian Revolution: Studies of the Inter-war Literature on Money, the Cycle, and Unemployment* (Cambridge: Cambridge University Press, 1999); Susan Howson, 'Keynes and the LSE Economists', *Journal of the History of Economic Thought*, 31 (2009), 257–80.

50 Fiorenza Belussi and Katia Caldari, 'The Lancashire Industrial District: Its Rise, Prosperity and Decline in the Analysis of British Economists', in Tiziano Raffaelli, Tamotsu Nishizawa, and Simon Cook (eds) *Marshall, Marshallians and Industrial Economics* (New York: Routledge, 2011), pp. 135–62.

51 'Obituary, Edward Harper Parker', *Manchester Guardian* (29 January 1926), p. 10. For information on Parker's work, see David Prager Branner, 'The Linguistic Ideas of Edward Harper Parker', *Journal of the American Oriental Society*, 119 (1999), 12–34.

52 For example, for the academic year 1921/22, his report to the University Council stated that he then had two students and expressed some excitement at the prospect of third starting in the next academic year. *Report of the Council* (November 1922), p. 38.

53 Manchester, University of Manchester Archives (hereafter, UoMA), VCA/7/314 (Professor Walter Moberly to Professor Jerome Greene, 3 April 1933).

54 UoMA, VCA/7/314 (W. L. Holland (Research Secretary Institute of Pacific Relations) to Walter H. Moberly, March 1933); VCA/7/314 (Jerome Greene to Walter H. Moberly, 27 April 1933). For details on Ho's life and career, see 'Dr Franklin Ho, Economist, Dies', *New York Times* (7 July 1975), p. 28.

55 In supporting Tayler for the new post, Hewlett Johnson (the Dean of Canterbury) wrote to Moberly noting that, in his opinion, there was no one who had 'a more thorough and first-hand knowledge of China's economic affairs than Mr. Tayler': UoMA, VCA/7/314 (Herbert Johnson to Walter H. Moberly, March 1933). For further information on Tayler's work in China, see Paul B. Trescott, 'John Bernard Tayler and the Development of Co-operatives in China, 1917–1945', *Annals of Public and Cooperative Economics*, 64 (1993), 209–26.

56 'Obituary: Mr E. W. Mead', *The Times* (9 January 1941), p. 9; 'Obituary: Mr E. W. Mead', *Manchester Guardian* (10 January 1941), p. 7.

57 Some early publications by Mead from this period included 'China', *Journal of the Royal United Service Institution*, 74 (1929), 847–51, and 'Chaos in China', *Journal of the Royal United Service Institution*, 75 (1930), 608–14.

58 UoMA, VCA/7/314 (Gilbert Hubbard to Walter H. Moberly, n.d. 1933).

59 *Ibid.*

60 'University of Manchester: Extending the Study of Chinese', *Manchester Guardian* (18 May 1933), p. 12.

61 'University of Manchester: Summer Term', *Manchester Guardian* (1 July 1933), p. 11.

62 'University of Manchester: New Session', *Manchester Guardian* (6 October 1933), p. 3.

63 It is worth recalling here that Frieda Utley's study of the cotton industry and the trade of Lancashire, China and Japan – *Lancashire and the Far East* – had been published in 1931.

64 These lectures covered, among other things, the history of the treaty port system in China, the international policy of the Chinese Nationalist Government, and the importance of peace for the prosecution of trade in the Far East. Summaries of some of Mead's lectures can be found in 'Foreign Traders in China: The First Eighty Years', *Manchester Guardian* (9 November 1933), p. 11; 'Foreign Trade in China: Extraterritoriality', *Manchester Guardian* (23 November 1933), p. 18; 'British Interests in Far East',

Manchester Guardian (12 February 1934); 'British Interests: No Territorial Designs on Asia', *South China Morning Post* (12 March 1934), p. 15.

65 *Report of the Council* (November 1934), p. 67; UoMA, VCA/7/315 ('Report by the Reader in Chinese Language and Commerce: Sessions 1933–34 and 1934–35').

66 See, for example, 'In Manchester', *Manchester Guardian* (30 September 1935), p. 11; 'China's Problems: The Special Privileges of Foreigners', *Manchester Guardian* (24 October 1935), p. 11; 'China and Japan's Policy: New Hopes in League?', *Manchester Guardian* (7 January 1936), p. 6; *Report of the Council* (November 1936), p. 69; 'China and Japan: Prestige and Economics', *Manchester Guardian* (28 February 1938), p. 13; *Report of the Council* (November 1938), p. 78. Short details of other public lectures – covering public finance in China, British trade prospects in China, and Sino-foreign relations – can be found in 'China Today: The Problem of Foreign Contracts', *Manchester Guardian* (8 December 1934), p. 16; 'Public Finance in China: Remodelled Methods', *Manchester Guardian* (13 December 1934), p. 20; *Report of the Council* (November 1935), p. 74.

67 'In Manchester: Contacts with China', *Manchester Guardian* (25 October 1935), p. 13; 'Anglo-Chinese Society: Promoting Friendship', *Manchester Guardian* (22 November 1935), p. 12; 'Chinese in England: Manchester Plan to Help Lonely Visitors', *South China Morning Post* (10 December 1935), p. 16. Despite his limited success in recruiting students to the course on Chinese language, history and institutions, Mead's energies were none the less widely recognised. In a speech to mark the opening of an exhibition of Chinese art at the Manchester Art Gallery in the spring of 1936, the Chinese Ambassador, Dr Quo Tai-chi noted: 'we Chinese also appreciate your maintenance in Manchester University of a Readership in Chinese, and we note with satisfaction how active Mr Mead, the holder, is': 'Chinese Art Exhibition: Opening Ceremony at Manchester Gallery – The Ambassador's Speech', *Manchester Guardian* (4 April 1936), p. 15.

68 'Lancashire and China: Language Question', *Manchester Guardian* (8 November 1934), p. 13.

69 'Russian Studies: Manchester's New Chair', *Manchester Guardian* (20 June 1919), p. 14. At the time of his appointment, Trofimov was Reader in Russian at King's College, University of London.

70 See, for example, 'The Study of Russian', *Manchester Guardian* (14 September 1918), p. 4.

71 Less than a year earlier, Mead had been appointed assistant to the Vice-Chancellor: 'University of Manchester', *Manchester Guardian* (23 December 1938), p. 18

72 'Obituary: Mr E. W. Mead', *Manchester Guardian* (10 January 1941), p. 7.

73 UoMA, VCA/7/1 (Minutes of Special Meeting – Manchester University Appointment Board and Manchester Chamber of Commerce (25 March 1935), Appointments Board).

74 For a list of Allison Peers's extensive publications, see H. B. Hall, 'E. Allison Peers: A Selective Bibliography', *Bulletin of Hispanic Studies*, 30 (1953), 12–19. See also 'University News', *The Times* (7 July 1922), p. 9; 'A Summer School in Spain', *The Times* (30 April 1932), p. 10; 'Obituary – Professor E. Allison Peers', *The Times*

(24 December 1952), p. 6; 'Obituary – Prof. Allison Peers', *Manchester Guardian* (29 December 1952), p. 2.

75 *Report of the Council* (November 1936), p. 69; *Report of the Council* (November 1937), p. 70; *Report of the Council* (November 1938), p. 78. Examples of Mead's reviews for the *Manchester Guardian* include 'A Surgeon's China', *Manchester Guardian* (19 September 1934), p. 5; 'In Search of Old Peking, *Manchester Guardian* (16 September 1935), p. 5; 'The New Culture in China, *Manchester Guardian* (24 July 1936), p. 7; 'The New Social Order in China', *Manchester Guardian* (23 March 1937), p. 7; 'Crisis in China', *Manchester Guardian* (30 November 1937), p. 7; 'Agrarian China', *Manchester Guardian* (18 August 1939), p, 5.

76 *Report of the Council* (November 1936), p. 69.

77 *Report of the Council* (November 1935), p. 74; *Report of the Council* (November (1937), p. 70; *Report of the Council* (November 1938), p. 78.

78 UoMA, VCA/7/315 ('Report by the Reader in Chinese Language and Commerce: Sessions 1933–34 and 1934–35'). Trofimov, like Mead, struggled due to external factors. Despite Trofimov's great efforts to promote the teaching of Russian, the Russian Revolution and the subsequent suspicion of Communism deterred students from studying his course. It also appears that Trofimov's public lectures tended to be much less focused on commerce and trade than Mead's, concentrating instead on Russian literature, various aspects of Soviet rule, and modern Russian history. See, for example, 'Prof. Trofimov's Lectures', *Manchester Guardian* (6 December 1919), p. 8; 'Professor Trofimov on Soviet Rule', *Manchester Guardian* (13 December 1920), p. 8; 'Soviet Russia', *Manchester Guardian* (5 February 1935), p. 14, 'Industrial Progress in Russia', *Manchester Guardian* (26 February 1935), p. 11; 'Landmarks in Russian History', *Manchester Guardian* (27 October 1933), p. 13.

79 See, for example, *Report of the Council* (November 1938), pp. 14–15.

80 'Trade Interests in China: Manchester's Chance', *Manchester Guardian* (23 January 1928), p. 6.

81 UoMA, VCA/7/315 (Minutes – Arrangements in Chinese (5 March 1941)).

82 The gift consisted of shares in the two Simon engineering businesses. The original dividend income – which grew substantially in real terms – was over £3,000 a year, equivalent to more than £100,000 in 2024: Jones and Godden, 'Burghers and Citizens', 263–4.

83 UoMA, VCA/7/732 ('Note for members of the Simon Fund Committee' (30 October 1944)).

Servicing the State: Municipality and the Military Industrial Complex

RICHARD BROOK, LANCASTER UNIVERSITY

Abstract

Following its charter of 1956, the Manchester Municipal College of Technology appointed a new principal, who oversaw the rapid expansion of the campus. The development of a suite of new buildings, on one of the city's most polluted and derelict tracts, required cooperation between the College, the Victoria University of Manchester, the Manchester Corporation, and a host of central government ministries. This initiative was driven by the recognition that technology and technological education were vital tools in the retention of Britain's global influence. Manchester was identified for the accelerated growth of higher technological education due to its history of engineering, manufacturing and the development of commercial computing. Founded on archival sources, this article explores the complex relationships between statecraft, Whitehall policy, municipal governance and space. Using the manifestation of urban planning and architecture, it argues that the 'Warfare State' had influence beyond overt military programmes, which informed certain civic and municipal local enterprise with objectives other than rearmament, such as education, employment and economic recovery.

Keywords: UMIST; urban renewal; post-war; planning; architecture; university

Post-war Britain demanded new technological education. Manchester was an obvious choice, owing to its industrial manufacturing history, and the clustering of computing and nuclear research and development in the north-west of the United Kingdom. In this article, I argue that David Edgerton's conception of the 'Warfare State' can be extended beyond its explicit military context, and that the existential threat of a Cold War was, in this case, leveraged by regional and municipal actors in pursuit of technological, economic and educational advancements.[1] I suggest that such development serviced central government agendas, but also satisfied local demands for growth in a post-industrial economy that languished in the face of globalisation, decolonisation, the economic downturn of the 1930s and the slow recovery, particularly in the North, in the immediate post-war years. The expansion of Manchester's College of Science and Technology was bound with rearmament and tied to a regional cluster of military industrial research, but was also intrinsic to the desires of local business and the local authority to enact urban renewal at a large scale. The major phases of its development, from 1957 to 1970, ran in tandem with the reconstruction of large parts of the city, and together they signalled economic recovery worthy of further investment by government and the private sector.

Atomic warfare was a powerful force shaping the government agenda in the late 1940s.[2] The political elite, in the face of diminishing global power, wanted to restate Britain's international authority. In the United States, the McMahon Act of 1946 denied Britain any further collaborative role in the development of the atomic bomb. The first controlled nuclear explosion by the Soviet Union in 1949, and the outbreak of war in Korea in 1950, made the rearmament programme and civil defence central to government activity. Welfare expenditure shrank and defence spending grew, feeding the 'Warfare State'. In the United Kingdom, civil and defence applications were interwoven – relationships that were underpinned by personnel who held military positions during wartime and parliamentary posts in the post-war period.

Earlier, in 1944, Ernest Bevin, Minister of Labour in the wartime cabinet, had brought attention to the lack of technically skilled workers. This was underlined by a series of reports, that considered the demand for retraining scientific workers, and the role of colleges and universities in this provision.[3] The Hankey committee (1945) 'identified the extent of Britain's (re)training needs'; the Percy committee (1945) looked at higher technological education; and the Barlow committee (1946) examined the demand for educated workers in the future.[4] Collectively, the outcome was a recommendation for a significant increase in student numbers, particularly in technological education. The Percy Report made the distinction between the provision of technological education in universities and colleges.[5] It also established the need for technical colleges to underpin the immediate expansion, since the universities were not then in a position to do so.[6] Technical colleges needed investment, and it was this dual purpose of expansion and improvement that drove the initiative for the first wave of new colleges of technology, amongst which was Manchester.

Networks

Defence and military research during the war, by Allied and German scientists alike, advanced knowledge for the technologies that would define the global political landscape for the rest of the twentieth century and beyond: the nuclear bomb, the rocket and the computer. Whilst directed from Whitehall, it was the regional military industrial structures that influenced the focus of nuclear and computing cultures in the north-west of England. The geography of regionally clustered nuclear research and development was a product of war. From as early as 1935, Cabinet had discussed the flight range of Luftwaffe bombers and the location of munitions factories.[7] Sites in the north-west were preferred owing to their distance from mainland Europe. Of the forty-four Royal Ordnance factories, nineteen were retained after 1945 for the peacetime production of arms, including the nuclear programme.[8] For atomic production facilities, 'a certain separation from centres of population had to be balanced against the accessibility of local labour. Within these constraints it was the proximity of industrial and academic organisations ... that led to the selection of North West England as the key location.'[9] These industrial and academic organisations were already collaborating on various aspects of research and development necessary to realise the delivery of a nuclear missile – the earliest uranium enrichment occurred at Rhydymwyn in North Wales, where Metropolitan Vickers (who also operated a large facility in Manchester) worked with Imperial Chemical Industries; pioneering nuclear research was undertaken jointly by the University of Manchester and the United Kingdom Atomic Energy Authority (UKAEA) at Risley near Warrington; guided missiles were developed by Ferranti in Wythenshawe; and an array of defence contracts were awarded to companies in the north-west, most notably at sites at Warton and Samlesbury near Preston, operated by English Electric (later British Aerospace).[10] Instrumental in the development of rockets and the nuclear programme was the computer. Manchester was one of three British centres where the earliest computing research was carried out, in this case by a group of scientists already known to one another from their wartime occupations.[11] Amongst them was Bertram Vivian Bowden, who was 42 years old and leading the computer sales division at Ferranti when he was appointed as Principal of the Manchester Municipal College of Technology (hereafter referred to as 'the College' and later, from 1966, known as the University of Manchester Institute of Science and Technology (UMIST)) in 1953.[12]

During the war, Bowden had been posted to Washington DC and the Massachusetts Institute of Technology (MIT) to work on the development of the radar. He led a British team in his role as principal scientific advisor to the Ministry of Supply's Telecommunications Research Establishment, where he worked with Freddie Williams, Tom Kilburn and Peter Hall.[13] On his return to the United Kingdom, Bowden joined the UKAEA.[14] His experience of military technological research in well-funded higher education institutions was a dramatic influence and shaped his collaborative approach in the future, including his stewardship of technological education in Manchester. Freddie Williams and his assistant Kilburn were electronic engineers, who found themselves rapidly without purpose in August 1945 as hostilities ended.[15] They gravitated towards the University of Manchester, where the Cambridge mathematician Max Newman had taken a post as Professor of Pure Mathematics in 1945. Following encouragement from Patrick Blackett, Williams was appointed by Newman as Chair of Electrical Engineering in November 1946, and Kilburn was 'on loan' from the Ministry of Supply.[16] By June 1948, the assembled group of mathematicians and electrical engineers achieved a global first in realising the 'stored program' computing principle, in the machine now popularly known as 'Baby'.[17] In October 1948, the Ministry of Supply asked Ferranti to help to build a computer, to designs by the group, funded by the Ministry of Defence and given technical support from the Telecommunications Research Establishment.[18] Shortly afterwards, Bowden and Hall took positions with Ferranti, also in Manchester.

Bowden's experience in the United States, combined with his personal proximity to technological research and development in Manchester, led to his appointment as principal. His advocacy for the development of the College was not far short of propaganda, a tactic in which he was well versed; in his introduction to an edited volume on British computer research, *Faster than Thought* (1953), a potted history helped to fix the narrative of Manchester as its birthplace. By 1956, in typically bombastic prose, he had penned his *Proposals for the Development of the Manchester College of Science and Technology*, asserting that '[t]he college will perform a vitally important service for the industry of the country as a whole and of this district in particular'.[19]

The College of Science and Technology

The origins of the College can be traced back to the foundation of the Manchester Mechanics' Institution, in 1824, in the Bridgewater public house. In 1902, the Institution relocated to a new home on Sackville Street, designed for them by Spalding and Cross, and latterly extended to designs by Bradshaw, Gass and Hope (1927–57). The Institution became the School of Technology (1902) and later the Municipal College of Technology (1918). The College gained its own charter in 1956, leading to an increased focus on degree-level academic courses (it was not until 1966 that the name UMIST was adopted). The College makes for an interesting case study for several reasons, most obviously its transition from locally resourced further education college to a nationally funded higher education facility. It was one of the first institutions to make such a move, and its development predated the wider post-war expansion programme for British universities. The processes for the rapid approval and funding of construction at the College helped the University Grants Committee to refine their policies and budgets as the rate of expansion in the sector accelerated.

Furthermore, the site dedicated for the growth of the institution, combined with Manchester's post-war plans, entangled it with the ambitions of the Corporation – its southern edge was bounded by a proposed aerial motorway that cut a swathe through existing, but condemned, dense terraced housing. As well as its position in the interplay of tiers of governance, the development of the campus was a collaborative exercise, where the Planning and Development Committee arrived at a consensus view that informed architectural decisions. In the ten years between 1959 and 1969, thirteen new buildings were realised on the complicated inner-city site, their design distributed between three local architectural practices. The ensuing suite of predominantly white concrete buildings, set amidst the lawns of a well-organised campus, whilst arguably mainstream, are broadly considered as a group to be amongst the best of the post-war campuses in the United Kingdom.[20]

Manchester's College, with Imperial College London, was one of the first significant investments in the expansion of higher education after 1945. Its growth does not align with the established architectural histories of university development in the United Kingdom, however; it was not 'ancient', 'redbrick' or 'plate-glass'.[21] The idiosyncratic situation of the institution lies in its creation, and the prevailing British attitude towards higher technical education. Historically, the College made an unusual provision for both further and higher education in science and technology subjects. Since 1905, a concordat with the University of Manchester had underwritten the awarding of higher degrees.[22] The College itself retained its funding structure from the Ministry of Education and the Manchester Corporation, whereas universities were independent, with their sole source of State funding coming from the University Grants Committee and, in varying degrees, controlled by the Treasury.[23] As early as 1936, and perhaps pre-empting the post-war organisational demands, the Manchester Corporation realised that logistical planning at a regional scale was required to 'organise a more rational use of equipment' (at the College), and to transfer less specialist courses to other local institutions.[24]

The local understanding of the regional, if not national, importance of the College was reinforced in the years following 1945, and, as the extension to the Sackville Street building neared completion in the mid-1950s, discussions between the University of Manchester, the City of Manchester Education Committee and the University Grants Committee were underway as to how best to develop the institution.[25] Part of this preparation involved the construction of new technical colleges by the Manchester Corporation, which would divert some of the more vocational courses away from the College and thus permit a greater focus on higher technological education at the inner-city site.[26]

The University Grants Committee was historically able to 'propagate without interference' from the Treasury and the Board of Education, and, until 1939, it was the universities that set the ideological tone within which their development took place.[27] At this time, the accepted consensus was that the State should be the 'subordinate partner' in this relationship.[28] The outbreak of war changed this situation, however, as buildings were requisitioned for alternative purposes, young men were enlisted, and institutions were evacuated in their entirety. The study of science was subject to particular intervention 'directly related to the various and developing needs of the war machine'.[29] The legacy of this type of direct instruction from the State, combined with the numerous reports produced in the mid-1940s that examined the educational needs of a range of professions, was a strengthening of the University Grants Committee's 'machinery'.[30] Nevertheless, the College was in a position to inform the policy and cost yardsticks of the University Grants Committee as it developed new and unique building types and was in advance of other university construction. Effectively, a generous budget was available to the College if it was able to justify its demands. Due in part to the lack of input from the Ministry of Education, the unprecedented new technological institutions had much more control of their own planning and building programmes than the plate-glass universities that would follow.

As well as recommending expansion in science and technological higher education, the Barlow Report, referring to the demand for educated workers, proposed that certain existing university colleges should become universities in their own right, and that a number of institutes of technology should be established. It advocated for the increased involvement of the University Grants Committee in planning for the development of the universities, and proposed that at least one new university was founded.[31] These factors, and the extant situation of the College in an industrial city with a history of innovation already delivering higher education courses, combined to make Manchester a prominent candidate for investment. Even so, despite the recommendations, the Labour government was slow to act, and did not consolidate its views until its 1951 pre-election statement in *Higher Technological Education*.[32] Labour lost the general election, but the case for expansion was clear, and the incoming Conservative administration had to address demand. Their policy response was not implemented until the White Paper on Technical Education (1956). In the meantime, necessity being the mother of invention, the plans for the College, its transition to exclusively Higher Education provision, and its full charter as a university, progressed, despite there being no agreed national framework.[33]

Reflective of the focus upon defence and rearmament in the region, in 1953–54 Manchester was in receipt of a greater proportion of central government funding for technical education than any other provincial city.[34] The grant of a Royal Charter to the College was publicly announced in March 1954 by the Conservative Party chairman, Lord Woolton, on a visit to Manchester, and endorsed by the city's Education Committee.[35] It was formally announced in the House of Commons on 1 August 1955, and one year later, the new governing body took control of the institution, replacing the Education Committee of the City Council who had been administrative guardians since 1892.[36] Bowden's description of the negotiations implies a degree of trust between central and local government; that each would adhere to implicit agreements concerning sources of funding for various acts of land assembly and purchase. This sentiment was mirrored by Rab Butler, Leader of the House of Commons (famously known for his promotion of political consensus in the post-war period), who described the Manchester Corporation as having 'shown the utmost forward-looking patriotism … to reserve an area of seventeen and a half acres for the development'.[37]

Following the royal assent of the Manchester Corporation Act, the transfer of the College was formalised. The new campus was to be built to the south of the Manchester South Junction and Altrincham railway viaduct. Thus, with the original College buildings to its north, efforts to unify the campus either side of the brick mass that cut a divisive east–west transect across the site were ambitious and complicated. Further design and construction challenges were encountered as the proposed site extended into Chorlton-upon-Medlock, an area that was one of the oldest industrial sectors of the city. The dark curves of the polluted River Medlock wound their way through the allotted land, and carved through the railway viaduct. The culverting and rerouting of the river was key to releasing the land, and initial plans envisioned exclusively new buildings on the site. The new aerial motorway, initially known as 'Link Road 17/7', would form the southernmost boundary. The Manchester Corporation Bill of 1957 was designed to achieve the major objectives of permission for the alignment of the road and the culverting of the River Medlock, both of which had a bearing on the plans for the College, but equally could be achieved independently. The cost of culverting the River Medlock was eventually shared between the local authority and the University Grants Committee.[38] In this instance, we can see the relations between local and national government that the planning historian Gordon Cherry reconciled as a dual system of 'shared responsibilities', and which John Davis explained as expanding the activities of local government whilst increasingly determining their financing.[39] It was the conflicts of the twentieth century that created the dispersed regional offices of government departments with devolved powers, yet increasingly, in the post-war period as peacetime advanced, local government was in direct communication with Whitehall, rather than relying on regional offices as a conduit. Thus, some of the powers invested in the regional ministerial offices were diminished, and local government responsibilities intensified.

The interrelationship of the various actors was further highlighted by delays in the approval of the Bill that followed in 1958. Its slow passage through Parliament had a direct impact on the construction schedule. This in turn required an 'exceptional' transfer of funds from one year's programme into another by the University Grants Committee.[40] As building projects were delayed, costs began to rise, placing phasing possibilities at odds with funding streams.[41] The University Grants Committee did not wish to be consulted on the design of buildings until the schemes reached a particular submission status, when proposed buildings could be costed in relation to other buildings of a similar type.[42] This was problematic in terms of the first major building on site, the lecture room block, since it was a 'new departure in educational building' and seen as risky to significantly develop without consultation.[43] It also meant that any plans for a phased sequence of development were routinely disrupted. As the University Grants Committee gained experience, costs would become much tighter, but in 1957 there was no indication that they would apply standardisation to the building models and subsequent expenditure on the Manchester campus. Indeed, any 'unimaginative cheeseparing' was deemed 'undesirable' if it limited the quality of new buildings.[44]

Generally, the University Grants Committee viewed the College's committee structures favourably, and valued their advice in design and procurement protocols.[45] The building programme itself was under constant adjustment, in line with parliamentary decisions that impacted upon the work of the University Grants Committee and ultimately the development of the College, where the content and organisation of the master plan was subject to both national advice and local interpretation. Indicative of its special status, and of the urgency for its services, the College secured an annual review of its construction budget, and was not subject to the quinquennial system applied elsewhere.[46]

Bowden was concerned with the site organisation in terms of its open space. His was a vision where buildings should 'be sited with dignity and propriety, and in such a way that the sun and air can penetrate the buildings and the spaces between them'.[47] Aligned with Bowden's view, and accounting for the overall appearance of the development, the Planning and Development Committee prepared a design-briefing document entitled 'Some Canons of Good Design'.[48] In a manner befitting a technological institution, the functional demands of spaces were assumed as the primary organising factor in the design of buildings. Their aesthetic treatment was also a concern, however, and was referred to under the banner of 'pleasing appearance'. This short treatise extended to the massing and proportion of new buildings, a tacit instruction as to the honesty of facades and to a simplicity informed by economy, lack of 'fuss', and the use of modern materials that would not deteriorate with age in the Manchester climate. The University of Manchester developed a range of 'neo-Georgian' buildings during the 1950s in a similar and unified style designed by H. S. Fairhurst & Sons on Brunswick Street, broadly aligned with the beaux-arts vision of Worthington's plan in 1945.[49] The architectural qualities of the Brunswick Street ensemble were unpopular with certain politicians; the visual appearance of the new buildings was regarded as insufficiently progressive, which may have influenced the directive for honesty and simplicity in the College buildings. A further clause stipulated that 'the use of modern materials, constructions and techniques is desirable', but also that 'they must have a raison d'etre [sic] other than a mere exercise in technological ingenuity'.[50]

Sir Hubert Worthington was appointed as the site architect in July 1955. The son of accomplished Victorian architect Thomas Worthington, he had spent some time training in Edwin Lutyens's office before the First World War, and was Professor of Architecture at the Royal College of Art and Slade Lecturer at Oxford.[51] He was responsible for the planning of the 'Educational Centre' component of City Surveyor and Engineer Rowland Nicholas's radically ambitious *City of Manchester Plan, 1945* (Figure 1), and designed several university buildings including the Arts Library (1937), Dental School (1940) and Museum extension (1952) for the University of Manchester, as well as an extension to the Radcliffe Science Library (1933–34) and buildings for Merton College (1940) and the Department of Botany (1952) at Oxford University.[52] It was proposed that Worthington would be joined by 'two or three Project Architects, every project for a building to be given to one or other member of the panel'.[53] The other appointed firms were H. S. Fairhurst & Sons, and Cruickshank & Seward.[54]

Representatives from all three practices were regularly in attendance at the Planning and Development Committee meetings of the institute, where the Corporation's interests were fostered by various parties including the powerful Rowland Nicholas. This association of the Mancunian architectural establishment of the day was extremely significant, and was perhaps one of the reasons for the considerable strength of the masterplan and the capacity to carve out a campus from the carcass of a knotted and crumbling part of the city. The architects held discussions with one another about their respective projects within the context of the broader vision. The production of the masterplans (Figures 2 and 3) continued through 1960 and 1961, but without any new contribution by Worthington's office, as Arthur Gibbon of Cruickshank & Seward asserted his authority and capitalised on a burgeoning friendship with Bowden; Gibbon saw Bowden as his patron, having been previously associated through his scheme for a missile factory in Wythenshawe for Ferranti. As site architects, Worthington's drawings simply

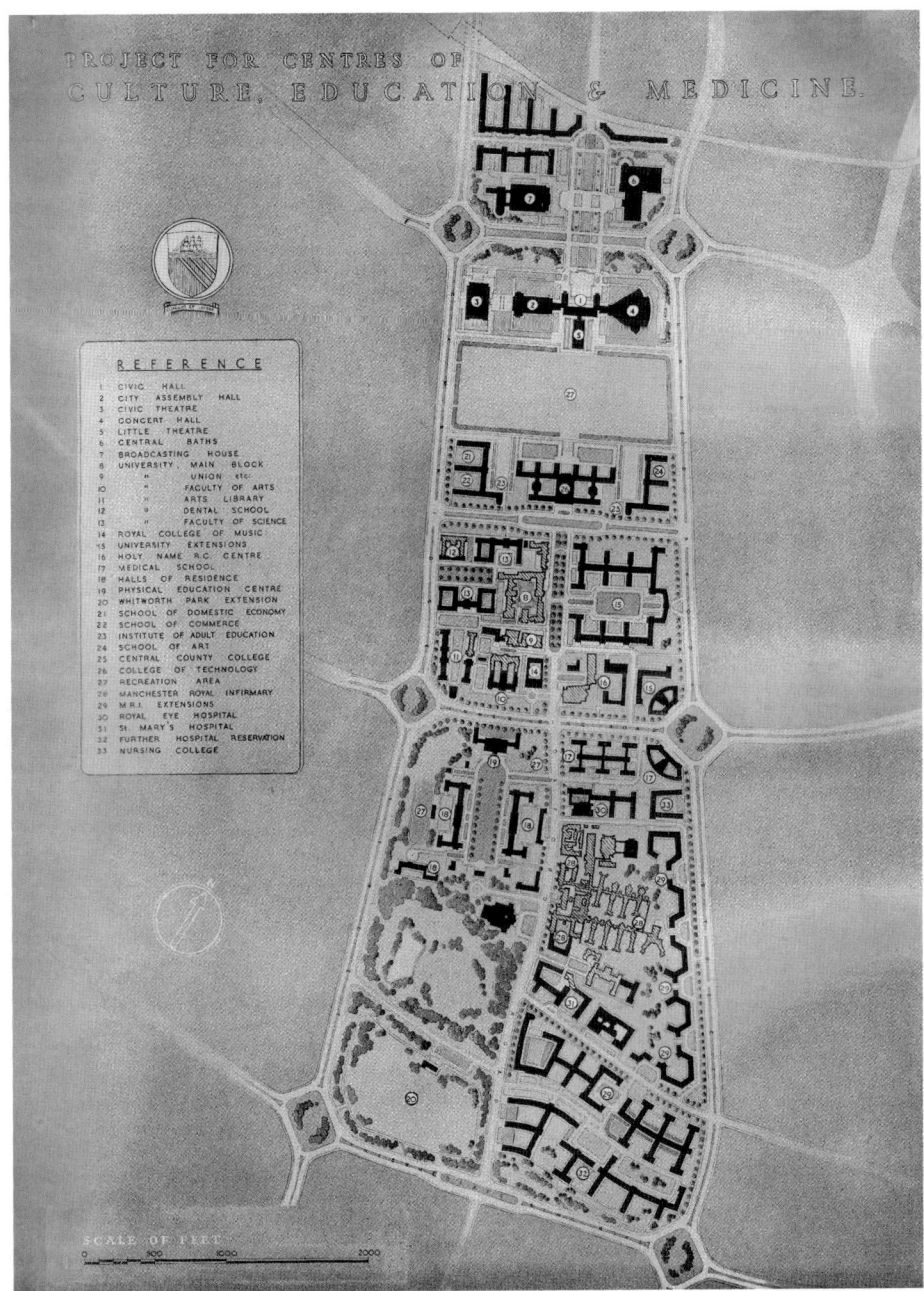

Figure 1 Hubert Worthington's plan for the Centre of Education, Culture and Medicine from Manchester's 1945 Plan. The strong axial and symmetrical planning was used to organise the buildings of the 1950s and 1960s along Brunswick Street (labelled '15' on the plan). R. Nicholas, (1945) City of Manchester Plan, Plate 30. Reproduced courtesy of Manchester Archives+.

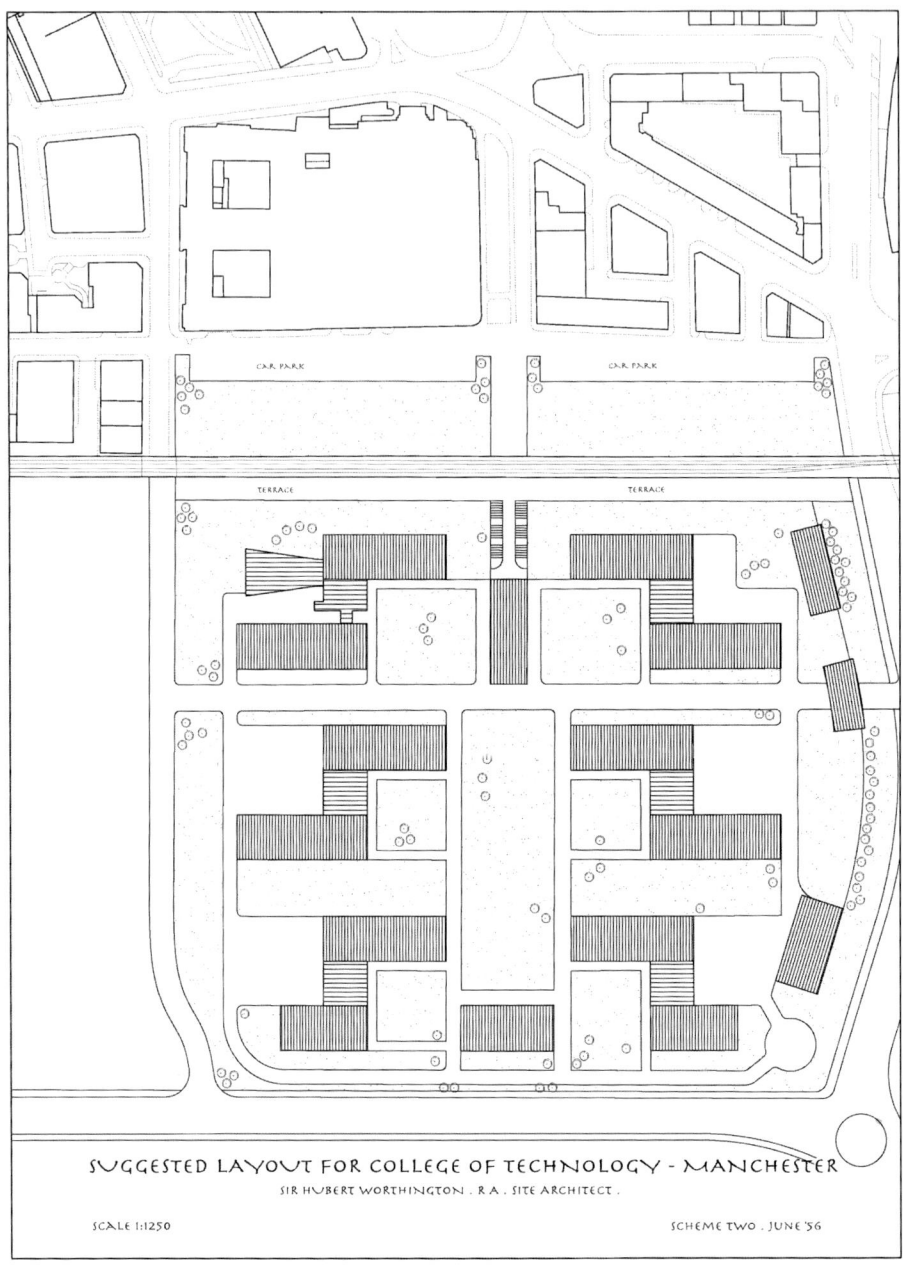

Figure 2 Scheme Two. Suggested layout for College of Technology from the office of Hubert Worthington, June 1956. The axial and symmetrical planning is reflective of the type employed by Worthington for the Centre of Education, Culture and Medicine in 1945, and for early iterations of his collaborative work at Imperial College, London. Redrawn by author based on drawing in the Minutes of the Planning and Development Committee (Manchester, University of Manchester Archives, TGB/2/5/1).

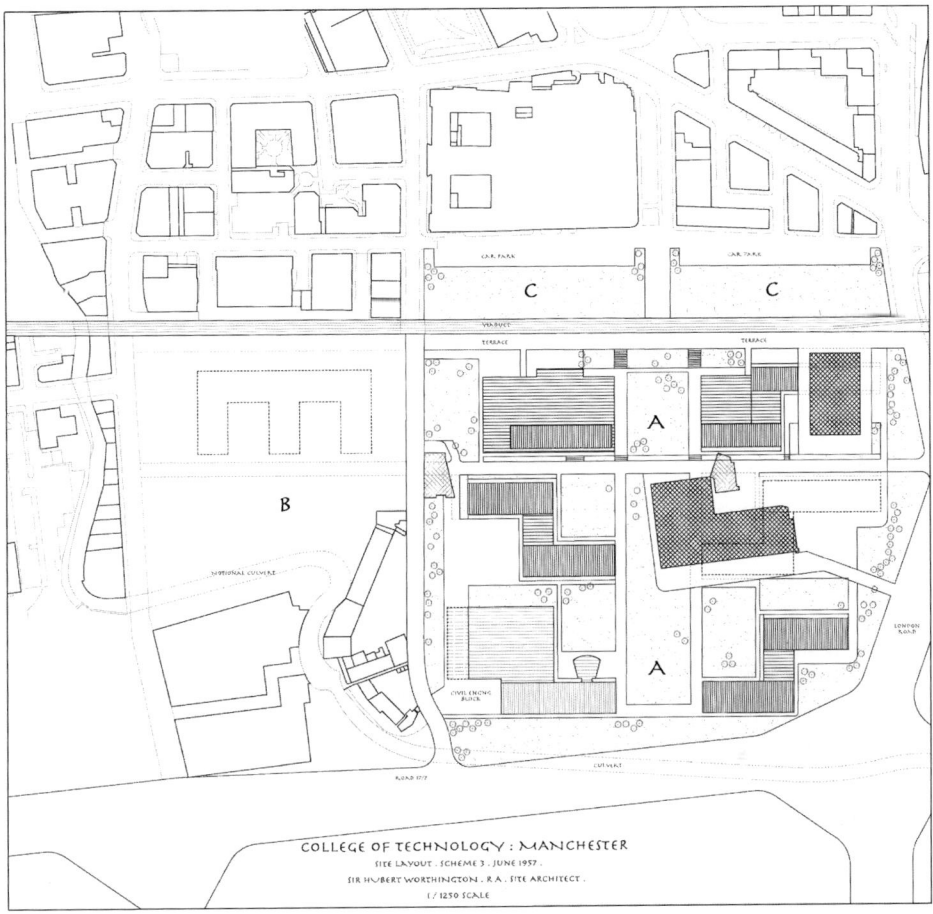

Figure 3 Scheme Three. Here is seen the decision to retain the existing mill building at the centre of the site and the emergence of the quads based on its retention. The tower and podium of the Renold Building (top left) reflects the need to site the tower element as far away from the noise of the railway as possible. Redrawn by author based on drawing in the Minutes of the Planning and Development Committee (Manchester, University of Manchester Archives, TGB/2/5/1).

reflected the detailed design work undertaken by the other two firms. It was important to keep the master plan up to date, since it accompanied the 'unusual' annual submissions to the University Grants Committee. As the dynamic masterplanning ran alongside the design of the buildings to populate it, form and appearance were decisions reached by consensus.

The first such agreement hinged upon the retention of Jackson Street Mill in the centre of the campus. The mid-nineteenth-century mill had been substantially remodelled in 1903, following a fire two years earlier. It was already in use by the College and its floor area was roughly equivalent to that required by the rapidly growing departments. Delays to the Manchester Corporation Bill meant that funds from the University Grants Committee were reallocated to protect the College building programme for 1959.[55] In quick and decisive mode, it was acknowledged that a small addition to the mill was the only construction project that could be achieved within the allotted period and for the designated sum.[56] Retaining the mill redefined the proportions of the open spaces envisaged in Worthington's early plans. The small extension was considered to 'form a more satisfactory southern boundary to the second court'.[57] It consolidated a series of implied squares, and created stronger orthogonal boundaries. Its development was viewed as an important element of the overall master plan, and it can be seen in Scheme 5 (Figure 4) adjoining the mill in the centre of the plan. The plan form of 'Staff House building with cloister and concourse' was intended to complete the two self-contained quads.[58] Here is the traditional language of an Oxbridge College – the cloister and quad – in combination with the development of contemporary modern architecture. It might be argued that the 'Some canons' document was a dilution of modernism to produce acceptable mainstream architecture; Staff House was the first new building to be completed on the campus, and could well fit this classification. Nevertheless, the College pioneered new and unique building types, including Europe's first lecture room block, one of the United Kingdom's first purpose-built halls of residence that used a prefabricated system, and a chemical engineering lab with a strong functional bias, putting its exposed pipes and wires on display. Emblematic of their novelty, the cost control exerted on the plate-glass universities of the 1960s was developed through the analysis of these prototypes in Manchester.

Following Hubert Worthington's death in 1963, Gibbon took control of the masterplan. Worthington's passing prompted the Planning and Development Committee to note his intentions in relation to the campus organisation. The separation of pedestrians and service vehicles by means of an 'outer ring', the planning of an interconnected series of squares, and the site layout as the 'agent' to unite the buildings into a cohesive campus were the three guiding principles. This was evidently an evolution from the earliest ideas, and was exemplar of both the consensus view and the motion away from axial planning to something more modular. The masterplan for the campus created a modern urban park from the ad hoc urban-industrial grain that had grown up around the river. Whilst adopting the use of the word 'quad' when describing external spaces, these were not the enclosed courts of Oxford colleges, but rather open lawns accessible to the citizenry. The campus was a new modern imposition, as if a clean slate, delimited by existing and proposed infrastructure. Its design did not take account of the existing grain of the streets, but instead sought to address the new and to adjust the existing to suit. The progressive sweep included the reordering of nature, as the river was diverted into an engineered culvert, literally and metaphorically moulding the city through concrete pours and assemblies. The series of towers defined the new formal logic of the site. Gibbon was responsible for the design of four of these, and the siting of the fifth. Most of the architectural precedent for the new buildings came from

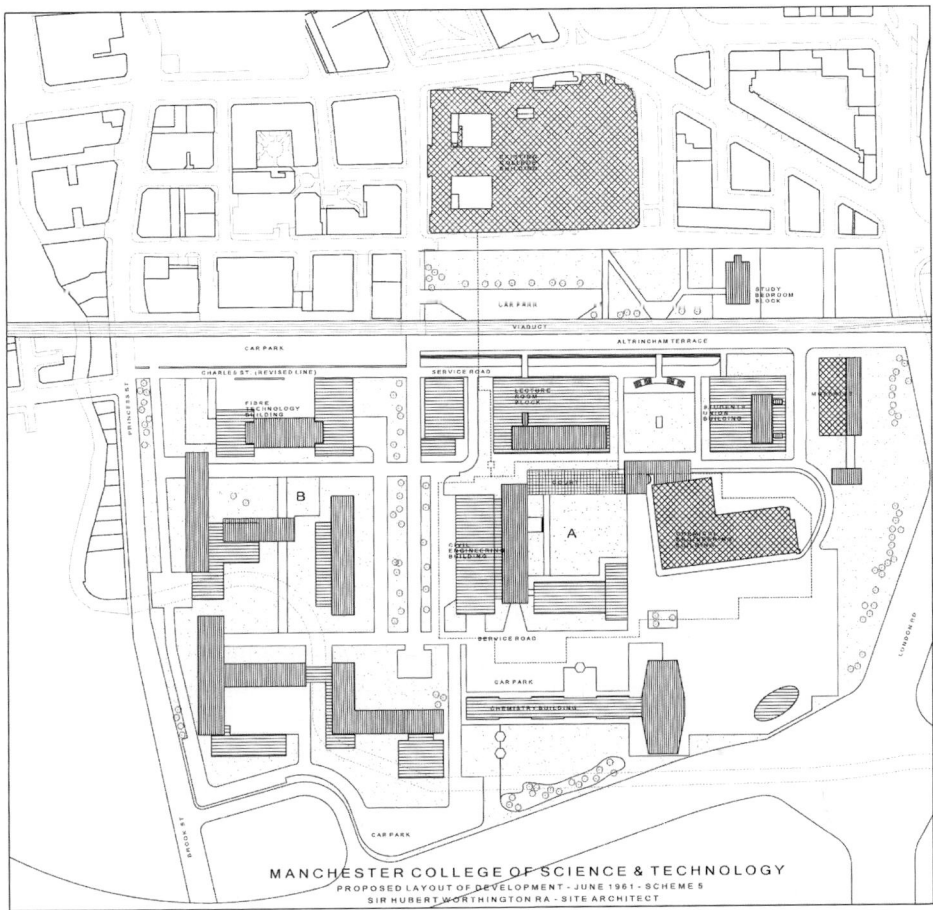

Figure 4 Scheme Five. This drawing shows the increasingly fixed forms of the Lecture Room Block (Renold Building), Students Union Building (Barnes Wallis) and Civil Engineering Building (Pariser Building). The addition of Staff House to the mill is also shown, and formalises the southern edge of the most northerly quad. Redrawn by author based on drawing in the Minutes of the Planning and Development Committee (Manchester, University of Manchester Archives, TGB/2/5/1).

continental Europe, but the precedent for campus planning was more closely tied to the United States.

In the architectural journals of the early 1950s that were accessible in Manchester, most published articles about university buildings were from the United States. The architects for the College must have been aware of the expansion and master plans in US institutions. In spirit, if not in scale, it is William Wurster's campus plans for the University of California, Berkeley (1951, 1955 and 1956) that can be compared to the College.[59] Wurster was Dean of the School of Architecture and Planning at MIT between 1944 and 1949, before assuming the equivalent post in California. He corresponded regularly with the Finnish architect Alvar Aalto, who was a proponent of more organic forms of modernism, and who described his own work as 'between Humanism and Materialism'.[60] Wurster was responsible for Aalto's appointment as professor at MIT, and for the subsequent commission of the Baker House dormitory block.[61] In his final year as Dean of MIT, Wurster delivered a talk about 'architecture as social art'.[62] It is this central concept that can be seen to underpin the 'utopianist' ideas of the various international post-war higher education programmes.[63] For Bowden, as well as connecting research to industry, the life of the students and their proximity to both study and amenity was crucial in his conception of a university. Like the College, Berkeley had to expand into adjacent urban fabric. Each institution protected its character from over-development, despite land premiums, by the preservation of open space, referred to as 'greenbelt' by both.[64] Wurster's plans were developed according to guidance from the Educational Facilities Laboratories and, it is suggested by Stefan Muthesius, informed by émigré architect and founder of the Bauhaus, Walter Gropius's imported form of Modernism at Harvard and MIT.[65]

The expansion of Berkeley required 'demolishing many older buildings and minimizing automobile circulation on the campus through perimeter parking', as well as the tower and open space programme, all strategies that emerged at the College as the campus plans developed in parallel with the new buildings.[66] These characteristics may not have been apparent in Worthington's early drawings, but it is fair to assume that Gibbon was familiar with Wurster's approach. The parallels extend beyond the organising devices of the plan; halls of residence in Berkeley and in Manchester were similarly designed using bespoke prefabricated systems. Further, the city of Berkeley aided the university expansion in a mutually beneficial deal that resonated with the assignation of land by the Manchester Corporation to the College. It was then, the physical as well as the political fabric with which the College engaged.

Following the death of Sir Hubert Worthington in 1963, Arthur Gibbon was commissioned with the design of the later stages of the campus organisation, formalising the role he had incrementally assumed. The systematic association of curriculum and building programme, later evident in the plate-glass universities programme and presented as 'socio-diagrams' in development plans, was not yet general visual currency or part of design processes.[67] In Manchester, the 'long-term development' of the site and buildings was a collaborative experiment. As such, its status would feed into and inform the University Grants Committee's policies for development and the evolution of the plate-glass universities.[68] When Sussex, the first of the plate-glass universities, was founded in 1958, the appointment of a consultant architect was regarded as essential.[69] The College's appointment of a professional team in 1956 was in advance of most national programmes. This could be partially attributed to the experience of the city of Manchester in promoting such ideas, and in their comprehensive approach led by Rowland Nicholas in his direction and authorship of the city's ambitious and comprehensive 1945 Plan.[70]

Figure 5 Perspective painting by Peter Sainsbury for Cruickshank & Seward of the new campus. The new white buildings contrast against the soot-blackened Victorian city in the background. Manchester, Manchester Metropolitan University Special Collections, Cruickshank and Seward Archive. Reproduced courtesy of Manchester Metropolitan University Special Collections.

When the Robbins Report was published in 1963, the expansion of the College was predominantly planned and already under construction.[71] It was unlike any campus, other than its immediate predecessor, Imperial College London.[72] Imperial, however, had involved more direct intervention into the existing Institute buildings (by the architect Thomas E. Collcutt, 1887–93) and the site, whilst slightly sloping, was not as polluted or knotted as that in Manchester. The first masterplan for Imperial (Norman and Dawbarn, 1956) was subject to substantial revisions intended to preserve more of the historic fabric, and its eventual composition was tighter and more introverted than that of the College.[73] Plans for the College also predated most of the redbrick university post-war development plans, and those for all the plate-glass universities. There is one image that seems to capture what the architects were trying to do at UMIST. It is a photographic print, in an elongated landscape format, of a painting by the architectural perspective artist Peter Sainsbury (Figure 5). The image is unusual in its format. Notable is the position from where the view was taken; it is from the south, and shows the proposed campus with the city of Manchester behind it, as approached from London Road, one of the city's main arteries. It is cleverly composed in two-point perspective; the centre is deliberately positioned at the south-east corner of the proposed maths tower. Two darker and domed Victorian towers (the Refuge Assurance Building and the London Road Fire Station) flank the bright white orthogonal volumes of the campus, and the modern city is recognisable by the white slabs of Rodwell Tower (Douglas Stephen & Partners, 1965) and Piccadilly Station (R. L. Moorcroft, 1964) set in the background, on the far right and above the shadowy viaduct that sinks into the campus mass. As the perspective indicates, the city and campus were combined at UMIST. The campus masterplan, as built, allowed the interface of 'town and gown'. Where the campus planning swept away the old grain, the city adjusted itself to the new form.

The new form is best articulated through two of the thirteen buildings, the Renold Building (a lecture room block) by Arthur Gibbon and Gordon Hodkinson for Cruickshank & Seward, completed in 1962, and the Chemical Engineering Pilot Plant, designed by Harry M. Fairhurst and completed in 1966. The Renold Building was a new type of university building, and the Pilot Plant was the most innovative scheme amongst Fairhurst's post-war work. In each is also seen the continuing influence of external factors, albeit progressively informed by the emergent context of the developing site, rather than the statute and governmental interplay that defined the site procurement and its limits. The following section outlines their development as integral to setting the architectural tone, and as innovative within their type, despite an evidently mainstream appearance.

The Renold Building

A scheme for the lecture room block, 'comprising eight storeys', was proposed in May 1957.[74] The overall master plan was still in flux, and responsibility was handed to Cruickshank & Seward to resolve the finer details of siting, in consultation with Worthington. In agreeing the alignment and general form, the architects consolidated the idea of 'quadrangles' as organising devices for a sequence of buildings.[75] The eastern and southern facades of the Renold Building formed edges to two new open spaces at the heart of the campus. The scheme itself eventually took the form of a podium and tower, and is one of the earliest examples of this arrangement in the country.[76] The podium housed large lecture theatres, and the tower contained smaller theatres and seminar rooms. The angled east facade of the tower was the result of an acoustic study, and followed the profile of the rear of the vertically stacked smaller theatres. The tower was positioned as far away from the adjacent railway viaduct as possible, and the podium was acoustically insulated by virtue of the significant topographical shift between the viaduct, the parallel street and the rest of the campus to the south.[77] The provision of two entrances, one at first floor level to the north side and one at ground level to the south, exploited this difference in datum. It also required the provision of a bridge link from Altrincham Street that traversed the site service road below.

Although the Renold Building was the second building to be completed, it had a longer period of gestation than the rapidly delivered Staff House. As such, the treatment of its facades was a forebear to the rest of the campus architecture. The building was first discussed in terms of its appearance after H. T. Seward tabled artist's impressions. Comments recorded in the minutes centred upon the style of the elevations, described as 'contemporary'.[78] Worthington emphasised the importance of the decisions attached to the lecture room block as 'it would tend to set the general style for the whole of our development'.[79] The Planning and Development Committee was 'strongly in favour' of Cruickshank & Seward's treatment, 'rather than an adherence to more traditional lines'.[80] The assembled group also

Figure 6 Artist's impression of the Renold Building by L. Tucker. Surprisingly, this shows cars in front of the building when the campus was eventually designed to be car free and serviced from its perimeter. Manchester, Manchester Metropolitan University Special Collections, Cruickshank and Seward Archive. Reproduced courtesy of Manchester Metropolitan University Special Collections.

decided that it was not necessary to finish each new building in the same material; harmony could be achieved in other ways, such as through the formal association of elements and the 'treatment of paths, paving and retaining walls which would draw the campus together' (Figure 6).[81]

Members of the Planning and Development Committee were invited to inspect other sites before making final decisions about the stylistic treatment.[82] A special meeting was held to discuss the material finishes for the lecture room block, and one outcome of these inspections appears to have affected the selection of material: Sir Charles Renold stated 'that there appeared to be a general opinion in favour of Portland stone'.[83] Any exposed concrete was white, to match the stone, as were the adjustable louvres on the south facade, deliberately manufactured in white fibre-cement.[84] The louvres are long gone, but one anecdote concerning their manufacture is redolent of the threshold between craft and mass production so often encountered during the mid-century. The project's architect, Gordon Hodkinson, visited the cement factory charged with making the louvres, and drew the S-curve of the profile on the factory floor with a piece of chalk, which was traced over and used as the template from which the louvres were formed.[85] Modern did not always mean machined, cold or monochromatic. Gibbon introduced a blue band of faience to the exterior of the ground floor, subtle colouration to the spandrel panels, and proposed the use of colour internally, to be glimpsed from the outside.[86] These materials and colours informed much of the proceeding development.

In the interior Gibbon wanted the vivacity of the student population to provide life and colour. The Planning and Development Committee embraced this approach, and the large circulation areas on the ground and first floor were seen as a 'valuable aid to creating a communal life'.[87] These spaces were treated neutrally with contrasting polished wood and simple rough concrete, and eventually provided the backdrop for a period, abstract mural, *Metamorphosis* by Victor Pasmore, in the lower of the two halls.[88] The visual separation of the tower was achieved by using elegant birdsmouth beams that facilitated the continuous clerestory window at the junction of the two formal elements. These 'cantilever pre-stressed reinforced concrete beams' were sufficiently experimental for the College, the architect and the engineer to test the solution on a model in the Department of Structural Engineering, and the results were published in a journal.[89] The Lecture Room Block subcommittee commented that '[a]n unusual feature of these beams is the slot which runs full length on both sides and into the cantilevered splayed ends. The slot is an architectural feature.'[90]

The most prominent device for display and circulation, however, was the stair tower, a perpendicular projection of perilously thin glazing bars. This element was part of the evolving modern language of the firm, and had its predecessors in their buildings at Wythenshawe and its growing family in the college and university buildings to come. Here, it was purposefully employed to encourage students to use the stairs, by affording excellent views, and in turn put the students on display.[91] Conscious that the lid of the podium would be exposed to those ascending and descending, Gibbon applied a diamond check pattern in bonded gravel to the roof, and positioned rooflights in a deliberate composition. In a final flourish for the exterior, and with a nod to eminent modernist architects Oscar Niemeyer and Pierre Luigi Nervi, Gibbon instructed Gordon Hodkinson, in full view of the design team, to define the curved profile of the rooftop plant enclosure. With a single freehand sweep, Hodkinson made his mark, and was then instructed to set out the curve.[92] Strong volumetric elements that housed plant equipment on roofs were another hallmark of Cruickshank & Seward schemes across Manchester and further afield.

The Chemical Engineering Pilot Plant

In the Chemical Engineering Pilot Plant (1966), Fairhurst realised their most adventurous project on the campus (Figure 7). The building, and the adjoining sculptural wall by the artist Antony Hollaway, formed the eastern boundary of the site.[93] The bold coloured volumes of the roof-mounted cooling plant had a plastic quality, and the floating fluid shapes above contrasted against the orthogonal form below. The building was effectively divided in two; this was expressed clearly

Figure 7 The Chemical Engineering Pilot Plant at night, with its scientific instruments on display. Manchester, Manchester Metropolitan University Special Collections, Visual Resource Centre Slide Collection (ref. ZW-2L-67). Reproduced courtesy of Manchester Metropolitan University Special Collections.

by the use of curtain-wall glazing to one end, and blue engineering brick to the other. The glazed section was open through all four floors, designed for undertaking large-scale experiments and handling large pieces of scientific equipment. It was intended to exhibit the students' experiments to those passing on London Road, perhaps with the earlier Daily Express Building (Sir Owen Williams, 1938) in mind, whose printing machines were on display to passers-by on Great Ancoats Street.[94] Specific colours defined the utility service runs, five years before Richard Rogers and Renzo Piano designed the Pompidou Centre in Paris. Without explicit design intent, driven primarily by function, the filigree lattice of kit, transoms and mullions and the reflective qualities of the glass provided a sense of science and its complexity, visible from London Road, a major arterial route of the city. On each floor, a narrow band within the curtain wall extended laterally across the brick facade to provide clerestory windows to the laboratories and offices. This lightened the whole building by defining the masonry as cladding rather than structure. The entire block was grounded using a plinth wall at grade that extended to enclose the service yard. This was the most functionally defined of Fairhurst's post-war schemes, and yet the most progressively modern.

The first wave of campus development was completed by 1970. Its southern edge, contained by 'Link Road 17/7' (known as the Mancunian Way from 1964), turned the gable ends of its towers to the road and offered blank, defensive facades in the Ferranti Building (Cruickshank & Seward, 1969) and the lecture block of the Maths and Social Sciences Building (Cruickshank & Seward, 1970). The architectural language established in the earliest buildings was evident in all the schemes that followed, despite tightening budgets. Gibbon also had a final contribution to make. The very first formal proposal for the campus included a stair from Altrincham Street to the first quad, and as the Site Architect, Worthington was originally responsible for the design of this stair. As the master plan developed and the lower-level service road required bridging, Worthington and Gibbon were to collaborate over the design of the bridges to ensure harmonious style.[95] Following Worthington's death, Gibbon assumed the role of designer for the stair, as well as the bridges to the Renold Building and the Union. He originally proposed the curved sweeping flights onto his 'great lawn' to be without a handrail – a beguiling Brazilian-style gesture, clearly referential to the work of architect Oscar Niemeyer.[96] Ultimately, handrails were added and made from bronze. The rail at the head of the flight, from where one has a commanding view across the campus, was inscribed 'The Sir Hubert Worthington Stair', a memorial that remains visible to this day.

Conclusion

UMIST was city and institution in a literal and in a metaphorical sense. Its first new buildings were civic in their function: communal spaces to learn, relax and refresh. Its position, as of and in the city, was advantageous as the nation sought to address its future through education, research and development in the technology sector. The assembled architects were senior figures of an architectural establishment that, until the mid-1950s, remained very traditional. Despite this, a consensual modernising agenda emerged, and this underwrote Arthur Gibbon's relationship with Bowden as the most influential agent in the production of the campus architecture. Expressive of his admiration, Bowden remarked:

> I have seen several of Aalto's buildings both in America and in Scandinavia, and I do not believe that any of them are any better, if as good, as the Renold Building which Mr. Gibbon designed for us. This of course is only the opinion of one amateur, but my own belief in the merit of this building has been supported by one of the city planners of Rotterdam, who told me it was the finest building he had seen in Europe.[97]

UMIST did not, however, stem from one good idea and did not have a sole champion, although Bowden undoubtedly had the vision actively sought by the Education Committee and the University Grants Committee when making the appointment. In 1993, he was described as 'a visionary and expansionist, who would have been quite frustrated in the present era of efficiency gains and tight budgetary control'.[98] It is perhaps fortunate then, that the University Grants Committee was inexperienced in the stewardship of large-scale development, and that cost targets for construction were less restrictive in the early years of building. Nor was the campus formed from a single source of precedent. It was an application of Continental and North American ideas in a collaborative atmosphere. In 1962, as the first wave of new buildings were about to be handed to the College for occupancy, the Planning and Development Committee proposed that the respective project architects be invited to comment upon *any* material proposals for new buildings, signage, furniture or landscape in the following two years.[99] This was symbolic of the spirit of shared endeavour, and in this sense UMIST could be described as 'utopianist'.[100]

In the development of the UMIST campus, the relationship between the networks of government and the governance of the institution affected the spatial and material outcomes. The central government demand for the expansion of technological education met with a strong local tradition and institutions with long histories. Whitehall and the Manchester Corporation had to cooperate with one another to achieve their collective aims. The local committees were in almost constant communication with the University Grants Committee. In the early stages of development, the University Grants Committee was learning from the active construction, and latterly it began to exert more financial control, which in turn impacted upon the architecture. There was considerable discussion locally between the various bodies charged with delivery and the local authority. The inner-urban motorway and river culvert determined certain massing and form, as did conditions imposed by British Railways. Political interplay, policy, planning and infrastructural conditions were all filtered through an assembled group of architects and other committees working in a very specific location, and composed of its own networks founded upon a military industrial complex, both shrouded and exploited by civic and civil undertakings.

Notes

1 D. Egerton, *Warfare State: Britain, 1920–1970* (Cambridge: Cambridge University Press, 2006). As well as Edgerton's treatise on warfare and the State, see M. Grant, *After the Bomb: Civil Defence and Nuclear War in Cold War Britain, 1945–68* (London: Palgrave Macmillan, 2009).

2 Edgerton, *Warfare State.*

3 For a detailed description of the Labour government's policy and response to these reports see J. Bocock and R. Taylor, 'The Labour Party and Higher Education: 1945–51', *Higher Education Quarterly*, 57 (2003), 249–65.

4 Lord Hankey, *Higher Appointments: Report of the Committee appointed by the Minister of Labour and National Service in July 1943 (Chairman Lord Hankey)* (London: HMSO, 1945), Cmnd. 6576; Percy Report, Ministry of Education, *Higher Technological Education. Report of a Special Committee* (London: HMSO, 1945); Barlow Report, Lord President of the Council, *Scientific Manpower*

(London: HMSO, 1946), Cmnd. 6824, para. 33. Quote from Bocock and Taylor, 'The Labour Party and Higher Education', p. 252.
5 Manchester was unusual in its delivery of both further and higher education courses in one institution.
6 Bocock and Taylor, 'The Labour Party and Higher Education'.
7 Cabinet papers. Kew, National Archives (hereafter NA), CAB 24-/55/82.
8 Gary Willis, 'Fields into Factories: The Impact on the Post-War Rural Landscape of Britain's Second World War, 1936–1946', Northumbria University, 'New Lives, New Landscapes: Rural Modernism in 20th Century Britain', 1–2 August 2019.
9 Julian Garratt, 'Atomic Spaces, North West England: 1945 to 1957' (MSc dissertation, University of Manchester, 2016), p. 8.
10 www.rhydymwynvalleyhistory.co.uk [accessed April 2023]; English Electric first moved to the site at Warton in 1948. C. G. Keil, 'Supersonic Wind Tunnels: Details of the Two New High-Speed Tunnels Operated by English Electric Aviation Ltd. at Wharton', *Aircraft Engineering and Aerospace Technology*, 32 (1960), 338; J. Aylen, 'Bloodhound on my Trail: Building the Ferranti Argus Process Control Computer', *The International Journal for the History of Engineering & Technology*, 82 (2012), 1–36.
11 The other two centres were at the University of Cambridge and Birkbeck College, London. In Cambridge the EDSAC stored program computer was developed, and Birkbeck's research connected it with the British Tabulating Machine Company. See M. Wilkes, *Memoirs of a Computer Pioneer* (Cambridge, Ma.: MIT Press, 1985), and Andrew D Booth, 'Computers in the University of London, 1945–1962', in Nicholas Metropolis, Jack Howlett and Gian-Carlo Rota (eds), *A History of Computing in the Twentieth Century* (Academic Press, New York, 1980), pp. 551–61.
12 'Proposed talks on future of College of Technology: Dr B. V. Bowden to be New Principal', *Manchester Guardian* (27 June 1953), p. 3.
13 *Ibid*.; D. Johnson, 'What Manchester did Yesterday', *Guardian* (15 December 1975), p. 5.
14 Geoffrey Tweedale, 'Bertram Vivian Bowden', *Annals of the History of Computing*, 12 (1990), 138–40.
15 Paul Drath, 'The relationship Between Science and Technology: University Research and the Computer Industry 1945–1962' (PhD thesis, University of Manchester, 1973).
16 Manchester, University of Manchester Archives (hereafter UoMA), GB 133 USC/4/1, p. 90.
17 S. Lavington, *A History of Manchester Computers* (Manchester: The National Computing Centre, 1975).
18 S. Lavington, *Early British Computers: The Story of Vintage Computers and the People Who Built Them* (Manchester: Manchester University Press, 1980).
19 B. V. Bowden, *Proposals for the Development of the Manchester College of Science and Technology* (Manchester: The Manchester College of Science and Technology, 1956), unpaginated preface.

20 Manchester Modernist Society celebrated the campus with 'Campus Day': http://umistcampus.wordpress.com/2012/06/26/manchester-modernist-society-designate-conservation-area-status-to-the-umist-campus/ [accessed 5 September 2024]; C. Hartwell, *Manchester* (New Haven, CT and London: Yale University Press, 2002), pp. 123–5.

21 The old universities fall into three descriptive classifications: 'ancient' (Oxford, Cambridge, St Andrews, Glasgow, Aberdeen, Edinburgh and Durham), 'redbrick' (Birmingham, Liverpool, Leeds, Sheffield, Bristol and Manchester) and 'plate-glass' (East Anglia, Essex, Kent, Lancaster, Sussex, Warwick and York – also known as the 'Shakespearian Seven') – attributed to the officers of the University Grants Committee: T. Birks, *Building the New Universities* (Newton Abbot: David & Charles, 1972), p. 15. The Colleges of Advanced Technology programme was instituted in 1956, and applied special status to ten colleges, which later became universities. See Robin Simmons, 'Science and Technology in England and Wales: The Lost Opportunity of the Colleges of Advanced Technology', *British Journal of Educational Studies*, 69 (2020), 735–51.

22 The 1905 agreement situated the University Faculty of Technology within the College.

23 Bowden, *Proposals*, p. 31.

24 The University of Manchester Institute of Science and Technology, *1824–1974, 150 Years of Progress at UMIST* (Manchester: University of Manchester/UMIST, 1974), p. 9.

25 NA, UGC 7 /895 (University Grants Committee, *Higher Technological Education – Development of Manchester College of Technology*).

26 In Manchester, the first phase of Openshaw Technical College (Halliday and Agate, 1954) was amongst the first post-war buildings in the city, and was later joined by the College of Building (1957), West Wythenshawe College of Further Education (1958), the Domestic and Trades College (1960), Moston College (1962), and John Dalton College (1964). See M. Steele, 'The Making of Manchester's Technical Colleges (1954–1964)' (MRes. thesis, Manchester Metropolitan University, 2014); NA, UGC 8/895 (Manchester Municipal College of Technology, *Application to the University Grants Committee for the Years 1952–1957, supplementary statement*).

27 B. Salter and T. Tapper, *The State and Higher Education* (Ilford: The Woburn Press, 1994), p. 107. See also Bocock and Taylor, 'The Labour Party and Higher Education'. For an excellent account of the University Grants Committee's changing relationship with the government in the post-war period, see M. Shattock, *The UGC and the Management of British Universities* (Buckingham: SRHE and Open University Press, 1994).

28 Salter and Tapper, *The State and Higher Education*, p. 107.

29 University Grants Committee, *University Development 1935 to 1946* (London: HMSO, 1948), para. 6. In the period 1939–45, the College was put to use as a research and training facility for the British and United States military, during which period the Textile Technology Department produced a thread for use with 'sticky bombs'.

30 The professions were served by the Goodenough Report (medicine), the Teviot Report (dentistry) and the Loveday Report (agriculture). The term 'machinery' is utilised in

the Barlow Report: Barlow Report, Lord President of the Council, *Scientific Manpower* (London: HMSO, 1946), Cmnd. 6824, para. 33. It seems unusual now that the Ministry of Education was not involved in either the advice or funding allocation in Higher Education provision; it was not until 1964 that responsibility for the University Grants Committee was transferred from the Treasury to the newly formed Department of Education and Science. Bocock and Taylor describe the 'furious lobbying' (p. 258) by both the universities and the University Grants Committee against any transfer of power to the Education Ministry as suggested in the Barlow Report. See also Shattock, *The UGC and the Management of British Universities*, p. 8.

31 This was eventually realised in Keele in 1949. Keele was in many ways an anomaly, rather than a test case. It was founded in 1949, and was a forerunner of greenfield campus development in Britain, but its architecture was called into question. It was the brainchild of A. D. Lindsay, former Master of Balliol College, Oxford and ardent Labour supporter. He had been interested in establishing a university in the Potteries since 1925, and saw the advice of the Barlow Report as an opportunity to test his ideas. See Birks, *Building the New Universities*, pp. 10–11; S. Muthesius, *The Postwar University: Utopianist Campus and College* (New Haven, CT: Yale University Press, 2000), p. 105; Bocock and Taylor, 'The Labour Party and Higher Education', pp. 260–1.

32 *Higher Technological Education: Statement of Government Policy* (London: HMSO, 1951), Cmnd. 8357. Bocock and Taylor argue that there was no strong tradition of Labour policy on universities, and that they also fought entrenched elite liberal views of what an English university should be, which did not include technological or eminently vocational study. They also describe the existing universities as 'reluctant expansionists': Bocock and Taylor, 'The Labour Party and Higher Education', p. 256.

33 The awarding of a separate independent charter to the College was championed by the vice chancellor of the University, John Stopford, in November 1951, only one month after the general election. Stopford was a physician and a leading member of the Joint Research Council that studied the relationships between industry and science. His primary concern was the continuing provision of higher education level technological teaching in Manchester, and his fear was that the Ministry of Education would push the College 'right down to the level of one of these colleges in neighbouring towns': NA, UGC 7 /895 (letter from John Stopford to Sir Arthur Trueman, Chair of the UGC, 26 November 1951 and letter from John Stopford to Sir Arthur Trueman, Chair of the UGC, 24 January 1952); Manchester Joint Research Council, *Industry and Science. A Study of their Relationship Based on a Survey of Firms in the Greater Manchester Area Carried out by the Manchester Joint Research Council, 1950–1953* (Manchester: Manchester University Press, 1954); NA, UGC 7 /895 (letter from John Stopford to Sir Arthur Trueman, Chair of the UGC, 30 November 1951).

34 'Technical Education (Comparative Expenditures)', House of Commons Debate, 16 December 1954, vol. 535, cc1954–5.

35 'Independence for College "Government Policy"', *Manchester Guardian* (13 March 1954), p. 2.

36 Bowden, *Proposals*, unpaginated preface.

37 'Technical Education' House of Commons Debate, 21 June 1956, vol. 554, cc1639–767.
38 UoMA, TGB/2/5/1, p. 331.
39 G. E. Cherry, *Town Planning in Britain Since 1900: The Rise and Fall of the Planning Ideal* (Oxford: Wiley-Blackwell, 1996), p. 16; J. Davis, 'Central Government and the Towns', in M. Daunton (ed.), *The Cambridge Urban History of Britain* (Cambridge: Cambridge University Press, 2001), pp. 261–86.
40 UoMA, TGB/2/5/1, p. 256.
41 Universities were obliged to submit five-year plans to the University Grants Committee that indicated their capital expenditure on buildings, staff and equipment. UoMA, TGB/2/5/1, p. 258.
42 'Schedule 1' was a set of key indicators in relation to areas and costs associated with conventional laboratory style education buildings.
43 UoMA, TGB/2/5/1, p. 78.
44 Three years later, as the plate-glass universities were in development, following the creation of an architects' department at the University Grants Committee to filter and disseminate construction and cost information, the tone began to change. The publication of *Methods Used by Universities of Contracting and of Recording and Controlling Expenditure* (University Grants Committee, December 1960) built upon the Gater Report on the financial control exercised by the University Grants Committee. The language used indicated a tightening of budgetary controls and the methods used to establish such. UoMA, TGB/2/5/1, p. 72.
45 UoMA, TGB/2/5/1, p. 571.
46 In a letter to Sir John Wolfenden, Bowden acknowledged the 'unusual' financing provision that the University Grants Committee had made to the College and that he hoped it could continue. He made clear that the situation had allowed the construction of buildings 'which cost considerably more than a single year's allocation: which take three years to complete': UoMA, TGB/2/1/3, p. 204.
47 Bowden, *Proposals*, p. 134.
48 UoMA, TGB/2/5/1, p. 83.
49 Hartwell, *Manchester*, p. 118.
50 UoMA, TGB/2/5/1, p. 83.
51 G. Tyack, *Oxford. An Architectural Guide* (Oxford: Oxford University Press, 1998), p. 290.
52 W. Whyte, '"A Pastiche or a Packing Case": Building in Twentieth-Century Oxford', *Twentieth Century Architecture*, 11 (2013), 24; 'Manchester University Library', *Design and Construction* (April 1937), p. 223; 'New Architecture at Oxford University', *Architectural Review* (June 1942), pp. 440–4; 'Department of Botany for University of Oxford', *Builder* (11 January 1952), pp. 63–9; 'Dental Hospital', *Architectural Review* (August 1940), p. 51.
53 A series of plans by Worthington from 1956 to 1961 are held in the files of Lord Bowden, UoMA, BVB papers. See also UoMA: TGB/2/5/1, p. 10, and VCA/7/386 Folder 1. For architects joining the panel, see UoMA, TGB/2/1/1, p. 78.

54 Fairhursts were a family firm established in 1895. Their heyday was during the Edwardian and inter-war periods, when they build substantially across the north-west of England. Cruickshank and Seward were established in Manchester in the 1920s, and through Arthur Gibbon in the post-war period had a very successful few years, with UMIST being their most significant contribution to the city. See W. Whittam (1986) *Fairhursts Architects: The History of a Manchester Practice* (Manchester: Department of History of Art and Design, Manchester Polytechnic, 1986); J. J. Parkinson-Bailey, *Manchester: An Architectural History* (Manchester: Manchester University Press, 2000); A. J. Pass, *Thomas Worthington. Architecture and Social Purpose* (Manchester: Literary and Philosophical Society, 1988).

55 The realignment of the culvert required an Act of Parliament, and if passed before Compulsory Purchase Orders had been completed would have artificially inflated prices on outstanding acquisitions.

56 UoMA, TGB/2/5/1, p. 297.

57 *Ibid.*, p. 212.

58 Worthington raised the accommodation to create a colonnaded cloister for sheltered transition between the lecture room block and the proposed Students' Union. Raising the staff areas afforded a greater sense of privacy, and had the dual function of masking 'a drab area of old and irregular brickwork' on the existing mill. The construction was steel-framed with precast concrete floor slabs. The external walls were metal units infilled with glass or wall panels, as required by the corresponding internal function. Its facade was described as an 'uncompromising frame of big squares', but it is its presence and formal configuration, rather than appearance, that is of note here. UoMA, TGB/2/5/1, pp. 403–4; Hartwell, *Manchester*, p. 125.

59 The scale of the two campuses is not comparable. Berkeley had 10,000 students before 1939, and the College had fewer than 1,000 full-time students by 1956. TA further 5,000 part-time students were engaged in 'non-university' level study: Bowden, *Proposals*, p. 137.

60 Alvar Aalto, 'Between Humanism and Materialism' (1955), lecture at Central Union of Architects, Vienna. First published in *Der Bau* 7/8 (1955), 174–6. Reprinted in G. Schildt (ed.), *Alvar Aalto: Sketches* (Cambridge: MIT, 1985), p. 130.

61 Marc Treib suggests Wurster's 'influence' on the campus planning at MIT. There was no overarching masterplan, but his patronage of Aalto and others meant a break from tradition. M. Treib (ed.), *An Everyday Modernism: The Houses of William Wurster* (Berkeley, CA: University of California Press, 1995), p. 96, n. 29.

62 *Ibid.*, p. 91.

63 Muthesius, *The Postwar University*.

64 UoMA, TGB/2/5/1, p. 579; W. Wurster, quoted by P. Allen, 'The End of Modernism', *Journal of the Society of Architectural Historians*, 70 (2011), 354–74.

65 The Educational Facilities Laboratory was founded by the American Institute of Architects in the late 1950s, and advocated modern planning and architecture. Muthesius introduces Wurster as having 'imbued' various European influences; Allen introduces the 'organic' nature of the master plan as well as the modernist tendencies

in the promotion of towers. See Muthesius, *The Postwar University*, p. 47; Allen, 'The End of Modernism'.

66 Allen, 'The End of Modernism', pp. 359–60.
67 Muthesius, *The Postwar University*, pp. 88–9.
68 The University Grants Committee was inexperienced in procuring large buildings, since there had been no similar period of expansion. In the post-war years, as well as appointing their own architects to assess work, they also began to collect and tabulate cost information that eventually led to standardisation of budgets for particular building types.
69 Birks, *Building the New Universities* p. 11. Sir Basil Spence was invited to submit a plan for the new university in 1959.
70 R. Nicholas, *City of Manchester Plan 1945* (Norwich: Jarrold & Sons, 1945).
71 The Robbins Report recommended the immediate expansion of universities, and that all colleges of advanced technology should be given the status of universities: Committee on Higher Education, *Higher Education. Report of the Committee Appointed by the Prime Minister under the Chairmanship of Lord Robbins 1961–63* (London: HMSO, 1963).
72 The growth of Imperial College was only slightly in advance of UMIST. The master plan by Norman and Dawbarn, in collaboration with Hubert Worthington, who for many years was consultant architect to Imperial, was published in 1956. 'Imperial College', *Survey of London: volume 38: South Kensington Museums Area* (1975), pp. 233–47. www.british-history.ac.uk/report.aspx?compid=47532 [accessed 5 September 2024].
73 'Save the Imperial Institute', *Country Life* (23 February 1956), pp. 329–30; 'Project in Kensington', *Architects' Journal* (6 February 1958), pp. 197–9.
74 UoMA, TGB/2/5/1, p. 43.
75 *Ibid.*, pp. 186–7.
76 Skidmore, Owings & Merrill's Lever Building (1952) is generally acknowledged as the first of this type. John Madin's Post and Mail building has also been cited as an early British example, but this was not completed until 1964. See A. Clawley, *John Madin* (London: RIBA, English Heritage, 2011).
77 W. A. Gibbon, 'Manchester College of Science and Technology', *Guardian* (9 April 1963), p. 12.
78 UoMA, TGB/2/5/1, p. 60.
79 *Ibid.*
80 In the first instance, the preferred cladding for the first new building was Travertine marble. In the event that the University Grants Committee vetoed this choice then a cheaper alternative, Portland stone, was envisaged. *Ibid.*
81 UoMA, TGB/2/5/1, p. 262.
82 Visits to Imperial Chemical Industries facilities were seen as able to provide insight for new technical spaces. Serge Chermayeff's celebrated laboratories (1936) at Blackley in Manchester were examined by the Committee, as were the new buildings of Imperial Chemical Industries' Plastics Division at Welwyn (E. D. Jefferiss Mathews, 1955). UoMA, TGB/2/5/1, p. 78.

83 *Ibid.*, pp. 107, 262.
84 *Ibid.*, p. 263.
85 Interview with Gordon Hodkinson (1 October 2012).
86 W. A. Gibbon, 'Manchester College of Science and Technology', *Guardian* (9 April 1963), p. 12.
87 UoMA, TGB/2/5/1, p. 157.
88 The Edwin Abbey Memorial Trust were consulted on funds to provide a mural in the Civil Engineering building in 1961. Vincent Harris inspected the site on behalf of the trust and rejected the proposed space, due to the poor quality of the space and its daylight conditions. The idea was not abandoned, however, and after Pasmore inspected the site himself and selected an area in which to work, the funds were provided. UoMA, TGB/2/5/2, pp. 235, 375; TGB/2/5/3, pp. 174, 509–10.
89 R. B. L. Smith and W. Merchant, 'Critical Loads of Tall Building Frames', *The Structural Engineer*, 34 (1956), 284–92.
90 UoMA, TGB/2/5/1, p. 621.
91 Interview with Gordon Hodkinson, 1 October 2012.
92 *Ibid.*
93 www.c20society.org.uk/botm/hollaway-wall-manchester/ [accessed 19 March 2014].
94 UoMA, TGB/2/5/2, p. 803.
95 *Ibid.*, pp. 658, 780.
96 *Ibid.*, p. 780.
97 UoMA, VCA/7/386 Folder 2 (letter from B. V. Bowden to W. Mansfield Cooper, 17 January 1963).
98 G. C. Wood, 'Conference Introductory Paper: Why Manchester?', *Corrosion Science*, 35 (1993), 1–12.
99 UoMA, TGB/2/5/2, p. 405.
100 With reference to Muthesius, *The Postwar University: Utopianist Campus and College*.

Forging the Future with the White Heat of the Past? Legacies of 'the Tech', and the Making of the Manchester Institute of Science and Technology, 1966–74

ERIN BEESTON, UNIVERSITY OF MANCHESTER

Abstract

The University of Manchester Institute of Science and Technology (UMIST) was created for the advancement of technical education in post-war Britain. Born of an existing technical college, fondly known as 'the Tech', UMIST represented optimism and Manchester's prominent position in the 'white heat' epoch. Historians have recognised the political and personal role of the first principal, Vivian Bowden, in the expansion of UMIST in Manchester's metropolitan and intellectual landscapes. Alongside colleagues and councillors, Bowden selectively harnessed Manchester's scientific reputation and industrial heritage to forge the future. The purpose of this article is to contextualise this and understand how historical narratives and acts of commemoration aided the rapid expansion of UMIST in Manchester's educational and civic realms. Considering the relationship of key actors with concepts of the past, present and future of technology underlines the significance of attitudes towards 'the Tech' in this process.

Keywords: Technology; heritage; commemoration; education; futures

In 1966, when the Manchester College of Technology – fondly known as 'the Tech' – was transformed into the University of Manchester Institute of Science and Technology (UMIST), its advocates shaped a distinctly modern institution. While the zeitgeist of 'white heat' was noticeable through UMIST's ongoing modernist campus building project and in the rhetoric of its ambitious principal, Vivian Bowden, I argue that the ethos of the institution was contingent on its relationality with the past. 'White heat' is a term taken from Harold Wilson's 1963 Labour Party conference speech, which heralded education and innovation in technology as the balsam to Britain's post-war malaise. As a historical category, 'white heat' is both useful and problematic, as David Edgerton has explored.[1] The phrase has become synonymous with concept of techno-declinism, despite Wilson's intention not to re-establish the industrial 'workshop of the world', but rather reposition Britain as the 'toolroom of the world'.[2] Wilson's government (1964–70) upheld the recommendations of the 1963 Robbins Report on Higher Education, which recommended that colleges of advanced technology receive university status.[3] How science and technology was conceptualised by key proponents is therefore significant in understanding the establishment of this institution. I argue that, by looking beyond the hyperbole of Bowden's declinist rhetoric, and through considering the actions of UMIST staff and civic supporters, it is apparent that affection for the industrial past – and thus a sense of historical continuity rather than re-birth – ensured Manchester's future as a centre for science and technology education. Moreover, industry, and industrial applications of knowledge, often characterised as inferior to the culture of 'pure' research, are explicitly embedded into the narrative of progress woven around UMIST.[4]

Manchester's civic identity, shaped by urban actors from local politicians to city planners, for the most part distanced the industrial past with city-centre improvement plans focused on slum clearance and reconstruction, beginning with the 1945 *City of Manchester Plan*.[5] The textiles industry, the backbone of the north-west economy, was in swift decline; indeed, Sven Beckert shows that, in a global sense, 1963 (the year of 'white heat' and the Robbins Report) marked the end of European dominance with the Bhakra Dam opening in India and providing water to 2.8 million acres of land, much of it cotton fields. Meanwhile, Beckert argues, the UK textiles industry died 'with a whimper' as Liverpool's Cotton Exchange sold off its furnishings.[6] In Manchester, the once proud free-traders of the Chamber of Commerce resorted to protecting British interests; nevertheless, by 1968, Manchester's Royal Exchange had closed.[7] It is perhaps unsurprising that celebrating Manchester's scientific and technological achievements of the previous century was in its infancy, but as Peter Shapely notes, Manchester's post-war planners occasionally looked to the past 'and used it as evidence of status and image'.[8] In this article, I emphasise how interpretations of Manchester's past innovations were also invoked to legitimise UMIST, while the city council's support for the project also highlights Manchester's enduring civic relationship with applied research. Contemporary perspectives on technology from Bowden, local politicians, university administrators, academics and, significantly, the students, provide a lens through which to interrogate the 'technocratic moment'. Moreover, I argue that visions of the past directly shaped Manchester's future in both subtle and dynamic ways through invoking the legacies of 'the Tech'.

As other articles in this volume show, institutional founding dates and delineations often create false breaks between the threads of the complex web of further and higher education networks in Greater Manchester. In Robert Kargon's 1977 evaluation of the mutually beneficial relationship between civic elites and scientists in Victorian Manchester, he reflected on the present: 'on one issue – the symbiotic relationship between science and modern society – its history provided apt preparation for the future'[9] Perceptions of scientific progress and technological futures with the ensuing hopes, anxieties and ambivalence remained relatively consistent across the mid-twentieth century.[10] This article shows similar continuities in public discourse on the future of scientific education in Manchester. The first section addresses the influence of Bowden, whose experiences in wartime state science and private industry, and his consciousness of local poverty, shaped the foundation of UMIST. The second section follows the commemoration of Manchester scientists and local worthies through new building names, highlighting a conspicuous exception. Student perspectives on technological progress were reflected in the naming of the Student Union for Barnes Wallis – well known for his wartime achievements but with no direct connections to the University, and chosen to distance the Union from Labour prime minister and long-term advocate of Bowden, Harold Wilson. In the third section, the tumultuous founding of Manchester's science museum shows how instrumental visions of UMIST and the 'university city' were to its success. Finally, in 1974, the new institution paid homage to its oldest iteration with the 150th anniversary celebrations of the Mechanics' Institution. Rhetoric surrounding this event reveals how legacies of the 'Tech' continued to influence perceptions of modern UMIST.

The Technocrat's University

As principal of the College of Technology, Vivian Bowden oversaw the granting of a Royal Charter to the College in August 1955, which shifted governance from the committee of the city council to an autonomous body. The College was granted a coat of arms designed by Ellis Tomlinson, which featured an open book flanked by two gold bees (since bees symbolise Manchester) and the motto 'scientia et labore' ('by knowledge and work'), evoking the principles of the Mechanics' Institution and the College's ongoing ethos of adult education.[11] The motto also bears close relation to the Manchester Corporation's motto, 'concilio et labore' ('by counsel and work'), a reminder of their entwined aspirations. In 1956, Bowden presented his vision for the College: plans for campus of around twenty-seven acres between 'the tech' and Victoria University, the physical realisation of his aspiration to grow technological research alongside commercial interests.[12] Publicly vocal, Bowden was prolific in decrying of the state of scientific education in Britain, exasperated at what he perceived as the relative lag behind America and Russia. In December 1955, Bowden had written a series of three articles on 'the scientist crisis' for the liberal-leaning *News Chronicle*, focusing on inadequate Higher Education programmes, insufficient funding and insufficient science education in schools.[13] Vivian Bowden's polemical speeches and writing on the advantages of scientific education were contemporaneous with the 'two cultures' debate, the starting point for which was the Rede Lecture given by C. P. Snow, a former chemist turned civil servant and novelist, at the University of Cambridge in 1959.[14] Snow argued that educated individuals required scientific comprehension as well as knowledge of high literature, and believed that the upper echelons of the civil service distinctly lacked the former. Bowden's position as a booster of scientific education in this context was additionally complicated by long-standing ambivalent perceptions of applied science, developed with industry, as opposed to pure science.[15] Moreover, the 1960s saw active opposition to unfettered scientific progress, with the looming threats of nuclear war, overpopulation and pollution.[16]

Bowden's plans to expand the College of Technology's intellectual and physical infrastructure was in steady progress ahead of the creation of UMIST. The College benefited from an elevation in status for its wartime role as an Anglo-American military research and development facility and was able to finally complete the oft-delayed extension of the Sackville Street Building in 1957. Significantly, Bowden had witnessed the might of United States technological research funding at MIT and in Washington DC during his time as the principal scientific advisor to the Ministry of Supply's Telecommunications Research Establishment, which Brook notes 'dramatically influenced Bowden and would come to shape his collaborative approach'.[17] Before joining the College as principal in 1953, Bowden held roles in industry, including a stint as what he later described as the world's 'first computer salesman' for Ferranti.[18] Bowden's talent for 'quotable aphorisms' and publicity for his work in education led Prime Minister Harold Wilson to bestow a peerage on him, making him Baron Bowden of Chesterfield in 1963.[19] One year later, Bowden was confronted with the machinery of the civil service – which he admitted guided him politically as he guided them practically – in the newly created role of Minister for Science and Education in Wilson's government.[20] Through Bowden, we see the influence of warfare state experience upon the educational sphere, and, as David Edgerton has highlighted, how techno-declinists shaped the early 1960s modernisation project.[21] It is difficult, however, to consider Bowden as a typical 'anti-historian' (Edgerton's concept of those techno-declinists who mobilised counter-factual narratives), given the importance that he attached to the College's tangible heritage and its historical links to local government and industry. These deep ties were an integral part of (and not just a pretext for) his vision for its future. In a 1960 profile, one reporter noted that 'his office, like the man, is a happy blend of old-old world charm and newest ideas'.[22] In May 1964, the *New Statesman* deliberated on his motivations ('there is more to Bowden than the scientist's familiar impatience with the ramshackle machinery of government'), while noting his experiences of state education and the depression in Chesterfield growing up ('a social conscience informs his passion for efficiency').[23] To Bowden, slum clearances should not have been confined to his patch of campus redevelopment, but become a city-wide endeavour.[24]

Enshrining and Challenging 'White Heat'

While campus expansion was a modernist endeavour, as Brook highlights in this volume, the creation of new buildings and public spaces provided ample opportunity to simultaneously historicise Manchester science.[25] The aesthetic of the campus collectively, which is relatively compact (Figure 1), presents a group of white, mostly concrete-clad buildings. The expansion was the masterplan of Hubert Worthington, with later buildings designed by either H. S. Fairhurst & Sons or by Cruickshank & Seward.[26] The contrast with the 1902 building of the Manchester Municipal School of Technology was stark; the red-brick and terracotta French Renaissance style Sackville Street Building, designed by Spalding and Cross, was

Figure 1 View of the south campus, including the Barnes Wallis Building (bottom left), 1971. Manchester, University of Manchester Archive, UPC/2/516.

an imposing reminder of the turn of the century style; even its 1957 extension appeared older, since its architects followed plans from 1927.

A common theme of electrical innovation connected figures chosen for building names from research in science and technology. In 1967, the new chemistry building was named for Michael Faraday (1791–1867), noted for his work on electricity and magnetism, while the 1969 Ferranti Building was named for the Manchester electrical manufacturing firm and pioneers of computer technology. Faraday had been a supporter of the Salfordian physicist James Prescott Joule (1818–89), positively reviewing his influential paper 'On the Mechanical Equivalent of Heat', a tangential connection to Manchester science.[27] The homage to the Ferranti family is more transparent: Bowden had worked for Ferranti between 1950 and 1953, compiling what he learnt and his expectations for digital computers in the work *Faster Than Thought*.[28]

New buildings for the most part memorialised men instrumental in the institution, such as the 1962 Renold Building, named for the engineer and innovator in management science, Charles Renold. Renold was the vice president of the College and was chairman of the planning committee that oversaw the campus expansion. Also in 1962, Chandos Hall was named for Oliver Lyttelton, first Viscount Chandos, President of the College in the 1950s. The 1963 Pariser Building was named for a local civic advocate, Sir Maurice Pariser, whose support as a councillor

Figure 2 Victor Pasmore (in dark clothes) directs the painting of his mural *Metamorphosis* in the Renold Building, 1968. Manchester, University of Manchester Archive, UPC/2/799.

was instrumental in the College expansion and the foundation of a science museum discussed further in the next section.

Beyond the building names, artworks commissioned around the campus represented a fragile synergy between art and science on campus. The Renold Building, designed as a central facility for students, had a vast, double-height, entrance hall spanning the ground and first floors; Brook highlights how the Building Committee envisaged the space for circulation, facilitating communal experiences. Aptly, the lower hall was selected by the artist himself, Victor Pasmore, for his *Metamorphosis* abstract mural in 1965 (Figure 2).[29] The Faraday Building was also adorned with a ceramic tiled mural, *The Alchemist's Elements* by Hans Tisdall, with this work visible on the exterior. A companion relief sculpture by Tisdall, *The Elements*, was also erected at the Victoria University of Manchester's chemistry building on Brunswick Street in 1967. The twin murals represent parity between the departments of the 'new' UMIST and the well-established university.

Less harmonious was the reception of art on campus, embodying the divisive rhetoric of Snow's 'two cultures'. Also in 1967, sculptures displayed by students at the Manchester College of Art and Design were vandalised across the UMIST campus. In February 1968, further displays fared better, and the *Manchester Evening News* reported that 'the thing braved science' ('The Thing' was the only sculpture to survive from the original display).[30] The Student Union then organised a three-day arts festival in March 1968, realising the long-held aspiration to better integrate the arts with science on campus, and the student magazine *The New Techknowledge* produced an 'art in technology' themed edition. This included a pop-art inspired collage, in which photographs of campus walkways, the Renolds Building, cranes and diggers were juxtaposed with images of students in labs and partying.[31]

While the magazine illustrator provided a modern pop-art take on campus, a distinctly traditional approach was taken by the wider student body who named the Students' Union building. Completed the same year the 'Tech' was transformed into UMIST, the Students' Union was later named by popular vote after Barnes Wallis, the creator of the bouncing bomb: a wartime hero of aeronautical engineering without any connection to Manchester or the institution. Wallis had become a popular figure in the post-war period, especially following the release of the film *The Dam Busters* in 1954, based on Paul Brickhill's 1951 book. Robin Higham, Wallis's biographer, has highlighted the influence that the film had on his public image: 'Michael Redgrave's representation of Wallis as the much-misunderstood genius, already quite similar to the way in which Wallis was accustomed to see himself, subsequently became ever more part of Wallis' public persona, continually redrawn in his many broadcast interviews.'[32] Students found a maverick hero of science and engineering in the cult status surrounding Wallis, but there were also political implications in this choice, given his overtly right-wing views.[33] In 1964, the Students' Union made Wallis an honorary lifetime member, but were disappointed when, one year later, ill health meant that Wallis was unable to give a visiting lecture on 'The Strength of England'.[34] The dogmatic lecture, which he had honed between the 1950s and the 1970s, drew on the contemporary perceptions of national decline following the Second World War – including a form of moral decline attributed to the incoming migration from Commonwealth countries.[35]

The decision to name the union after Wallis appears in opposition to Harold Wilson, who the university had initially invited to open the Student Union building. The Student Union rejected this in March 1967, and its president, John Carrell, claimed that this was to avert demonstrations over recent decisions on higher education.[36] Parliament had ratified the proposed fee rises recommended in the Robbins Report (to cover 20 per cent of the course costs), and in February 1967 also debated an increase in fees for overseas students.[37] Indeed, when Wilson visited Manchester on 5 May 1967, his speech in the Renold Building was apparently greeted with 'traditional Tech barracking from students outside the lecture theatre'.[38] The unpopularity of Wilson around campus also relates to perceptions of the vice principal, especially given Bowden's prior role in Wilson's government from 1964 to 1965. Moreover, Bowden was attacked for his views on student loans by socialist students in 1968.[39]

Whilst UMIST's union was 'apolitical' as a body, student politics rippled across campus. Support for honouring Wallis provides an insight into the prevalence of his popularity, despite the strain of left-wing activism on campus. Wallis's right-wing activism ranged from supporting Conservative parliamentary candidates to delivering his 'Strength of England' talk to elite societies, including the extreme right-wing Conservative Monday Club in the later 1960s.[40] Wallis was the only named individual proposed by students, with only Carrell tempering fervour by suggesting that a student hall take the name instead.[41] Student democracy prevailed, and the official naming was formalised in February 1969.[42] It is difficult to ascertain the political perspectives of Student Union members keen to hear from Wallis and later name the building for him. Was it his wartime reputation, the excitement surrounding *The Dam Busters* during their childhood, or some level of sympathy with the right-wing politics he espoused that acted as the main draw? The naming for a man of technology is entirely unsurprising, given the gender skew in the subject areas taught at UMIST. The Institute presented a highly masculine environment, with women who proved to be the exception in studying subjects at UMIST singled out in the press.[43]

The UMIST Student Union were constitutionally not permitted to debate politics, thereby obscuring the record of their motivations in selecting Wallis, but what is clear is that this unique example of the student influence upon campus memorialisation subverted the official histories espoused by UMIST.[44] Indeed, Wilson had a long-standing relationship not only with Bowden, but with Manchester and the College of Technology; he was therefore an obvious choice. His father, Herbert Wilson, had studied chemistry at the Tech, and Harold's son was rumoured to attend the College in 1965.[45] Although he was raised in Huddersfield, Wilson's parents returned him to Openshaw specifically to baptise him in Manchester.[46] Ironically, given Wallis's lack of connections, the rejection of Wilson for the official opening was expressed as a desire to invite 'someone closer to the institution'.[47] Bowden's biographer, K. M. Entwistle, noted that he pioneered the inclusion of students in decision-making bodies, and permitting the Student Union to name their own building is a visible example of this.[48]

A Science Museum for the 'University City'

In tandem with ambitions specifically for 'the Tech' were wider visions for Manchester as a modern city that integrated 'town and gown'. Brook demonstrates the role of the relationality between city and campus specifically in architectural plans; in this section, I show how the academics themselves envisaged Manchester as a 'university city' and sought to establish a museum, with South Kensington's closely aligned Imperial College London and the Science Museum as a model.[49] It swiftly became apparent to Bowden that the transformation of 'the Tech' into UMIST provided the opportunity to establish this long-sought-after museum. As with the campus development, this aim was already articulated formally from the mid-1950s by a group of academics, city councillors and industry representatives.[50] However, the museum plan had roots in even earlier aspirations throughout the history of 'the Tech', from the nineteenth century onwards.[51]

During the interwar period, public exhibitions in the Sculpture Hall of the ornate Sackville Street Building had provided space for Manchester's scientific and industrial achievements. Remarkably, while nineteenth-century learned societies gathered ad hoc collections, Manchester did not boast a science museum despite the idea being regularly mooted by scientists and civic figures; the concept continually failed to gain adequate financial support. James Joule had himself decried the absence of a regional science museum (beyond the natural sciences) in 1870.[52] The absence of a dedicated museum is particularly noticeable considering Kargon's characterisation of the symbiotic relationship between scientific institutions and civic pride: 'practitioners of science developed a view of science which was at once civic and cosmopolitan'.[53] At the turn of the century, the professor of Electrical Engineering at the College, W. W. Haldane Gee, alongside the renowned physicist and advocate of technical education, Silvanus P. Thompson, tried to establish a museum with the support of Sir William Bailey. This was intended to be based in Piccadilly, the new municipal centre of Manchester.[54] Displays during the Municipal College of Technology period (1918–55) provided a public interface for the teaching and increasingly research work of the institution, although how open this was to the citizens of Manchester is unclear. A long-term 'War Works' exhibition opened on 3 October 1919, and was removed from the Sculpture Hall four years later to make way for the 1924 'Coming of Age' exhibition. The organisers hoped that wartime objects would form the 'nucleus of a museum' elsewhere, potentially at Heaton Park.[55] As with the earlier museum plans, this ambition was never realised.

In 1955, a committee was formed with the Victoria University and the city council to establish a science museum, the same year that the College received its Royal Charter. The primary site considered for the museum was Quarry Bank Mill, which was instead later preserved through the creation of Quarry Bank Mill Trust Ltd as tenants of the National Trust in the mid-1970s.[56] Meetings of this committee reveal a loss of momentum by late 1957, conceding Quarry Bank and finding little support from the city council. The hiatus was brief, however, since most members re-convened in 1959 to enter into talks with Sir Gerald Barry. Barry, widely known as the architect of the 1951 Festival of Britain, was working for Granada Television as executive of educational programming. Sophie Forgan characterised the science displayed at the festival as 'optimistic, technocratic in spirit and, moreover, was "official" science'.[57] For Manchester, Barry proposed a museum of 'two revolutions'.[58] This framed the 'two revolutions' as the industrial revolution and the 'atomic revolution', promoting British exceptionalism in rhetorical terms defined by Robert Bud as 'defiant modernism'.[59] The notational museum would have highlighted Manchester as a centre for atomic physics, a familiar narrative in a place where John Dalton (1766–1844), the 'father' of atomic physics, was heralded as a hero of science and celebrated in his lifetime.[60] In living memory, the Victoria University's Langworthy Chair was occupied by three consecutive Nobel prize winners, beginning with Ernest Rutherford, who performed the first artificially induced nuclear reaction – 'splitting the atom' – at the university in 1917. Even more recently, in mechanical engineering, Jack Diamond had overseen Europe's first nuclear engineering programme in 1954. Later sources show that he was directly involved in the hunt for a museum site in the 1960s, another indication that scientists were concerned with industrial heritage.[61]

Barry was instrumental in shaping perceptions of British technology through the Festival of Britain, and, while details of his Manchester vision are scant, the framing of an atomic 'revolution' relates to contemporary anticipation of nuclear futures.[62] This scheme nevertheless collapsed, apparently owing to the inflexibility of the Victoria University, whose planners wished to incorporate the museum into a scheme for a concrete-clad laboratory.[63] Negotiations between universities and the city council, with their differing priorities and financial clout, led to several false starts to the museum project. Meanwhile, the Sackville Street Building continued to be the place where the public, industry and academics interacted. Perhaps the closest Manchester came to a museum of the 'atomic revolution' at the College of Technology was in spring 1963, with the 'Atoms at Work' exhibition by the Atomic Energy Authority. The temporary exhibition was directly aimed at schoolchildren, welcoming 119 school visits across ten days.[64] Established in 1954, the Risley-based Atomic Energy Authority were research partners with the Victoria University of Manchester, a collaboration that may have also inspired Barry's 'two revolutions' concept.[65]

National developments in Further and Higher Education enhanced lobbying for the science museum alongside ambitions for the College of Technology. As early as October 1963, Professor Johnson of the Engineering Department cited the Robbins Report as a justification for the museum.[66] The creation of a museum at the height of the College's transformation into UMIST heralded an opportunity for status as well as science communication; in personal correspondence and public interviews, Bowden vociferously campaigned for the expansion of science education in schools, as well as pushing for higher graduate ratios in science across his tenure. A key asset to the museum project was Donald Cardwell, the first reader in the History of Science and Technology at the College, and head of the department from January 1963. In the original advertisement for the role, the appointee was charged with 'saving history'.[67] The teaching of the history of science and technology to undergraduates demonstrates that Bowden was concerned with the inclusion of 'liberal arts' in the curriculum, while students lamented that there was not enough plurality in teaching across the 1960s.[68] A significant step towards the realisation of the museum was Cardwell's appointment of a research assistant in textiles history, Richard Hills, to work on the project in the autumn of 1965.[69] Less than a year after the College became UMIST, a working party report set out the foundations of a new museum, which was then formally instated in the Manchester Corporation Bill 1966–67.[70]

Bowden developed a clear vision for the future of scientific education in the city, which also safeguarded Manchester's industrial past; this was a situation with growing urgency, since textile mills and engineering firms were rapidly folding. The message that he honed to advocate for the science museum always underlined the significance of preserving artefacts and demonstrating applied science. Bowden declared: 'We do not think that the past and present of technology and science can be separated without a danger of the former being rather too antiquarian in nature and the latter too ephemeral.'[71] Bowden framed the significance of preserving technology against the danger of present science becoming too 'ephemeral', and thus no longer demonstrable to future scientists. Through championing history at the institution, Bowden also spoke to the two cultures dichotomy between arts and science subjects in public discourse. Indeed, Bowden was self-taught in the history of science, with his contribution to *Faster Than Thought* including archival research into Ada Lovelace and Charles Babbage.[72] The desire to preserve 'old Manchester' extended beyond the material culture (which Richard Hills was actively collecting), to sites and structures of industry, with all but one proposal for the new museum involving the re-purposing of an industrial complex.

The power of place was conceived by the actors involved in the museum project, who considered many potential sites, often in response to plans by Manchester City's Architects Department. The museum was expected to enhance the relationship between 'town and gown'; proximity to the UMIST and Victoria Universities was regularly advocated by academics and university administrators in negotiations. Preferred options were often located close to Piccadilly Station and the campus. Councillor Maurice Pariser, whom Cardwell credited with providing much momentum in the early museum, envisaged a 'cultural quarter' on the corner of Princess Street and Portland Street.[73] In 1966, 101 Princess Street was proposed and later abandoned, owing to a new road scheme that would have affected the warehouse (a project later abandoned).[74] Another warehouse, the ornate Cook and Watts building on Portland Street, was considered for several years. York House, a 1911 warehouse, was a favourite with the Manchester College of Art and Design academics, since it was 'central to the city, adjacent to both arts and education precincts, alongside a canal in a part of the city very much in need of redevelopment'.[75] This was considered too expensive, however, and the Council decided to take no further action in October 1967.[76] The Working Party were wary of the limitations of space between pillars inside the warehouses, and were concerned that the floors would not support the heavy engineering exhibits already collected by the eager historians and technicians at the Department for the History of Science.

Ultimately, temporary premises were found in the Oddfellows Hall on Grosvenor Street (Figure 3), conveniently equidistant from the Victoria University and UMIST's main campus, a space shared with the Victoria University's methodist chaplaincy. The Hall is an Edwardian Baroque-style building, which originally housed the Oddfellows Friendly Society and was scheduled for demolition to make way for the metallurgy building in the campus redevelopment. Richard Hills, in his reminiscences, illuminated the network that influenced the commandeering of the Oddfellows Hall in the mid-1960s, when even temporary accommodation seemed unlikely: 'I was living in one of the National Trust properties of Styal while the UMIST Bursar, Geoffrey McComas, lived near-by … we discussed progress on the museum … he had close contact with the Principal, Lord Bowden.'[77]

Figure 3 The North-Western Museum of Science and Industry at the Oddfellows Hall; the mural along the side of the building was created by Walter Kershaw and Ken Billyard in 1977. Image courtesy of David Dixon.

Hills emphasised that he was not privy to information 'behind the scenes', but it seems that this friendship, formed on a commute into Manchester, enabled the researcher to build momentum for the museum with McComas.

The Manchester Museum of Science and Technology eventually opened on 20 October 1969, and was renamed the North Western Museum of Science and Industry by 1971, to reflect the regional nature of the collections.[78] The new name also projected Manchester as a regional centre, and aligned with the bolder claim that the city was the 'capital of the North', which appeared across local news in the 1960s.[79] The search for a permanent museum site accelerated across the 1970s, as objects were salvaged from more defunct industries. In 1970, Donald Cardwell's preferred option was the vast iron-framed Central Station opened in 1880, but another proposal for a purpose-built museum on campus gained momentum as the Education Precinct expanded.[80] In 1972, a notional design was drawn up by the Manchester Education Precinct architects, Hugh Wilson and Lewis Womersley. The design shows a three-storey museum with a basement, ground floor, and a first floor with a series of skylight windows, which resemble the peaked windows of weaving sheds in the north of England, although industry was an unlikely inspiration for the pair who were known for their modernist experiments in urban renewal across Manchester.[81] This was to be located at the corner of Oxford Road and Booth Street East, near the Oddfellows Hall site and along the main thoroughfare conceptualised as the 'education corridor' of Oxford Road. Since lobbying for the Central

Station had failed, Cardwell advocated for the campus site, suggesting that the public might be drawn into the campus area, thus minimising social distinctions between 'town and gown'.[82] Ultimately, a change in governance – from the financial support of the city council to the newly formed Greater Manchester Council in 1975 – quashed hopes for the museum as part of a 'university city'. The North Western Museum remained in the Oddfellows Hall until its collections were transferred to Greater Manchester Council's chosen site at Liverpool Road Station in the early 1980s. Re-made as the Greater Manchester Museum of Science and Industry, the museum's civic role would ultimately lead the regeneration of Castlefield rather than contribute to the 'education corridor'.[83]

Remembering the Mechanics' Institution and Promoting UMIST

In 1974, the 150th anniversary of the founding of the Mechanics' Institution provided a publicity boom for UMIST, and an opportunity to present a narrative of historical progress that legitimised recent developments. Although there is little research on the 'cult of centenary' beyond the 1960s, the form continued as a popular vehicle for public history.[84] Those involved in the anniversary looked back at the interwar period centenary for inspiration. This period witnessed a peak in historical pageantry, civic weeks (established for the British Empire Exhibition) and various centenaries of the towns and cities incorporated in the nineteenth century. At the College, a public 'Coming of Age' conversazione marked the twenty-first year of the latest iteration of the institution in 1923, followed by an exhibition for the 'centenary' of the Mechanics' Institution in 1924.[85] Conversely, in 1952, a jubilee marked the fiftieth anniversary of the opening of the Sackville Street Building. This provided publicity for civic ambition; 'Manchester has a college to be proud of', boasted H. D. Wheeler, as he declared the Municipal College 'the birthplace of science in industry'.[86]

Centenary speeches at the Sackville Street Building were an interactive affair, with visitors furnished with copies of the speeches printed immediately by staff and students of the Printing and Photographic Department.[87] Events for the 150th anniversary included a schools' open day on 12 July, and a public open day on 13 July, with talks and displays from the university's nineteen departments, as well an evening lecture series. Adverting pamphlets explained why the public were welcome to attend: 'the Institute is very conscious that its development over so many years has depended upon public support'.[88] While the new acronym, UMIST, was used liberally in publicity materials and adorned the University's new crest (derived from the College's 1956 coat of arms), the familiar slang term – 'the Tech' – remained in use locally. D. E. Hodgson, who worked for the bureau of industrial liaison at UMIST, noted that the acronym 'now enjoys quasi-official status', appearing on letterheads, a neon sign on the Mathematics Tower, and direction signs.[89]

The celebrations also allowed academics to historicise their own experiences, crafting institutional histories, most notably in the volume *Artisan to Graduate* edited by Cardwell. As James Sumner has highlighted in his exploration of the complex lineage of the current University of Manchester, the Mechanics' Institution provided the starting point for several establishments.[90] Created in 1824 out of exasperation at the exclusivity of the Manchester Institute, a group of radical businessmen, including several Unitarians and three future Members of Parliament resolved to instruct artisans 'in those branches of science and art which are of practical application'.[91] This was not instructional education around specific professions, but rather the opportunity for skilled workers to gain elevated education in subjects underlying their professions. The representation of this in the 1974 commemoration reveals that key UMIST figures used the overt connection with the practical application of knowledge as a point of continuity. As Hodgson reflected, 'there is little evidence of loss of vocation, and no sign of modifying, or dissenting from, the founder's purpose'.[92] This sense of continuity built upon Bowden's polemical speeches of the 1950s and 1960s, in which the industrial past was considered an asset rather than a point of divergence for the modern institution – a further indication that in the local context, Bowden bucked the technocrat's tendency for anti-histories.

As with the distant lineage to the Mechanics' Institution, the long-standing identity of the former college as 'the Tech' was combined into UMIST's identity. Key actors were aware of the negative connotations of this. Discussions among the Student Union council members on the renaming of the Student Union building in 1967 show the unease with their old naming; one student, D. A. Filson, noted that 'it was difficult to maintain a position in the university world when one was known as "Manchester Tech"'.[93] In a booklet produced for the 150th anniversary, Margaret Geake of the European Studies and Modern Languages Department commented that the connotations of the 'the Tech' were 'homely', and academically 'not quite respectable'.[94] Bowden continued to use the term; as late as 1969, he told the Manchester Evening News (in a moment of modesty) that 'the Tech has been an extraordinary place for over 150 years, and I just happened to be here when the government decided to spend some money'.[95] Bowden's use of 'the Tech' – especially in Manchester contexts – evoked longevity and continuity, rather than presenting the College as an interim institution between the Mechanics' Institution and UMIST. Geake felt that the name change would 'finally convince everyone that the Institute is part of the University of Manchester', highlighting the 1905 concordat that granted the Faculty of Technology to award degrees at the Municipal School of Technology.[96] The inclusion of these comments in the university's official publicity material is surprising, since much of the emphasis from Bowden and others highlighted UMIST's autonomy, rather than its collaborative role with the Victoria University of Manchester.[97] Geake also highlighted how the twenty-fifth anniversary of the degree awarding Faculty of Technology was commemorated in 1930, when a concert organ was donated by friends of the College.[98] In Geake's narrative, the phasing out of non-university courses in 1966 is highlighted, while Bowden lamented the finality of this in *Artisan to Graduate*.[99] Bowden's regret at the loss of evening classes and part-time adult courses indicates, again, that he did not wish to break with the past to forge future education, and that the legacy of 'the Tech' continued to influence his leadership of UMIST.

Conclusion

By the time that the 150th anniversary of the Mechanics' Institution was commemorated in 1974, UMIST was only eight years old. The projection of UMIST was so grounded in past achievements and perceptions of industrial Manchester that Bowden oversaw a relatively seamless transition from 'the Tech' to a vast teaching and research complex. Against the backdrop of the divisive 'two cultures' debate, the students writing in *The New Techknowledge* and their public criticism of Bowden showed a desire to expand the rigid focus of 'the Tech' on teaching for industry to a broader, more liberal education. While these students criticised Bowden's prioritising of building projects over a broader syllabus, Bowden worked tenaciously to preserve the city's past, with the creation of a new museum and a department dedicated to the history of science, whose activities proved integral to the realisation of this ambition. Views of 'the Tech' appear throughout UMIST's publicity material, and simultaneously offered a break with the past and a cosy option to reassure the public of the new institution's long-standing relationship with the city.

Steeped in the familiar spirit of Manchester exceptionalism, the views of key actors in this process demonstrate that the broader collective conceptualisation of Manchester and its place within the history of technology shaped UMIST as a 'modern' institution with a philosophical relationship with the past. Bowden may have been technocratic in action, but his concept of the past, present and future of science was imbued with civic consciousness and grasp of the potential for heritage in shaping the city. In this, he pre-empted the industrial heritage movement of the 1980s when the next iteration of the North Western Museum of Science and Industry would perform a major role in the regeneration of post-industrial Manchester.[100]

Notes

1 David Edgerton, *Warfare State Britain, 1920–1970* (Cambridge: Cambridge University Press, 2006).

2 James Sumner, 'Defiance to Compliance: Visions of the Computer in Postwar Britain', *History and Technology: An International Journal*, 30 (2014), 323. For historiographic scrutiny of post-war declinist rhetoric, see Jim Tomlinson, *The Politics of Decline: Understanding Postwar Britain* (London: Routledge, 2001).

3 *Higher Education: Report of the Committee Appointed by the Prime Minister under the Chairmanship of Lord Robbins, 1961–1963* (London: HMSO, 1963).

4 Robert Bud, 'Modernity and the Ambivalent Significance of Applied Science: Motors, Wireless, Telephones and Poison Gas', in Robert Bud, Paul Greenhalgh, Frank James

and Morag Shiach (eds), *Being Modern: The Cultural Impact of Science in the Early Twentieth Century* (London: University College London Press, 2018), pp. 95–129.

5. R. Nicholas, *City of Manchester Plan* (Jarrold & Sons: London, 1945), https://issuu.com/cyberbadger/docs/city_of_manchester_plan_1945 [accessed 29 January 2024].

6. Sven Beckert, *Empire of Cotton: A Global History* (New York: Vintage Books, 2015), pp. 427–8.

7. Terry Wyke, 'Rise and Decline of Cottonopolis', in Alan Kidd and Terry Wyke (eds), *Manchester: Making the Modern City* (Liverpool: Liverpool University Press, 2015), pp. 108–15.

8. Peter Shapely, 'Civic Pride and Redevelopment in the Post-War British City', *Urban History*, 39 (2012), 317.

9. Robert H. Kargon, *Science in Victorian Manchester: Enterprise and Expertise* (London: Routledge, 2010), p. 237.

10. Peter J. Bowler, *A History of the Future: Prophets of Progress from H. G. Wells to Isaac Asimov* (Cambridge: Cambridge University Press, 2017), pp. 204–9; Frank A. J. L James and Robert Bud, 'Epilogue: Science after Modernity' in Bud, Greenhalgh, James and Shiach (eds), *Being Modern*, pp. 386–93.

11. B. V. Bowden, *Proposals for the Development of Manchester College of Science and Technology* (Manchester: Manchester College of Science and Technology, 1956); Tomlinson also designed the College's ceremonial mace in 1957: Our own Reporter, 'Mace as Mark of Progress', *Guardian* (26 October 1957), p. 10.

12. *Ibid.*

13. Manchester, Manchester Archives, Biographical Cuttings Box 26 (Dr Bertram Vivian Bowden, cuttings from *News Chronicle/Daily Dispatch*, 14 December 1955, 15 December 1955 and 16 December 1955).

14. C. P. Snow, *The Two Cultures and the Scientific Revolution* (Cambridge: Cambridge University Press, 1959).

15. Bud, 'Modernity', p. 121.

16. Bowler, *A History of the Future*, pp. 207–8.

17. Richard Brook, 'UMIST, the Evolution of an Institution: Personnel and Politics', *The Modernist*, 5 (2012), 13–14.

18. James Sumner, 'Science, Technology and Medicine', in Kidd and Wyke (eds), *Manchester*, p. 158.

19. K. M. Entwistle, 'Bowden, (Bertram) Vivian, Baron Bowden (1910–1989), scientist and educationist', *Oxford Dictionary of National Biography*, https://doi.org/10.1093/ref:odnb/40199 [accessed 17 September 2024].

20. 'Meet Lord Bowden', *Manchester Evening News* (11 November 1969), p. 8.

21. Edgerton, *Warfare State Britain*, p. 247.

22. Manchester, Manchester Archives, Biographical Cuttings Box 26 (BOW-BRAD, 'Profile of Dr B. V. Bowden', cutting annotated as *Manchester Evening Chronicle* (28 January 1960)).

23. 'Labour's New Men of Power: the Computer Man', *New Statesman* (8 May 1964), pp. 722–3.

24. Entwistle, 'Bowden'.

25 Richard Brook, 'Servicing the State: Municipality and the Military Industrial Complex', *Bulletin of the John Rylands Library* 100:2 (2024), 97–124.
26 Brook, 'UMIST, the Evolution of an Institution', 14.
27 Crosbie W. Smith, 'Faraday as Referee of Joule's Royal Society Paper "On the Mechanical Equivalent of Heat"', *Isis*, 67 (1976), 444–9; Joule was later commemorated by UMIST, naming the refurbished library in the Sackville Street Building after him in 1987.
28 B. V. Bowden (ed.), *Faster Than Thought: a Symposium on Digital Computing Machines* (London: Sir Isaac Pitman & Sons, 1953).
29 Brook, 'Servicing the State', 114.
30 'Where the Thing Braved Science', *Manchester Evening News* (9 February 1968).
31 'Pop-Art in Technology', *The New Technowledge*, 4:4 (1968), unpaginated collage in centre.
32 R. Higham, 'Wallis, Sir Barnes Neville (1887–1979), aeronautical designer and engineer', *Oxford Dictionary of National Biography*, https://doi.org/10.1093/ref:odnb/31795 [accessed 17 September 2024]; Robert A. Jones, 'The Boffin: a Stereotype of Scientists in Post-war British Films (1945–1970)', *Public Understanding of Science*, 6 (1997), 34–6.
33 Edgerton, *Warfare State*, p. 227; S. W. H. Zaidi, 'The Janus-Face of Techno-Nationalism: Barnes Wallis and the "Strength of England"', *Technology and Culture*, 49 (2008), 62–88.
34 Manchester, Manchester Archives, Newspaper Cuttings Box 160, (UMIST, cutting annotated with *Manchester Evening News* (8 March 1965).
35 Zaidi, 'The Janus-Face of Techno-Nationalism'.
36 Our Own Reporter, 'Students Oppose Invitation to Mr Wilson', *Guardian* (23 March 1967), p. 20.
37 Hansard, vol. 741, col. 1981: Overseas Students (Increased Fees), 23 February 1967, https://hansard.parliament.uk/Commons/1967-02-23/debates/9dcdf6ff-4a9c-4701-be0b-d41568a272b7/OrdersOfTheDay#contribution-3a4f7989-7691-4a50-9bc8-96c2c9b33273 [accessed 8 January 2024].
38 'Opening at the Computer Laboratory of the National Computing Centre', *The New Technowledge*, 3:7 (June 1967), p. 17.
39 William Hanley, 'Lord Bowden Faces 7 Page Socialist Attack by Students', *Guardian* (1 November 1968), p. 22.
40 Edgerton, *Warfare* State, p. 227.
41 Manchester, University of Manchester Archive (hereafter UoMA), TSU/1/20 (UMIST Union Minutes of Council Executive and Finance Committee, Executive Committee motions, 28 September 1968).
42 Our Own Reporter, 'Honour for Dr Wallis', *Guardian* (26 February 1969), p. 20.
43 Press coverage ranged from ridicule to intrigue, for example, 'Odd girls in', *Manchester Evening News* (19 February 1971), p. 10.
44 Terry Wallis, 'An Introduction to Owen's Union', *The New Technowledge*, 1:6 (1962), p. 14, highlights the absence of political societies from the Tech, aside from the

non-party political CND; 'Union Bid Rejected', *Manchester Evening News* (30 January 1970), p. 6, confirms that the Union continued to be 'non-political' to 1970.

45 Our Own Reporter, 'Premier's Son for Manchester College?', *Guardian* (10 December 1965), p. 3.

46 Our Own Reporter, '"Gate of Heaven" in Openshaw: Where Mr Wilson was Baptised', *The Guardian* (29 November 1963), p. 9.

47 UoMA, TSU/1/20 (UMIST Union Minutes, Extraordinary Meeting, 20 March 1967).

48 Entwistle, 'Bowden'.

49 UoMA, TPA/1/32 (Cardwell and Johnson paper on 'The Manchester Museum of Science and Technology', attached to memo to Bowden, 25 October 1963).

50 Manchester, Science Museum Group Corporate Archive, CORP/SIM/15/1/2024/001/0005 (Corporate Management: Museum of Science and Technology for the North-West of England, Minute Book, 1955–1957).

51 For further background on the nascent science museum, see E. Beeston, 'A Science Museum "to rival South Kensington": Industrial Legacies, 'Modern' Science Education and Civic Aspiration in Post-War Manchester', *British Journal for the History of Science* (forthcoming).

52 *Report of the Royal Commission on Scientific Instruction and the Advancement of Science*, vol. 2 (1872–75), cited by D. S. L. Cardwell, 'Castlefield, Past and Present: A Personal View together with an Account of the History of the Manchester Science Museum', *Manchester Memoirs* (new series), 3 (1983), 92.

53 Kargon, *Science in Victorian Manchester*, p. 235.

54 Cardwell, 'Castlefield', 92–3.

55 UoMA, TGB/1/1/5 (College of Technology, Management Sub-committee minute book 1918–1919; 1919–1920, Sub-committee War Works Exhibition, 25 July 1919); TGB/1/1/8 (College of Technology, Minutes of Sectional Committee meetings 1923–1925, Textile Sectional Committee 12 March 1923 and 4 June 1923).

56 R. Angus Buchanan, 'Landscape with Engines', in David Morgan Evans, David Thackray and Peter Salway (eds), *The Remains of Distant Times: Archaeology and the National Trust* (Woodbridge: Boydell Press, 1996), p. 85. Buchanan noted that a feasibility study, 'Styal', written by Richard Hills in the early 1970s, laid the foundations for the mill's transformation. Keen-eyed readers will note that Hills's recollections of around 1966 (quoted later in this section) indicate that he lived on the premises at Styal for a period.

57 Sophie Forgan, 'Festivals of Science and the Two Cultures: Science, Design and Display in the Festival of Britain, 1951', *British Journal for the History of Science*, 31 (1998), 240.

58 UoMA, VCA/7/8/11 (1/2) (Museum of Science and Technology file, Statement from Professor J. A. L. Matheson cites TV company interest in a museum of two revolutions (July 1959); Matheson to the Vice Chancellor (24 August 1959); Lennox-Kerr to the Vice Chancellor (Victoria) University re. Sir Gerald Barry (13 October 1959)).

59 Robert Bud, 'Penicillin and the New Elizabethans', *British Journal for the History of Science*, 31 (1998), 313.

60 Sumner, 'Science, Technology and Medicine', pp. 123–5.

61 *Ibid.*, pp. 147–50. Ernest Rutherford, Lawrence Bragg and Patrick Blackett were consecutive Langworthy Professors from 1907 to 1953; Hills, *The North-Western Museum of Science and Industry: Some Reminiscences* (Manchester: Chetham's Library), digital resource: https://library.chethams.com/collections/digital-resources/the-north-western-museum-of-science-and-industry-some-reminiscences-by-richard-hills/ [accessed 4 January 2024].

62 Bowler, *A History of the Future*, p. 207.

63 UoMA, VCA/7/8/11 (1/2) (Professor Louis Matheson to the Vice Chancellor of Manchester (Victoria) University, 24 August 1959; Peter Lennox-Kerr to the Vice Chancellor re. Sir Gerald Barry, 13 October 1959).

64 'Atoms at work', *Guardian* (22 March 1963), p. 24.

65 See Brook, 'Servicing the State', 99, on the post-war nuclear research context.

66 UoMA, TPA/1/32 ('Proposed Museum', memo from Johnson to Bowden, 25 October 1963).

67 'Saving History', *Manchester Evening News* (2 March 1962), p. 6.

68 Colin Smith, 'We Need Time', *The New Technowledge*, 9:3 (1960), pp. 12–13, argued that the rapid expansion of the College had created a student body indifferent to culture; Hanley, 'Lord Bowden Faces 7 Page Socialist Attack by Students', p. 22, attacked Bowden directly on the lack of liberal studies at the 'knowledge factory'.

69 Hills, *The North-Western Museum*, p. 11.

70 UoMA, TPA/1/32 ('City of Manchester, proposed museum of science and technology: the report of the working party appointed by the Joint Committee of representatives of the University of Manchester, UMIST and the City Council', 31 October 1966); House of Commons, Manchester Corporation Bill (Bills 1966–1967) (London: HMSO), clause 47.

71 UoMA, TPA/1/32, (Proposed Museum, memo by Cardwell to Bowden re. upcoming meeting with the Ministry of Technology, 7 October 1968).

72 UoMA, BVB/1/82, 152, 163, 166–7, 169 (Papers of Vivian Bowden, files on Charles Babbage and Ada Lovelace); Bowden (ed.), *Faster Than Thought*.

73 Cardwell, 'Castlefield', pp. 93–4; Manchester, Manchester Archives, RA1(A).1.3 (Museum correspondence, Cardwell, 'Report on the History of the NWMSI').

74 UoMA, TPA/1/32 (Proposed Museum, appendix to meeting of the Joint Committee, 9 November 1967).

75 *Ibid.* (Proposed Museum, John Bishop and Joseph Paul D'uras to Bowden, 14 January 1968).

76 *Ibid.* (Appendix to meeting of the Joint Committee, 9 November 1967).

77 Hills, *The North-Western Museum*, p. 11.

78 Manchester, Chetham's Library, Richard Hills Personal Archive, 16.K.2.24, R. L. Hills 'NWMSI: A Brief History up to December 1973', p. 4.

79 Peter Shapely, 'The Continuing Tradition of Civic Pride: Municipal Culture in Post-War Manchester', in Melanie Tebbutt and Alan Kidd (eds), *People, Places and Identities: Themes in British Social and Cultural History, 1700s–1980s* (Manchester: Manchester University Press, 2017), p. 163.

80 Tony Aldous, 'Station as Museum Plea', *The Times* (31 August 1970).

81 UoMA TPA/1/70 (1/2) (Museum of Science and Technology file, plan dated March 1972); Hugh Wilson and Lewis Womersley, *Manchester Education Precinct: Summary of a Review of the Plan 1974* (Manchester: Wilson & Womersley, 1974), p. 7; Richard Brook, 'Levelling Up: The Aerial Environments of Wilson Womersley', *The Modernist*, 40 (2021), 28–31.

82 Manchester, Manchester Archives, RA1(A).1.3 (Museum Correspondence, D.S.L Cardwell, Report on the History of the NWMSI).

83 Erin Beeston, 'Spaces of Industrial Heritage: A History of Uses, Perceptions and the Remaking of Liverpool Road Station, Manchester' (PhD thesis, University of Manchester, 2020), pp. 206–12.

84 Later twentieth-century commemoration is largely framed against national events, like the 1977 Silver Jubilee; see David Cannadine, 'The Context, Performance and Meaning of Ritual: The British Monarchy and the 'Invention of Tradition', c.1820–1977', in Eric Hobsbawm and Terence Ranger (eds), *The Invention of Tradition* (Cambridge: Cambridge University Press, repr. 2015), pp. 101–65. Thomas Hulme (*After the Shock City: Urban Culture and the Making of Modern Citizenship* (Woodbridge: Boydell Press, 2019), pp. 205–6) has argued that civic culture was usurped as new forms of citizenship emerged under the welfare state.

85 UoMA, UMIST Rare Book Collection, 607.42 MAN (Manchester City Education Committee, 'Programme of a conversazione held at the Municipal College of Technology, Manchester, to celebrate the coming of age of the college buildings', 1923).

86 H. D. Wheeler, 'The Birthplace of Science in Industry', *Manchester Evening News* (25 September 1952), p. 2.

87 M. Geake, *UMIST: 150th Anniversary Celebrations* (Manchester: C. Nicholls & Co., 1974), unpaginated.

88 Manchester, Manchester Archives, MSC 378/U (UMIST ephemera, 'Open Days' and 'Public Lectures' leaflet, 1974).

89 D. E. Hodgson, 'UMIST today', in D. S. L. Cardwell (ed.), *Artisan to Graduate: Essays to Commemorate the Foundation in 1824 of the Manchester Mechanics' Institution, now in 1974 the University of Manchester Institute of Science and Technology* (Manchester: Manchester University Press, 1974), p. 232.

90 Sumner, 'Science, Technology and Medicine', p. 160.

91 Kargon, *Science in Victorian Manchester*, p. 20.

92 Hodgson, 'UMIST Today', p. 245.

93 UoMA, TSU/1/19 (UMIST Union Minutes of Council Executive and Finance Committee, annual extraordinary meeting, 30 November 1967).

94 Geake, *UMIST*.

95 'Meet Lord Bowden', *Manchester Evening News* (11 November 1969), p. 8.

96 Geake, *UMIST*.

97 Lord Bowden, 'The Present Situation', in Cardwell (ed.), *Artisan to Graduate*, pp. 248–57. Bowden opened his chapter with the autonomy afforded by the 1956 Royal Charter, framing the establishment of the Faculty of Technology in 1905 as a 'take over'.

98 Geake, *UMIST*.
99 Entwistle, 'Bowden'.
100 On the re-making of the North Western Museum at Liverpool Road Station, see Beeston, 'Spaces of Industrial Heritage', pp. 181–220.

EU authorised representative for GPSR:
Easy Access System Europe,Mustamäe tee 50, 10621 Tallinn, Estonia
gpsr.requests@easproject.com